HOW GOOD PARENTS RAISE GREAT KIDS

It's not magic. It doesn't take a college education or a library full of books by so-called experts. Instead, good parenting is a matter of practicality, common sense, sensitivity, and a few acquired skills. Now find out just how to put it all together, by sharing the secrets of success with other parents like you.

Use this book to look at the lives of other families whose kids are doing well. Find out how to resolve the arguments, how to respond to "out-of-bounds" behavior, and how to open the channels of communication and keep them open. This book will show you why:

- Good parents don't try to win every fight.
- Good parents aren't perfect—and they admit their mistakes.
- Good parents often feel more uncomfortable talking about sex than their kids do—but they do it anyway.
- Good parents prepare for trouble before it happens.

"Refreshing....Presents the collective wisdom of parents in their own words...I recommend this book to any parent."
—Michael E. Bernard, associate pr[illegible] California State University, Long Beach, Department of Educat[illegible]on

[illegible]e...

"Filled with warmth, wit, and wisdom....A wonderful resource that helps guide today's parents to support the authentic development of children."
—*Eileen Paris, Ph.D., and Thomas Paris, Ph.D., authors of* **"I'll Never Do to My Kids What My Parents Did To Me!": A Guide to Conscious Parenting**

"Alan and Robert Davidson have produced an invaluable tool for all parents....If you want dynamic adolescents in your life, follow the practices of the successful parents described in HOW GOOD PARENTS RAISE GREAT KIDS. These six elements of success in child rearing should be in every adult's bag of tricks."
—*Robert E. Palazzi, past president, California Association of Teachers of English*

"A very special book. By the love and respect for fundamental human values, the authors imbue the book with a total commitment to helping parents to actualize their children's potential…a sense of morality, and purpose in life. If I were asked to recommend one book on parenting, I would recommend this one."
—*Thomas R. Verney, M.D., author of* **The Secret Life of the Unborn Child** *and* **Gifts to Our Fathers,** *and founder of the Association for Pre- and Perinatal Psychology and Health*

"Should help parents from birth through college. The title captures the spirit of the book: a successful parent is a good parent (not a perfect parent) who has great kids. This book presents the results of multiple field trials done by the true experts—successful parents."
—*Susan Reid, M.D., chief of psychiatry, Portsmouth Hospital, NH*

HOW GOOD PARENTS RAISE GREAT KIDS

The Six Essential Habits of Highly Successful Parents

ALAN DAVIDSON, Ph.D., and
ROBERT DAVIDSON

A Time Warner Company

Warner Books, Inc., 1271 Avenue of the Americas, New York, NY 10020
A Time Warner Company

Printed in the United States of America

First Printing: June 1996

10 9 8 7 6 5 4 3

Library of Congress Cataloging-in-Publication Data
Davidson, Alan.
How good parents raise great kids : the six essential habits of highly successful parents / Alan Davidson and Robert Davidson.
p. cm.
ISBN 0-446-67137-1
1. Parenting—United States. 2. Parents—Attitudes.
I. Davidson, Robert. II. Title.
HQ755.8.D37 1996
649'.1—dc20 95-43147
CIP

Interior design by Charles Sutherland
Cover design by Susan Newman

To the parents who opened their homes and hearts to us.
Thank you and congratulations on a job well done.

Acknowledgments

One of the first high school counselors we spoke with, Barry Miller, convinced us of the need for this project when he said, "This book is just what today's parents need." We thank him for his contagious enthusiasm.

Author and devoted friend Susan Page encouraged us to write this book and assisted us in numerous ways throughout the project. All writers should be so lucky.

Our literary agent, Shelley Roth, believed in this project from the beginning and offered excellent, insightful editing and organizational suggestions in the early stages. It was a real plus having not only an extremely qualified agent, but one who is also a top-notch writer.

Our editor, Colleen Kapklein, saw the importance of this book and made several astute editing suggestions, as did copy editor Libby Kessman, whose red pencil was always welcome. Thank you both.

Thank you Naomi Wise, whose wit and editing wisdom helped us develop our proposal. Her words, "Kill that passive voice!" will resound in our heads forever.

Thanks also to Jean Nattkemper who said, after reviewing our proposal, "You have a publishable book here." She was right.

We also want to acknowledge several other people who helped us in their own ways: Steve deLaet, Jim Nunan, Brad Bunnin, Ruth Davidson, Walter Rubenstein, our parents Joan and Milt Davidson, Howard Gurevitz, M.D., Grace Timpanero, Harold and Pauline Allen, Greg and Cleo Filias, Ceil and Tony Mirto and their "great kid" Jeanne—a shining example of what can happen through love, tolerance, and respect. May all children turn out as wonderful as she did.

Table of Contents

FOREWORD

There could not be a better time for this remarkable book. It is designed to help children not just survive, but *thrive* in our fast-paced, complex society. It shows parents that despite the tremendous distractions kids face today, they can grow up happy and do exceedingly well.

With so many contradicting child-rearing styles espoused in the various parenting books, this book is a welcome contribution. The Davidsons studied the families of children who achieved all-around success. By reading how skilled parents did it and why their methods worked, parents will gain fascinating insights that could not have been obtained any other way.

Perhaps most important, readers will learn how wise parents taught their children the important distinction between being a material "success" and being internally *successful,* between what they *have* and what they have *become.*

What they have become—and what all children can become when their parents follow the guidance in this wonderful book—are delightful kids who enjoy life by functioning at their maximum potential.

Way back in the 1930s, pioneer psychiatrist Karl Menninger sated in his landmark work, *The Human Mind*:

> Let us define mental health as the adjustment of human beings to the world and to each other with a maximum of effectiveness and happiness. Not just efficiency, or just contentment—or the grace of obeying the rules of the game cheerfully. It is all of these together. It is the ability to maintain an even temper, an alert intelligence, socially consider-

ate behavior, and a happy disposition. This, I think, is a healthy mind.

The Davidsons help parents develop these qualities in their children with a book that makes its own pioneering breakthrough. By looking not at the neuroses, compulsions, and phobias and how to "solve" them, but at healthy cases, parents can model their guidance accordingly. Whether addressing parents of infants or adolescents, this valuable book finally offers intelligent solutions to the parenting puzzle.

Howard Gurevitz, M.D., F.A.P.A.

INTRODUCTION:

Preliminary Parenting Principles

This book brings together a collection of valuable advice on successful child rearing from a wide cross section of highly successful parents. Based on a large array of interviews with the parents of children who were identified by high school administrators as "great kids," this book offers an intimate glimpse into the homes of all types of families—upper-class, lower-income, and single-parent—who found that six key elements were essential to quality child rearing. These elements, upon which this book is founded, are: *Communicate, Encourage Intellectual Development, Discipline, Instill Self-Esteem, Teach Values,* and *Support Socialization.*

Our book differs from other parenting books in one significant way: It does not rehash hackneyed child-rearing problems and the psychodynamics of dysfunctional families, nor espouse theories based on the authors' tribulations raising children. Rather, it relies only on genuine, unbiased evidence gleaned from eighteen months of interviews with "true experts"—the parents of extremely well-adjusted, well-rounded, happy children.

Inner contentment, self-reliance, and competence were the hallmarks of these kids whose perceptive parents focused less on cognitive milestones like first words, growth charts, or straight-A report cards and more on helping them explore their own creativity, develop individuality, and realize their potential.

As we considered doing this project and began some preliminary research, we observed something very interesting, which convinced us even more that a book like ours was needed. Neither libraries nor bookstores offered books containing real-life, in-depth investigations exclusively with the parents of happy, well-rounded children. The only books available were "theory" books based on authors' opinions, medical practices, or personal experiences raising their own children. Over and over, they discussed various predictable parenting problems such as sibling rivalry, bed-wetting, whining, disobedience, and so on, in books with titles such as *Tough Love, Teen Is a Four-Letter Word, Parents' Survival Training,* and *When Good Kids Do Bad Things.* We wanted to study the exact opposite: healthy families and their secrets of success.

We wanted an answer to the big question: What makes a few kids such standouts? So, we headed directly to the source. That's when we struck gold. In every home of every exceptional child we found, we discovered a treasure trove of valuable information—information that began to form an interesting consensus on the child-rearing methods used by highly effective parents.

OUR SEARCH FOR TRUE EXPERTS

This book investigates how parents raised children who not only were excellent students, but also, more importantly, possessed self-confidence and a genuine love of life. They stood out because they were friendly, sociable, and beautifully well-adjusted. They were popular, likable, and active, and they relished the learning experience. Teachers prefer working with these types of students because they are inquisitive, responsive, and ambitious. Even their friends' parents like having them around. They aren't particularly bookish and they are not unusually gifted, Mensa-bound children. They're just great kids—with a difference.

As soon as we approached school officials to help us find these kids, we knew we were on to something exciting. Principals, counselors, and deans responded to our inquiries with unbridled enthusiasm and, without exception, instantly knew which students would make excellent subjects for our book. "Your book is a great idea," said numerous counselors. "I've got just the kid for you." One dean said, "Boy, could parents use a book like this! I can think of three kids right off the bat who would be perfect for you."

One difference between the students they recommended and average students was obvious during a telephone call to one school official. The counselor had just recommended a student for our study when she coincidentally walked into his office. Since she was right there, we asked if we could talk to her for a moment. He said that would be fine and handed her the phone. Knowing that the average American child watches between four and six hours of television per day, we asked one quick question: "How many hours of television do you watch?"

"Oh, around four," she replied.

"Four?" we asked incredulously.

"Per week," she added, to our great relief. Here was one small indication of why her counselor selected her over the other students. She watched nearly *90 percent less* television than they did, leaving *90 percent more* time to stimulate her brain positively rather than passively.

Another difference was these kids' uncanny ability to excel in spite of some very tough conditions. Jerry Jones, for example, had no family structure at all, living alone as a high school senior, cooking and cleaning for himself in a tiny one-room apartment, but still passing with honors and planning to attend a major university. His parents were in another part of the country where they had found jobs. They were too poor even to attend his graduation and give him a commencement hug and congratulatory handshake. What had his parents done during his critical early years to allow him such self-sufficiency?

Tami Woo lived with her mother, father, grandmother, and great-grandmother—none of whom could speak a word of English! They lived in a low-income suburb of San Francisco where the homes all had bars on the windows and dirty sidewalks for front yards. Her parents owned a small corner market, yet they were now sending their second daughter off to a large, prestigious university. Tami spoke impeccable English (as well as Mandarin, Cantonese, and French) and interpreted for her parents during our interview, which we conducted wearing the Chinese slippers they had provided for us at the front door.

Something occurred during these children's childhoods that helped them attain attributes other children didn't, that helped them past the normal pressures and tribulations that so often derail kids. What was it? How was it different? Why was it so effective? And how can other children benefit from it? These are the questions the following chapters will answer.

We spent hundreds of hours sitting on an eclectic assortment of furniture ranging from fine, Danish leather sofas to old, split-and-taped Naugahyde recliners. We sipped coffee, ginseng tea, diet sodas, carrot juice, and even Ovaltine in kitchens and dining rooms of tiny apartments in the inner city and spacious homes in the hills, trying to find out what the parents in our study did differently from other parents. Our findings demolish the myth that raising children is destined to be a tortuous, nail-biting, fist-pounding experience. Not all toddlers go through the "terrible twos," nor do all adolescents become surly troublemakers.

During our interviews, we prodded and scraped, searching for the "big problems" we thought parents might be concealing. But we could not uncover them. Why? Because there really weren't any. The successful parents we came to know intimately did not encounter the child-rearing horrors described in so many of the parenting books we came across (one lists in alphabetical order all the nightmares parents are likely to face, starting with A: Aggression, Alcoholism, Anorexia; B: Bed-wetting, Biting, Brain Damage!).

Through instinct, research, or their own upbringings, our "true experts" found ways to raise happy, competent kids—without fear or catastrophes. In this book, we highlight those ways and the similarities between these parents' child-rearing philosophies. One mother's philosophy was straightforward:

> Parenting is much more like baking a cake than a delicate soufflé. You put in all the right ingredients, throw it in the oven, and forget about it for a while. Let it rise and do its own thing. You can put the icing and finishing touches on later. Don't keep opening the door, sticking toothpicks in it, and worrying about it. It'll come out fine.

What we found was that none of the parents we met were perfect, nor were their children Goody Two-shoes. We specified to school officials at the outset that we were not looking for perfectly packaged, little darling, straight-A superkids, but rather kids who went through all the normal stages any kids do.

As you will see in the following chapters, the critical differences between these parents and less effective parents were: (1) they were aware, insightful, and "tuned-in"; (2) they knew their roles and actively participated when necessary and appropriate; (3) they were relaxed in their roles as parents; and, perhaps most important; (4) they respected their children as living, breathing, thinking, feeling, highly intelligent, genuine *people*—at all ages.

The parents we interviewed found that communication was the foundation of their parenting programs. Only by communicating effectively could they encourage intellectual development, discipline appropriately, or instill self-esteem. To teach the values we discuss in Chapter 5, and help support their children's socialization, the sixth habit, our parents drew on and applied all of the other habits that define successful parenting.

You will see what was behind this top-notch parenting and how you, too, can develop the six habits and apply those same skills, ideas, and philosophies to your own situations, regardless of your child's grade or competency level. When we asked one parent about the age at which children are most receptive to guidance, she said emphatically, "*Now!* Now is the time to jump in! It is never too late for kids to improve, grow, and succeed." Her husband went on to explain that during junior high school, their son had been only mildly interested in his classes. But upon entering high school, he decided to switch tracks and take college prep courses.

> It certainly was not too late, as some would think. Suddenly Rick was receptive to us in a way he had never been before. We helped him develop new, healthy study habits, upgrade his reading skills, and get special tutoring for math. With new direction and guidance, he graduated in the upper levels of his class—just like we always told him he could.

Conversely, if your daughter is inclined to become an artist or musician, rather than the professional or businessperson you may have hoped for, you can help her realize her dream. One father put it this way:

> Rather than clutching steadfastly to our preconceived notion that Rhonda should pursue an MBA or premed program, we finally realized that we needed to support her efforts to enroll in a good art school. We now know that she was right all along because when she came home for Christmas break, she thanked us for being there for her, and with tears in her eyes, said she had never been happier in her life.

By learning the rules of the parenting game and following the advice of the coaches we found, you can raise delightful, competent children like those we met. The game metaphor may be a key in itself: Rather than seeing child rearing as a humorless, lifelong task, make it an interesting, exciting, rewarding challenge. As in any sports game, the parenting game includes delays, fouls, penalties, uncertainty about strategies, lots of mistakes, and yes, touchdowns!

The parents you will meet in this book were like good coaches: disciplined, confident, and willing to try new plays. The more the plays worked, the more they melded into habits—the six habits of highly successful parents.

A BAD TIME FOR GOOD KIDS

One school principal said:

> Many hopeful parents depend on the educational system to teach the rudiments that should be taught at home. But teachers have neither the time nor the inclination to *raise* children—they want to *educate* them.

Today, as educational budgets are slashed and teachers face the Herculean task of disciplining rather than teaching, many of them are losing heart. Some have even left the profession, making your role more critical than ever. Teachers prefer working with self-disciplined, motivated students who can absorb new material.

The principal continued:

> If parents don't watch the rules and get involved in the education process in earnest, students will lose every time. They need to enter the arena *prepared,* and that is exclusively the parents' role.

She went on to say that in order for today's parents to be successful, they had to learn how to deal with today's more complex issues and "counter whatever forces were undermining their children's efforts to survive and thrive." She, and the vast majority of parents we met, believed the most powerful of these forces was the media.

PRIME TIME FOR PROBLEMS

Over and over again, we heard parents decry the uncontrolled use of the media—especially television. They firmly believed that the negative influence of today's permissive media can have a ruinous effect on developing children. "How do violent, scary, and sexually suggestive programs affect kids' self-images? Their values? Their concept of reality? Their *behavior?*" one parent asked rhetorically. Another parent we spoke with did not have to worry about that; he just didn't own a television.

> When something is so earth-shattering or newsworthy that we have to see what's going on because reading about it isn't adequate—like a Superbowl or election or whatnot—we rent a television for a day or two. Otherwise, we find better things to do besides sit for hours in front of the usual mindless drivel that's offered today.

The other parents we met did not exclude television completely, but they did not give their kids carte blanche privileges either. Several said emphatically that when their kids were nine and ten, MTV was "off limits, period." One father went on a bit of a tirade about the merits of watching rock and roll band members strut around "like made-up peacocks," beseeching the crowd to adore them. "Where [in this programming] is the generosity and humility I'm trying to instill in my kids?" he asked. Another parent pointed out how Madison Avenue advertising pros know which buttons to push:

> Our job as parents is to stay nearby and deactivate those buttons. If we don't, our children will find it harder and harder to grow up at their own pace, without their visions of what's real and what's important becoming badly distorted.

Children are not prepared to deal with relentless messages that scream: "Looks are vital to happiness." "Casual, even random sex is the norm." "Violence is a way of life." "Skip childhood! Make yourself over and be an adult *now*!"

Adults may be able to segregate the reality from the fantasy, but when grade school kids flip through television channels and magazine pages designed for mature audiences, what goes on in their malleable minds? One mother said good child rearing requires that parents counter the media's messages aggressively, not passively:

> We've got a fight on our hands and to win it, we have to make bold statements that break through all the hype. Parents have to tell their kids in no uncertain terms that looks, clothing, makeup, trends—all the things our society idolizes—are *not* what matter! Fight back! Tell kids to get with it, get those ideas out of their minds because they're

> not true. The only thing that really matters is what's in your head and your heart.

Confusing for kids? Yes. Who do they listen to? That depends. Parents selected *communication* as the very first of the six keys—and for good reason.

One father said:

> If you can't get through to your children, or worse, they can't get through to you, society will take great liberties with them because they're so ill prepared to distinguish truth from fiction. Illusion then turns into *de*lusion—and sometimes it never ends.

But such problems can be avoided. Using the six habits of highly successful parents, you can wean children out of bad habits such as endless television viewing, chronic consumption, and emphasis on plastic veneers, and lead them into fulfilling activities like reading, hobbies, sports, or playing musical instruments.

Our true experts had ways of introducing positive stimulation without overdoing it. They did not take the lead and decide for their children what was important and where their interests *should* lie; they helped them discover where they *did* lie. They did not impose their own goals on their kids, but many heard of other parents who did just that. Some, they told us, demanded coloring book perfection, 1400+ SAT scores, and participation in every conceivable activity from music appreciation to ballet to art to French to horseback to soccer. One father told us how he, too, fell into this pattern and had a hard time letting go of his high expectations until he realized the problem: They were *his*—not his son's—expectations:

> I was nominated to coach my six-year-old son's team of pint-sized Pelés. I resisted at first, but eventually I found myself looking forward to Saturday afternoons with great anticipation. I started leaving work early on Friday afternoons to go over, for the umpteenth time, ever-so-clever plays I'd devised during the week, praying they would lead our team to victory. But it didn't take long for me to realize that the games were becoming more important to me than to my son. They were actually affecting our relationship. My palpitations over every missed goal should have signaled a red flag that something was all too serious about this activity. Parental perseverance is one thing; obsession with winning is quite another. One comment by my son was the last nail in my coaching coffin: "Dad, I don't want to play soccer this weekend. Couldn't we go fishing or something? I don't really like soccer that much anymore."

So, with this eye-opener, Coach Wilson became Dad again, as he gave up his coaching duties—and his weekend laryngitis—to another eager father who was destined to learn the hard way.

THE SUBPRINCIPLES

Infants need little more than food, sleep, and cuddling; five-year-olds need assurance that their first day of class is not abandonment for life; high school juniors need solid arguments as to why they can't have the car keys to "practice their driving skills"—especially on Friday nights! And if your teenager's cohorts (the ones he'll pick up the moment he dashes out the door with those keys) were raised by parents who let them smoke at thirteen or drink "a few beers" at fifteen, how can you counter those negative influences? How can you fortify your children with the courage to take unpopular stands and say, "No, thanks" to more daring peers whose idea of a good time is a hit of LSD? In short, how can you raise kids to be "great kids" like those we studied, kids with self-reliance, self-control, and solid morals, not to mention proper manners and excellent study habits?

You'll find the answers to these questions as you read about the six habits of highly successful parenting. But before we get to them, it may be helpful to know what other preliminary "subprinciples" were always working within those major issues. These principles are not new, deeply held secrets—but watch closely, for many of their *applications* are.

Heading the list is a greatly undervalued tenet that was one of the mainstays of the families we came to know. Let's look at Respect first.

• ***Respect***

When we asked the question, "What do you think is the most important aspect of raising happy, well-behaved kids?" the most common answers were similar to this parent's: "Treating them with the respect we enjoy as adults, even when they're very young." One mother said, "We never spoke baby talk to our children—even when they were in the crib and didn't understand anything we said."

Another mother told a similar story:

> When Liz was an infant in the hospital, I was holding her and talking away to her. The nurse walked in and said, "You're a good mother." I turned around and asked her what she meant. She said she was amazed at how many mothers didn't say a word to their newborn children. She felt that they didn't respect their babies as highly intelligent little people who were anxious to learn about the world and who deserved dignity from day one.

One father said that when he had serious disagreements with his older children, he would sit down with them and discuss what they thought it meant to be a good child and what they thought *he* should do to be a good father:

> It may seem that I left myself open for abuse with this seemingly lenient system—and believe me, there is such a thing as parent abuse too—but it rarely occurred. My kids knew better and they knew I would call them on it if they pushed their limits. It never happened, though, I'm sure because of the mutual respect we had for each other.

This father asked for—and *listened* to—his children's opinions, which, he said, not only led to a better understanding between them, but to their appreciation of his role as parent and guide.

- ***Admiration***

The magic of admiration is hard to describe. It, too, instills respect, but it does even more. It instills *self*-respect and further secures parent/child bonds. Though it always came from their hearts, the true experts acknowledged that one of the unintended results of their admiration was better behavior by their kids. The mother of one fifteen-year-old boy said that regularly, but not too frequently, she would just blurt out, "You're a neat kid! We really enjoy having you around." That was it. Then she would go about her business.

As we discuss in Chapter 4 on self-esteem, the key to having admiration mean something is that it has to be truly genuine and not contrived to bolster a child's ego. If her demeanor doesn't warrant such a comment, she'll be the first to spot it.

• *Unconditional Love*

Unconditional love—with no strings attached—combined with empathy and understanding strengthens the bonds between parent and child. Mr. Phelan, the father of a high school student body president, told us that when his daughter was fifteen years old, it was his policy to allow her to practice driving the family car up and down the driveway. While putting the car in the garage after one driving session, she accidentally hit the accelerator instead of the brake, crashing the Country Squire through the back wall—and Sapphire the parrot's cage.

> When the feathers settled and Susie crept into the house, pale and quivering like a frightened puppy, she was sobbing and sniffling, trying to explain what happened. I just pulled her close, hugged her, and told her not to try and explain, it didn't make any difference at all. "Now you'll never forget where the brake pedal is. And I'm sure glad, because you're a lot harder to fix than the car—or Sapphire."

• *Expectancy*

Having their kids in the top percentage of the class was not a compulsion with the true experts. There was no money-for-grades policy, nor did they pressure their children to compete. Instead, there was an implied "quiet expectancy" in these high-achievement homes that suggested, "Since you're capable, and you're putting the time in anyway, why not get an A while you're at it?"

One grandmother who lived with the family told us that when her daughter, Mrs. Hopper (Dixie's mother), would say, "Oh, that's good enough," she would quickly counter with, "Good enough is never good enough!" It must have sunk in. When we interviewed the group, Dixie was preparing to leave for UCLA, having achieved straight A's in her honors classes without any pressure other than Mrs. Hopper's motto: "We don't have *medium* in our vocabulary."

Whether the issue was scholastic performance, chores around the house, or sibling cohabitation, because of the expectancy that prevailed in the homes we visited, children tried to do well. They were not told to do well; they were told they were *capable.*

Cheryl Yee was another student who had just graduated from high school when we interviewed her and her parents. She was preparing to leave for college a few weeks later where she was to begin courses in a premed program. Though she finished at the top of her senior class, she started years earlier at the *bottom* of her first-grade class:

> I was born in China and since I was the third child, I wasn't allowed to go to school. Only two were allowed to go. We moved so I could enroll, but when I did, I had a very difficult time. I could speak only Mandarin and the classes were in Cantonese. After my first year, I came in thirty-second out

of thirty-three kids! I was very unhappy. But my parents did not worry. They said I would do well and they expected me to. When we came to this country and I could see the struggle they went through to provide a home and opportunity to learn, I understood very well why they viewed a B grade as just average. They believed A's were normal and attainable. When there was an honors class offered, my parents wanted me in it, and they expected me to be in the top 10 percent. I always was.

• ***Friendship***

When we asked Dixie why she thought she had such a smooth childhood and needed so little intervention as she grew up, she responded without any hesitation and with her mother sitting right beside her:

> My mom's my best friend, and you respect your friends. We've always been really tight. I could always go to her no matter what, and like any loyal friend, I never wanted to disappoint her. Plus, she trusted me. I didn't want to let her down.

Sometimes such a relationship can make it difficult to separate friendship from parenting duties. Fortunately, Mrs. Hopper rarely needed to discipline Dixie. But as we talked, she remembered one of those few occasions when Dixie was a young teenager and had to be restricted for something (she couldn't remember what). She recalled blurting out, "You're grounded for a week!" but then she panicked and quickly asked, "You didn't have anything planned for this weekend, did you?" As she and Dixie laughed uproariously, remembering the incident well, we could see they were indeed great companions who enjoyed each other very much. They were friends far more than they were authority figure and child, and it was obvious that their friendship was a big factor in Dixie's success.

Another parent put it succinctly: "Harmony and a pleasant home life—everything comes from that."

Adding to this philosophy, a mother of three highly successful children continued:

> Fairness is the fountain of ethics required for good parenting. Always keep that in mind. Ask yourself before reprimanding or disciplining: Is this fair? Is it reasonable? Would *I* like it? Will this better our relations and keep peace in the family, or am I out to prove I'm the parent and that I won't take any flak from my kids?

Another mother stated her parenting philosophy this way: "It's a feeling of friendship—more than any strategies you can devise—that makes good kids."

- ***Balance***

A high percentage of two-parent families had the same equation: rather strict fathers and considerably more lenient, flexible mothers. But the coupling worked because *compromise* and *communication* prevented either extreme from prevailing. One mother, for example, described herself as a "very liberal Democrat" who was always willing to listen to her son, while her husband was a staunch "conservative Republican" who rarely did. When we entered their home for our interview, we could immediately see their different personalities reflected in their hobbies. The father was quite an accomplished sculptor and had displayed large, ornately carved birds around the living room. His rigid, disciplined style came through clearly in the detailed works. The mother, on the other hand, was a free-spirited type who enjoyed gardening and outdoor activities. She enjoyed watching things grow naturally (including her son), but felt she was too loose with him at times. She felt coupling her liberalism with her husband's stricter style balanced their parenting effort, resulting in sensible decisions neither would have made alone.

Another couple had the opposite dispositions. The mother was the authority figure and the father was a folksy, relaxed type who called things as he saw them. Here's an example:

> One night I came home a little late. Joan had already served dinner, but there was a sullen cloud hanging over the table. "Hi, gang!" I said. Then Barbara, who was about ten then, looks over with a long face. Trudy, her eight-year-old sister, had a sour puss, too. "What's going on, gang?" I asked. And Joan says, "They don't want to eat their asparagus, Walt." Then I saw why. She had served *canned* asparagus, you know, those sort of yellowish-white ones. I took one look at those things and said, "Well, who can *blame* them, honey? Eating those slimy things is like eating banana slugs!" You could hear the cheer go up all the way down the street!

One German father, who met us at the door wearing a starched white dress shirt and slicked-back salt-and-pepper hair, described himself, in a heavy German accent, as an old country parent and admitted that he tended toward rigidity. His wife, on the other hand, a delightful, smiling woman of South American descent, was full of warmth, forgiveness, and love. She was highly religious and made several references to God and Jesus during our talk. (Spirituality was high on the majority of parents' lists, as we will discuss in Chapter 5.) She said one of her main goals was family harmony, and she went to great lengths to maintain it.

Once, when her daughter was fourteen and wanted to go to the movie with a boy for the first time, she had to excuse herself and her husband from the debate, and physically yank him into the kitchen to convince him that his staunch refusal to give his permission was fear-based and unreasonable.

> "Claus!" I said in an impassioned "whisper" that you could hear throughout the house. "She's old enough! She's fourteen. You'll *never* think she's old enough, but this is part of her growing up. Now we *have* to let her go! And besides, we're driving her, picking her up, and taking her for ice cream after. What in the world can go wrong?"

After an animated-but-destined-to-fail rebuttal, it was agreed that yes, daughters do grow up and yes, fathers have to, too.

We found one final element to maintaining a balance between parents: When you aren't sure about an admonishment or are not prepared for an unusual request from your kids, *put off* making that decision. The parents we met did not allow their children to pressure them into a hasty decision. They maintained control and decided the issue on their terms and their timetables. Despite differences in their own personalities, this helped them to arrive at mutually supported decisions.

THE PARENTING JOURNEY

If you are a new parent and just beginning your journey, you no doubt feel some trepidation as you survey the "parenting jungle." If you have ventured into it before—only to fight python and piranha at every turn—you probably didn't realize that it doesn't have to be that way!

Use this book as a reference guide from those who have traversed the terrain already. The parents we interviewed have been where you are going, so they can caution you in advance on where the trail narrows. Though they arrived at their destinations relatively unscathed, the going wasn't always a breeze. It got rough in spots, they suffered a few blisters and twisted ankles, and they had to slay a few unexpected beasts along the way. But that's the point of this book: They have done it so you won't have to; they have erected the guideposts to keep you on track.

Perhaps the best approach to your parenting expedition is to see the years ahead as miles on the trail. As with most backpacking trips, the first few miles are usually uphill—and heavy. The pack is loaded and the vertical elevation is dead ahead. But by mile eight or ten, you've hit your stride. Things have leveled off and you're moving along at a jaunty clip. Mile thirteen might be a killer, but around mile eighteen, a meadow appears in the distance with lush green grass and a cool brook babbling over the rocks. Time to set up base camp and pull out the old fly rod; the journey is over.

And what about the great kid who hiked alongside you? She'll return to camp from time to time, but for now, she's off to "bag a peak," as climbers say. She's got granite cliffs to scale and thanks to you, she'll be well equipped to tackle them. After having learned from you to believe in herself enough to take calculated risks, handle the stress, and then forge ahead, determined to meet her goals, she will gain a sense of purpose to her life. Rather than struggling to cope with the world, she will stand on her mountaintop and welcome it with open arms.

Before starting on the first chapter, you may find it interesting, as we did, to read the personal essay of one delightful young woman who was preparing to leave home for her first year at college. It was submitted to her college admissions board who, like employers, friends, future spouses, and society in general, were looking for well-rounded, likeable people. This essay exemplifies the strong character, vivacity, charm, and appreciation that can develop in a child when she is raised in a caring family—regardless of its structure and apparent disadvantages.

> Divorce. The big "D" word. No one likes to mention it. It's the terrible ordeal that scars families for life. But not for me. My parents' divorce, when I was six months old, turned out to be one of the best things that could have happened to me.
>
> My mom and I moved into my grandparents' home. It was a center of activity, filled with love and the bustle of people of all ages. I never lacked for a father figure because my grandfather and uncles helped to instill in me a sense of security. I always had a lap to sit on and a friend to play cards with. Their unconditional love and support was always with me. They were understanding and nonjudgmental, treating my views and opinions as important, rather than discarding them because I was young.

The strongest support came from my best friend—my mom. She developed in me a love for music, books, and life. We went to the *Nutcracker* every year, and I became interested in the performing arts. With the confidence she and my family instilled in me, I got the part of Mona in our school musical, *Chicago.* My mom and grandfather came to the play every night. Mom took an active role in the behind-the-scenes preparations, and my grandfather unfailingly started the standing ovation after each and every performance! I love them very much.

It's funny. I always assumed that every family was like mine. Only recently have I realized that not everybody sits down to a family dinner each night like we did, and not every child receives the kind of love and support that I did.

In the end, my parent's divorce really didn't have a negative impact on my achievements—it had a positive one! After all, not every kid had a wonderful grandfather who coached her softball team, practiced her positioning on the basketball court, or helped her with her homework—and even made it fun!

CHAPTER 1

COMMUNICATE

With only seconds of fuel left, Mission Control urgently radioed astronaut Neil Armstrong, imploring him to land the *Eagle* at once or risk crashing onto the moon's craggy surface. Responding immediately, Armstrong snapped off the autopilot, grabbed the controls, and manually guided the spacecraft to a smooth, safe landing. Successful communications, a successful mission. Without good communication, there would have been a tragedy.

Tragic, too, are the longings of children who cry out for guidance in their own journeys through life, only to find no one is listening. How long will a toddler tug at her parent's sleeve before giving up? How long will a sensitive adolescent try to share her joys and sorrows, her fears and aspirations, with parents who are too absorbed in their own frenetic lives? What happens to these once-eager children when they are not allowed to *communicate*?

Though all six habits of successful child rearing are integrally related, we have put communication first because it is the starting point, the bedrock upon which the other five rest. What is the very first thing a parent does with a newborn baby? Try to develop her intellect? Discipline her? Teach her values? No, these things come later, as do our chapters discussing them. Immediately upon seeing her infant for the first time, a mother tries to *communicate* with her. And in the families we met, the process never stopped.

Of all the parenting skills we will discuss in this book, communication is probably the most difficult—and the most neglected. When we broached this subject with one mother, shortly after the birth of her first son, she recalled the time her feisty, eighty-five-year-old neighbor stopped by. When the new mother asked the woman for any child-rearing tips she might wish to offer, without hesitation, the elderly grandmother trumpeted out one great parenting proclamation in her loud, cackling voice: "You TALK to him, THAT'S what you do!"

At the beginning of this and the other five key chapters, we examine the problems most parents face. Then, we move on to show through snippets of everyday life how the parents we met resolved—or headed off—those problems. In this chapter you will see the many ways in which communication is accomplished, such as being available, reserving special times for talking, listening and responding effectively, knowing when *not* to help your child express herself, and communicating your own messages when necessary. You will see that communicating—and child rearing in general—does not have to be the exhausting, somber, troubling experience it is for so many. One mother's sage advice exemplifies this point:

When you're raising kids, don't make the mistake so many parents do. Don't take things too personally. Your kids will say things for reasons they, you, *no one* understands. Case in point: Tom was growing about an inch a month and was always ravenously hungry. One day he came in the door giving lip. Do you think I listened? Do you think I got upset? No. I just ignored it, sat him down, and fed him! After that, he was the same pussycat he always is.

DEFINING COMMUNICATION AND ITS PROBLEMS

What is communication? "*Communicate: To reveal; to convey; to have connection with; interchange of thoughts or information.*" This definition is right out of Webster's dictionary, but it might as well be Swahili for most American families.

If astronauts floating on a barren rock in outer space can communicate so clearly with Houston's Mission Control, why is it so difficult to connect with kids in the next room? Probably because they have retreated into their own lunar atmospheres where they don't have to listen to parents anymore! Webster's "interchange of information" often deteriorates into indifference and confrontation between parents and children. "Interchange" becomes aggression, criticism, judgment, and blame. The result? Parents broadcast away on AM while kids tune into FM. Messages received? Zero. If by some quirk, parents and kids do cross wires and connect on the same wavelength, the reception is so loaded with static, it's unbearable to listen to. And what do you do with scratchy radio stations? You shut them off. *Static occurs when children's needs develop faster than their parent's communication skills.*

Listening. Talking. Not talking. Being there when necessary. Not being there when appropriate. Respecting children's right to privacy—and their right to *not* communicate. These are the communication skills you must develop if you want to raise great kids.

Before we go on, try asking yourself the following questions honestly and make a note of the areas you think may need improvement. As you read the anecdotes from the true experts, refer back to these questions and compare what you might have done with what they actually did:

- Whether she is five or fifteen, can you really look at your child and hear what she is saying? Are you sure you grasp the *meaning* behind her words?
- Have you let go of preconceived notions of what your child means or what, in your view, she *should* mean?
- Can your child understand *you* or is she threatened and intimidated by you?
- Does your child have the right to say what she needs to say and is she comfortable doing it?
- Has your communication developed to the point where you trust each other enough to honestly express your hopes, your joys, your secrets, *and* your failings?

Let's start by taking a look at one of the biggest problems today's parents and kids face: the communication gap. In some families it may be only a small fissure; in others, it dwarfs the Grand Canyon.

THE COMMUNICATION GAP

Some years ago, a group of seven thousand preteen and teenaged students wrote anonymous letters for a national PTA project. When all the letters were considered, the prominent message was: "We wish we could talk to our parents, but we don't know how. Neither do they." Such a communication gap forms because (1) parents talk too much and (2) they fail to listen to their kids. One top student put it this way:

> Instead of opening up and listening to what is going on with kids, parents are busy with their own agendas. They're set in their own ways. When they won't listen to their kids, they send the message: "Keep quiet, your views are not important." So kids take their advice and stop talking. While they're at it, they stop listening, too, just like their Moms and Dads.

What's the solution? Close the communication gap. How? We asked the experts.

> When this happens to other parents—and it will—they've got to begin closing the communication gap by making the *first overture.* Show a *willingness* to listen. Listen to new ideas, to new ways of looking at kids' problems, even to silence. When people are considerate enough to listen to your point of view, you're more willing to listen to theirs.

Keep the following thoughts in mind as you try to narrow the communication chasm—or better yet, prevent one from forming:

- If you are moving too fast in your own world, it is impossible to see into your child's world. It is like looking out of the window of a train as another one speeds by in the opposite direction: Everything's a blur. Your child needs you to slow down and explore both worlds with her.
- As we will say many times in this book, your child needs to know that you have experienced what she is experiencing. Communicate your feelings, your thoughts, and your emotions to her. Tell her that even you, her protector and guide, have made mistakes and suffered failures, too. But in the end, they turned out to be learning experiences.

> When Audrey was struggling with something, I'd relate a similar circumstance that happened to me at that age. Kids don't want advice at times like that, they want compassion, understanding. When she fell off her tricycle once, she came in bleeding from a skinned hand. But that wasn't what hurt. She felt she was a terrible tricycle rider. She said, "I can't ride my bike!" and then started crying. I said, "Look," and showed her the scar under my chin from when I fell off my own tricycle and hit the metal bell ringer. She stopped crying right away. She was fascinated by the scar, by the fact that her own mother did the exact same thing she just did. She felt a lot better knowing I fell off too.

- When your child learns she can come to you for little things when she is little, she will come to you for big things when she is big. One mother reminisced laughingly about the time her son, a college freshman, did just that.

> When his pile of dirty clothes got so big he couldn't move around his dorm room, he called home and said, "Okay, Mom. I've got to do the laundry. Was it clothes first, then detergent, or detergent first, then clothes?"

- Your child needs to know that you will consider her ideas and her requests. When she desires something very much, she relies on you to help her get it. It is when she doesn't think you are listening to her needs that frustrations mount. The following vignette is a case in point. When a sixteen-year-old high schooler asked—for the hundredth time—to borrow her mother's coveted down vest, the answer was, as usual, "No." But that wasn't the end of the story:

> I remember Anne asking again for the down vest about a week before. Then suddenly one night when she went out to the county fair with her friends, I noticed it was gone. It wasn't hanging on the coat rack by the front door anymore. She had made no attempt to put another jacket in its place or hide the fact that she took my down vest. I couldn't believe it! Then, as the blood was starting to boil, it struck me like a ton of bricks: She really, really, *really* wanted to wear that vest! I had no idea it was so important to her until that night. Sitting there staring at where it used to be, I realized she just *had* to have it! It was like, earthshaking to her—and I hadn't been hearing that. I calmed down and never said a word about it. Neither did she.

Mrs. Goldberg went on to give us a critically important bit of parenting wisdom—one that, if parents really grasped it, would mitigate all kinds of child-rearing problems: *Kids don't intend to hurt their parents, so don't take what they do personally.*

Thinking about their own needs instead of their parents', as in Anne's case, may be immature or selfish, but it is a very different thing from intentional disobedience.

Contributing to the communication gap is the *generation gap.* If you have ever tried arguing the merits of Beethoven or even the Beatles over the latest rap or heavy metal group, you know how wide that gap can be. Sure, every generation believes the one before it was square and out of touch, but today's teenagers seem to be the most inventive to date.

Those perfect Norman Rockwell poster kids, who once wore starched white shorts and polished leather shoes, now "hang" at the mall in shredded blue jeans, combat boots, reverse-billed baseball caps, and CD players permanently transplanted to half-shaved heads. If your kid is one of them, give thanks that she hasn't come home with an infected, red nostril from a trendy new nose ring. (Better check her navel, too.)

One father told us neither he nor his wife interfered with their fourteen-year-old daughter's need to "express herself" through what she called "awesomely outrageous" clothing, which, of course, was in total conformance with the rest of her group:

> Tina went through the army-fatigue-jacket-black-lipstick stage about the same time she discovered boys. She was

moody and nonresponsive, didn't want to do her chores, lived on the phone, and all the rest. But her grades were fine, so who were we to strap her into a straitjacket of our own making? She had her own identity—or was trying to—so it really wasn't our job to get in the way of that process. Anyway, somewhere between fifteen and sixteen, she went up to her room one day, wiped off the makeup, took off the rows of bracelets and earrings, and came down transformed into a natural, mature young woman, suddenly interested in talking politics and college.

Take a look at what is going on between you and your child. See the dynamics. Are you both relaxed and open, free to say whatever is on your mind? Do you let your child express herself as she sees fit? Or are you strained and tense like two circling tigers, constantly growling and swiping at each other? If you are, pay special attention to this next section.

CONTROLLING EMOTIONS

We use communication to instruct, to learn, to relate to one another, but most important, to *express our feelings.* To a significant degree, how we control our emotions determines how successful that expression will be. Our state of mind—anger, sadness, anxiety—can affect what we intend to say and can dramatically distort what we *think* we hear.

Kids of all ages employ an array of parent-irritating tactics. One mother called it "parent abuse": Three-year-olds screech and whine, seven-year-olds interrupt; then, by thirteen, the once-clingy kids decide it's "uncool" even to be seen with their parents, let alone comply with the simplest of requests. During trying times like these, when parents have been pushed to their limits, unplanned emotional outbursts can devastate insecure kids.

"Get out of my sight!" "You're such an idiot!" "You're more trouble than you're worth!" Such inflammatory blasts are attacks, and attacks draw defensive responses and foster deeply felt resentment, as Mrs. Scarpelli found out when she laced into her fifteen-year-old daughter, Jina:

> I don't remember what she did, but she made me absolutely nuts one day and I screamed out in a rage, "I hate you!" Suddenly the argument was over. Dead silence. She walked into her room and held me to that stupid comment, which, of course, I didn't mean. It lasted for months! I couldn't believe she wouldn't forgive me. I kept saying to her, "How many times do I have to tell you I love you? Doesn't that count for anything?" But Jina was just devastated by my comment even though she knew I was in a snit at the time. I had no idea a slip like that could have such an impact.

The following statement is one we will repeat often. It should not become trite because it is the very essence of parenting: *More than anything else, children learn their behaviors by watching their parents.*

Because your child will try to emulate you so closely, be sure your communication with everyone—her, your spouse, friends, strangers—is *calm* and *considerate.* Try to stay rational—even when it is a Herculean effort—because if your young child sees you arguing and yelling, she will learn that this is how people communicate. Not only does emotion-laden language block communication, it may cause a child to feel *she* is the cause of the conflict. Or worse, she may feel that at any moment, either she will be abandoned by her parents or they are going to destroy each other.

The following story comes from a couple who had bickered regularly in front of their child until one day they were stunned by something their child did. It finally woke them up to the realization that their abusive combat was terribly disturbing to their young son.

> I'll never forget when Aaron was only six, and as usual, Mort and I were at it in the kitchen, screaming and yelling, trying to force each other to change our minds. It got pretty hot and heavy and then Aaron leaps in between us and physically pushes us apart, screaming at the top of his lungs, "STOP FIGHTING! STOP FIGHTING!" Suddenly, Mort and I were silent and just looked at each other. Then we looked down at this little guy with swollen red eyes and outspread arms holding us apart. It was pitiful. We never, as long as we lived, argued in front of that child again.

A parent we interviewed held to one immutable rule, one that could have prevented the scene described above.

> The most important rule of communication in our house, one that we just would not tolerate any deviation from, was simply this: No yelling, period. We just didn't allow it and we would not condone it—ever.

She went on to explain how her own mother always used a calm-but-persuasive tone of voice with the grandchildren, and it never failed to get results.

> Mom just had to say in her slow, no-nonsense way, "Put that down, and you know I mean it," and like magic, the kids just, well, put it down! I don't know what it was, but they understood her and knew darn well she wasn't kidding. She was always calm, never raised her voice. It was amazing how they respected that.

She adhered to another rule just as strictly as she did the "No Yelling Rule." It was called the "Polite Rule."

> Whether the kids were in the mood to talk or not, the rule was, they had to at least acknowledge the other members of the family with a "Hello" when they came into the room or a "Good-bye" or "Good night" when they left. I didn't care what their problem was or why they were in a bad mood, they still had to be decent enough to be part of the family to this degree.

TALKING TURNOFFS

Parents seldom realize how noxious some of their comments are. If they dared videotape a typical dinner, they would be shocked to see how much negativity spews forth during an average meal: "Get those elbows off the table!" "You're not going anywhere until you finish those peas!" "Who do I look like, the *maid*?"

Here are some of the most common forms of negative communication, all of which hurt children, sometimes very deeply. Try to avoid them:

Criticism

Negative criticism is toxic. It creates anger and a desire for revenge, and it teaches children that faultfinding is perfectly acceptable. After constantly criticizing her fourteen-year-old about being underweight, Mrs. Dunn's son one day turned the tables and devastated her with a comment about her own weight problem:

> It was bad enough that I couldn't eat anything without feeling guilty, but then Jeremy strolls in with his buddies after school one day just as I was finishing, of all things, the bottom of the ice cream container! "Why are you eating that if you don't want to be fat?" he asked with a smirk. I was mortified. All his friends were standing there waiting, along with him, for an answer. And there I was in a pair of stretch pants I had no business in, thirty pounds overweight, just scarfing up about a thousand extra calories—and getting caught by my own kid and his lynch mob! I couldn't help believe it was because I was always all over him for being too skinny and *not* eating enough at dinner. I guess I got my just desserts, pardon the pun.

Accusations

"You're lazy." When parents keep this one up, guess what? Kids get lazier and lazier. "You're dumb." Response? Grades drop. One teacher we talked with said:

> Accusations are attacks, and it takes awfully good—and rare—ethics to just turn the other cheek and take it. Kids respond with counterattacks, so the battles go on and on.

A father we talked to described what his boy's reaction was when he accused him of mismanaging his summer earnings:

> It was obvious: I made a mistake. Gunnar was hoping to rent a nice apartment when he went off to Dartmouth, but when it came time to leave, he told me he hadn't saved enough for the one he wanted. I blurted out that if he hadn't blown his money on a new saxophone and a bunch of other stuff he didn't need—according to me—he wouldn't have this problem now. Well, I saw his face go white and he shut down completely. I knew I blew it. When I went back into his room and asked him if he was all right, he said yes, but I knew he was hurting.

Instructing

The first reason to avoid "teaching" is, your information might be flawed. If you have been *talking* instead of *listening,* you may not even understand your child's problem. Worse yet, if she already knows what you're telling her, why put her through a laborious lecture again? Unnecessary monologues block her from participating in the conversation and lessen the likelihood that she will be receptive next time. Unless you have some important new facts to impart to an eager audience, let professional teachers do the teaching. Said one mother:

> Rinnie had been driving over a year, but I still put her through driver's ed every time she took the car out at night—seatbelts, gas, watching out for crazies. This is when Rinnie would start rolling her eyes and twirling her hair. And she was justified. How many times did she have to say, "I know," before I got it?

Helping

By "helping" your child finish sentences she is perfectly capable of finishing herself, you tell her she is incapable of thinking things out, and you *decrease* her ability to deal with problems. Resist the urge to help—one of the hardest habits to break—and you will see she is quite capable of handling what *you* think are difficult situations. Sometimes the issue she first presents may not even be the real problem, so give her time to get there. Here's advice from another counselor we spoke with who worked with high-achieving students:

> Wait patiently when your child is trying to communicate. She may lose her thought or just plain stop in midsentence. Kids hem and haw or sometimes just gibber away or take off on wild soliloquies. What they're doing is testing the waters to see if you're in a receptive mood before plunging in. "What's the matter, dear?" is *not* what she needs to hear.

The counselor went on to suggest the following tips that he believed would be useful when tempted to help inappropriately:

- Remember that when you "help" your child by asking "What's the matter?" at a time when she is obviously not ready to divulge what the matter is, she will interpret it as prying, and she'll be right.
- Don't hurry your child along or try to project what *you* think she might be trying to say. For one thing, you might be wrong. Then what? Just keep guessing? "Is it . . . ? Well then, is it . . . ? O.K. How about . . . ?"
- Accept her decision to change the subject, hesitate, or drop the whole thing. If it's important, she'll bring it up again—*if* you've created a hassle-free environment.

- Kids rarely want to pour out the entire contents of their minds for parental examination—and the lambasting that comes with it. Don't ask them to do it.

Nagging

If you play back that tape recorder you had running at dinner, you will hear what you *thought* was "reminding," but it won't sound like it. A mother we spoke with told us:

> After three years of trying to get Tyler to wear matching socks to no avail, I just gave up and realized that he was perfectly content to wear whatever he wanted. I was a whole lot happier when I let go of the issue. He ended up in engineering at MIT anyway, and he's still as color-blind—and happy—as ever.

Here's a potpourri of nagging techniques to avoid. Our parents found them to be futile for changing behavior and often damaging to relationships:

- *Warning.* "Once more and you'll be in real trouble." Since these rarely get any follow-up, kids usually respond mentally with, "Oh, wow, I'm really scared."
- *Interrogating.* "I want to know where you were and what you did all this time!" Do you really think your fifteen-year-old is going to give you a detailed account of her day?
- *Threatening.* "You're going to be grounded for a month if you don't get this C up to an A!" Not exactly an incentive to try harder. Many an adolescent would test such a threat with a mental. "We'll just see about that," and abruptly drop the C to a D.

- *Judging.* A friend of one father told him she knew she had blundered when she told her eleven-year-old daughter, "Don't worry, Wendy, when you get older, we'll get that nose of yours fixed." (Great, Mom. What do I do in the meantime?)

ACCEPTING SILENCE

"How was your algebra test today?"
"O.K."
"What did your friend call about?"
"Nothing."
"Are you going to the game this weekend?"
Shrug.

Not getting anywhere? That's because you are more interested in talking than your child is. Before you can have an intelligible conversation, your child has to be present—physically, mentally, and emotionally. If any of the three are missing, he is not ready to talk, so accept his reticence; such understanding is the one thing that *will* bring him closer later. In the meantime, prepare yourself for one of the most irritating, sometimes frightening behaviors of all: silence.

To allay your fears that your son must be dealing drugs or your daughter is surely pregnant, recognize silence as a normal, natural mechanism kids use at various stages of development. They often need desperately to retreat into their own clamshells for their own reasons. Our experts' advice? Don't worry about those reasons.

One high school principal said:

> Don't play Sherlock Holmes and go snooping around trying to dig up hidden meanings every time your kid is less at-

> tentive than you think he should be. Worry more about entering where you are not welcome—a disrespectful intrusion based more on curiosity than anything else.

One parent explained her daughter's technique for avoiding unwanted conversation when she was not in the mood. When Louise was a little girl and was mad about something and did not want to talk, she would talk through her stuffed animals.

> Louise had one teddy bear in particular that she referred to as her sister. When I came in to talk, she would put her bear in front of her face and say, "Sister is not talking today. She doesn't want to talk to anybody." So I'd play along and ask, "Why doesn't Sister want to talk?" And she'd usually answer, "Because Sister just doesn't want to," or "Because Sister's mad at you." And with that I'd say fine and ask why she was mad or whatever. Sometimes I'd get a dialogue going, sometimes I wouldn't. But I wouldn't push.

Children must be allowed to retreat into their own worlds without parental intrusion. Only when a child feels it is safe, and the predator is gone, will she open her shell a crack and take a peek around. Don't be standing there with a crowbar ready to pry her open!

On the other hand, if the silence goes on longer than usual, and you feel it really is time to make some connection, try another one of the experts' strategies: *reverse psychology.* Rather than pry, back off. Show *less* interest. Prodding children at the wrong time is about as effective as coaxing new puppies to come to you. As you may recall if you've ever tried it, pups are nervous, uncertain what to do.

Instead of coming when you call them, they go off in the opposite direction. But if you sit down and do nothing—no whistling, no clapping, no hand extending, no funny kissing sounds—they eventually come sniffing around. Why? Because you're *not* interested!

MAKING COMMUNICATION POSSIBLE

How do you make your child feel comfortable coming to you and then open up when she gets there? *Attitude.* External signs communicate internal feelings. Facial expressions, body postures, and tone of voice are clues, without which your child can only guess at your willingness to interact. For example, when spoken in a flat, unenthusiastic tone, the words *I love you* impart little sincerity. But when a mother throws open her arms, opens her mouth in a gleaming smile of joy, with eyebrows arched and eyes twinkling, she at once expresses to her child how much he means to her—without uttering a word!

To send sincere messages, delay discussions when you are in a bad mood or preoccupied with something else. Just saying, "That's great, honey," or "I'm so glad" is not convincing. You have to *be* glad. You have to *feel* it and *express* it. Make your delight equal to your child's. Put yourself in her shoes for a moment and see life from her perspective.

Before you can express yourself, though, you have to be *available*—the next step to closing the communication gap. This means setting aside special times for talking and being ready to discuss uncomfortable subjects. Our experts had plenty to say about both issues.

BE AVAILABLE

If parents had a video camera running during a typical morning, the tape would show just how unavailable they sometimes are. It might look something like this: the coffee is brewing and the paper just landed on the front steps. Details of your upcoming business meeting buzz in your head as your four-year-old silently watches you shave from just beyond the bathroom door. He knows this is not the time to try talking to Daddy. Cut. Next scene: The paper is open, you're wolfing down your toast, gulping your coffee, rapidly scanning the news. No chance for Junior here either. As you zoom off in your car, your son watches silently from the living room window. Whatever thoughts he had fade away as your car fades into the distance.

How would you edit this tape and correct the situation? Perhaps by first recognizing your child's need to interact with you, busy or not, and by *making yourself available.* As we discovered when we related the above example to one father, his solution is really quite simple:

> Drink your coffee, eat breakfast, read the paper, talk to your spouse, pet the dog, call the office, and listen to your kid—all at the same time! Sound tough? It's not as hard as it seems. And hey, this is what raising kids is all about. No one said it would be easy, no one said you'd have the same time to yourself as you did before you had kids. That's just one of the sacrifices—if you really see it as one.

Another parent explained how, over the years, you will find your child needing more and more of your time:

> When kids are very young, all they usually need is a tight snuggle and a lot of smiles. They need assurance that they're loved. Later, they need more recognition and a good sounding board. That's the problem a lot of parents have—*they* make all the sounds instead of letting their kids bounce things off them. If kids aren't heard, they feel pushed off to the side. You've got to pay attention to their needs or you'll plant the seeds of resentment that can bring untold problems later on.

Younger children don't need detailed, intellectual conversations. They just need to know you are there and that you care about their army men's fatalities or their dolly's cold. A little sympathy is very reassuring. But if you seem unavailable—or worse, *uninterested*—young children can feel insignificant or even burdensome to their busy parents.

The bigger danger in not being available is: Sometimes children have things to discuss that really *are* important. Since you are the only one they can depend on to listen, what happens if you've tuned them out? Who can they turn to then? Such was the case with one eight-year-old who was suffering from nightmares. In the following anecdote, his mother explains how inept she had been in taking clues about a serious, underlying disturbance:

> At first I shrugged off John's mention of devil dreams because, for one, I didn't want to encourage them and two, I thought they might just be a passing thing. I didn't take them seriously and I even ignored them for a while. But after a few days, I realized something more might be going on, so each night after I tucked him in, I sat awhile and slowly and gently coaxed him a little. I was very careful not

> to move too quickly, and over and over I told John, "You know, there's nothing you can't tell me if you ever think you want to. If something's bothering you, I want to help you get over it. That's what moms are for. But if not, that's okay, too." It took several nights, but after he was comfortable with our bedtime routine, he finally came out with the fact that an older boy had molested him near the schoolyard and the dreams of the devil were really about this boy. I immediately called a counselor, and therapy helped him get over the incident.

A student we talked with explained how vital it is for parents to be available when things go wrong. She told us how relieved she was when someone finally stopped and listened to her. But she had worked herself into a panic before anyone did.

> When I was starting kindergarten, I had a terrible experience my first day of school. The neighbor girl, Amy, was supposed to walk me to my class when we got off the bus, but she didn't. She ran off and left me! I was petrified. I was crying and all upset. The next morning I didn't want to go to school, but I didn't say why, so my mom and dad had no idea. They probably thought it was normal butterflies. But I was scared to death of getting left alone again. No way was I getting back on that bus! When the bus came, I was holding on to the kitchen cabinet knobs so hard that when my dad tried to pull me away, I ripped them right off! Thank God he realized something was really wrong and didn't make me get on that bus. When he drove me to school, I told him what had happened the day before.

SPECIAL TIMES FOR TALKING

Kids are astute. If you are genuinely unavailable to talk, such as when you are running to a dentist appointment, children understand this. One couple explained how they learned a simple technique to handle this problem from their own parents in Hong Kong:

> When Lydia was very young and had to tell us something at a time when we were too busy to talk, we allowed her to talk, as we said, "Just a little bit," [mother gestures with thumb and first finger]. Instead of making her keep it all in, we let her tell us the basics, enough to make her feel better, and then we told her we would discuss it later when we weren't so busy. She accepted this and always felt better getting whatever it was off her mind. Most of the time she never brought it up again anyway.

As we saw with John's mother, when children are younger, the quiet period around bedtime is ideal for offering your undivided attention. Since their concerns are usually less complex than adolescents', a few minutes together may be all they need. One busy lawyer mother we met relied heavily on these bedtime meetings until her children were eight. She called them "staysies." During these private moments, she would lay down beside them, turn off the lights, and just "stay" for a while as her children told her whatever was on their mind, good or bad. This was a time for *listening*, not *talking*.

> First, I would say, "Tell me one good thing that happened today," and they would tell me about their school day or

what they did with their friend after school, you know, that kind of thing. Then, after they told their story, I would say, "Tell me one bad thing that happened today." I felt that if I gave the two equal billing without suggesting there were problems, anything that might be bothering them would be more likely to come to the surface, and it often did. Then without showing too much concern, I'd discuss it with the same interest as the good thing they'd brought up. Whatever the problem, it was always much easier for them to bring up during our quiet, staysies time. Maybe it's because it was all dark and quiet and we weren't looking at each other. All I know is, if I ever thought I could skip a staysies, I'd be sorely reminded with, "Maaaaaa, when are you coming up?"

Adolescents' meetings need to be of greater length because their concerns are of greater complexity. And they need to be *uninterrupted.* Don't try to hold summit meetings at the kitchen sink, in front of the television, while telephones are ringing, or when other siblings vie for your attention—the effort is destined to fail. *Preplan* your special times for talking. Set regular times to drive to the market, shop together, do laundry, go to ball games or other activities so your adolescent can look forward to having you all to herself. More important, she can let her ideas incubate during the week. When the meeting takes place, she knows (1) you will be receptive and (2) she will be prepared.

One father made "dinner dates" once a month with his teenaged daughter. He believed ardently that these special dates were instrumental to her later success. When we interviewed him, he was glowing from the recent news that she had just been selected from over two hundred other applicants for a high-ranking position in a major computer company.

> When Kathy was fifteen, we started on our dates. She would get all dressed up, I'd put on a suit and tie, and we'd go out to the finest restaurant—wherever she wanted to go. It was our night out. Just Kathy and me. Sometimes she'd have nothing in particular to talk about and we'd just have a good time. But she knew that, rain or shine, we were going out, and if there ever was anything on her mind—which there usually was—she had my undivided attention.

Special, preplanned times for talking are not optional.

The following are anecdotes from two other families who also relied on special times for talking:

> When Allison was in grade school, I would always meet her after class and walk her home. It was a bit of a distance, and most other parents drove, but I took advantage of the time to find out how things were going from day to day. Mostly we talked about school and Allison's lessons, but occasionally she would be upset about something. One time, for instance, another bigger girl who was bullying everyone—and Allison was very slight for her age—made Allison do a book report for her, saying she would tell everyone else not to be Alli's friend if she didn't. Well, Alli did the report, but that wasn't the end of it. She was blackmailed into doing another assignment and then another. This went on for two or three weeks, as I remember it, and then on the way home one day Alli broke down and spilled the whole thing. A quick phone call to the girl's mother took care of the problem. The girl had to get on the phone and apologize to both of us.

* * *

When I wanted to get something into his thick skull, I'd take Charley for a ride in the car. Only he'd hop in the back seat so we wouldn't be looking at each other. I think he felt kind of anonymous back there, and a little less intimidated. Then we'd talk while driving. When I tried talking face to face about anything heavy, it never failed: He'd clam up. But the back seat seemed to open the floodgates.

Important things to remember about the setting and timing for substantive, heart-to-heart talks are:

- *Both* parties must be willing to converse.
- *Both* parties must be in a cool, calm, unemotional state. Anger impairs parents' sense of justice and it fosters children's defensiveness.
- Don't let interruptions, distractions, or rushing compete with your talk. Dinner, for example, is the *worst* (but unfortunately, most common) time for families to start important discussions.
- Make appointments to talk with your children and *stick to them* like you would business appointments—they're equally important.

UNCOMFORTABLE SUBJECTS

Drugs. Sex. It is not the kids, but the parents who are reluctant to discuss these types of subjects. Why? They are immobilized by fear: "How much do my kids know about sex? Have they experimented with drugs? Don't tell me—I don't want to know!" One parent said:

> This is the end of the twentieth century. Like it or not, kids *do* know; they know more about drugs than their parents do, and they're gaining fast in the sex department, too. Bury your head in the sand if you must, but if you've got any sense, you'll take a periscope down with you!

The parents we met overcame their fears, informed themselves, and tuned into the program. For example, they knew that research shows most kids have been pressured to try drugs by the fourth grade. And they knew that sexual terms, sexual acts, and jokes about body parts were inevitably going to be part of normal, schoolyard jargon. One father said:

> You can't fight it, and you can't put your kids in a convent, so prepare them for what they're going to face in the real world. Sex isn't dirty or disgusting, but what they're going to hear about it will be. Beat them to the punch and tell them what they're in for. After all, you're a better teacher than the kids on the playground, so take a gulp and tackle the tough subjects.

One mother spoke for several other parents when she explained her stand on sex education this way:

> The way I figured it, when Randy was growing up, I was doing a community service by explaining the facts of life to him. When we started discussing sex, I knew he had heard a thousand different stories from different kids. I figured if he got it straight, at least one in twelve would have it right and the word would spread.

If your children are approaching or in adolescence, arm them with a thorough understanding of sexually transmitted diseases, pregnancy, and the like. With AIDS as prevalent as it is, this can be a life-or-death action on your part. Even six-year-olds are capable of understanding the facts of reproduction. Sex is a natural and wonderful part of life. Handle it as such. If you are uncomfortable discussing sex, your child can't help but be suspicious—and confused. One parent chuckled as she quoted something she remembered from an article she had read:

> Don't be surprised if after your talk, your child responds with, "Let's see, Mom. I think I understand what you said. Sex is normal, natural, and pleasurable, but it's also depressing, scary, and fatal, right?"

Another parent explained how she gently introduced reading material on sex:

> For years I left a good book—one with full color illustrations and clear explanations about reproduction, disease, etc.—on the bottom shelf of our bookshelves. We didn't make sex a hush-hush thing, and the book was always clearly visible because I didn't know when he'd be ready for it. Kids who are beginning to get interested in sex don't usually make a formal announcement. Then one day the book was gone; I found it under his bed.

We will discuss sex and other sensitive subjects in more detail in Chapter 6. In this chapter, though, the successful parents' primary message is: *No matter how uncomfortable you may be with them, you* have *to address the tough subjects.*

Difficult as they are, the important issues youngsters are likely to face cannot be left to chance or for the schools to handle. After all, who do you want your child to come to first if he has a problem, his teachers, his school chums, or you?

LISTENING AND TALKING TECHNIQUES

Therapists rely not on talking, but on *listening*, and for good reasons. First, people need to vent their feelings so they can dissipate the pressures building inside. Second, unless she listens, a therapist cannot possibly know what her patients' problems are. What works for a therapist in a clinical setting can work for you at home.

If your child needs to vent, lecturing him will only block him. Talking when you should be listening sends the message: "What *you* have to say doesn't matter. *I'm* the smart parent, and *you're* the dumb kid, so keep quiet and listen to me." Parents who take this stance miss the point completely: Their child doesn't *want* any answers! All he wants is to release steam. And when the lectures start, the valves shut closed.

Remember, when your child is under pressure, he's in pain. Don't take offense at what he is saying, because in any other circumstances, he wouldn't be saying it! Instead, heed these next pointers, for which there was great unanimity among the parents we spoke to:

- Wait until things cool down before approaching a child who feels hurt or unheard. Ask him to explain his problem and show him you are truly willing to listen—without interruption. This is not the time for questions; it is the time to *respond to emotions.* Instead of, "What are you upset about?" say, "You seem upset."

- Tell your child up front that you don't want to misinterpret what you *think* he means. Tell him, "I'm not sure what is bothering you, but I want to hear what you have to say. Then we'll discuss it so I'm sure I understand you." You want to avoid making assumptions or jumping to false conclusions.
- Instead of letting pressure build up in your family, get out of the way and let members have their say. Sometimes their "say" may take a strange form, as Mrs. Villanueva discovered. But she swore by the way her family kept peace for a month at a time.

> With three boys, there was going to be fighting whether I liked it or not. And fighting there was. Until I came up with the Monthly Nut Party. Basically, we all went berserk one night a month by pulling all the pots and pans out of the cupboard and beating them with wooden spoons and screaming at the top of our lungs like raving lunatics! Tony had his own snare drum and an old trumpet too, so the noise level really did reach quite a pitch. I always wondered what the neighbors must have thought. I'll tell you, these kids looked forward to that party every month and did they ever burn energy! Whatever might have been bothering them didn't have a chance.

Letting kids vent instead of trying to solve their problems for them makes the best sense because most of their problems can't be "solved" anyway—they're just part of growing up. Instead of intervening inappropriately, the parents we interviewed used a more relaxed communication style based on the primary tenet that *less is more.* Here are some of the basics they subscribed to:

- Wait until children ask questions before offering solutions to "problems."
- Be more willing to *receive* than to send messages. Writer Leo Buscaglia said, "Those who think they know it all have no way of finding out they don't."
- Don't appear overly anxious when talking or give the impression that the conversation is more important to you than your child. Interested, yes, but don't hang on every word as if they are critical clues to deep, dark mysteries—they're not.
- Relax. The more at ease you are, the more approachable you seem. A poised, easygoing demeanor assures your child that you are ready to listen—and it encourages her to come back again.

LISTENING AND RESPONDING

The parents we met encouraged their children to talk by adhering to the following six "listening basics."[7] Watch how they gradually progress from nonverbal, passive listening—which encourages children to talk—to more active participation after children have opened up.

Posture

To show you are there to bond, not fight, literally bring yourself down to your child's level. Rather than tower menacingly over your child, physically position yourself *lower* than her. A counselor one father spoke with said:

> If she's sitting on the bed, sit on the floor. Your *physical* posture and an open *mental* attitude express your willingness to talk on nondominating terms.

Pay Attention

There is an art to listening, and as with any art, competence requires practice. Really *tune in* to your child's frequency, and then *concentrate* on what he is saying as if he were an important speaker at a seminar. Nothing is more disconcerting to someone about to spill their innermost thoughts than a listener who is only half here. One father, the CEO of a large corporation, said:

> Think back to a cocktail party where you were speaking to someone whose eyes were constantly breaking away and scanning the room. Didn't it feel like they were searching for someone else to talk to?

Keep an Open Mind

Put your own opinions on hold and earnestly consider your child's views. Critical judgments kill communication. Encourage your child to form his own beliefs, even if they are clearly way off base; there is plenty of time later to steer him back on course. Rather than restrain his expression, keep things flowing by allowing him to speak without criticism.

Listen Quietly

If uninterrupted, your child will move from a superficial, warm-up stage, to a deeper, more intense level where the real feelings lie. By listening quietly, you help her reach that level while sending these nonverbal messages: "*You* can determine what you want to share." "I'm interested in hearing whatever you want to say." "I empathize with your feelings." This is worlds away from the dominant stance, "*I'm* the parent and *you're* the kid, so listen to me. I've got it all figured out!"

Listening quietly, however, does not require total silence. Respond to what is being said with simple nods, smiles, or an occasional "uh-huh," which assures your child that you are listening—and keeps him talking. As he does, his concerns will become clear. That is the time to move into the next level, where you can engage in more interaction and dialogue.

Participate

Now you can use a more active listening style, starting with small invitations to open up further. Softly coax your child with *open-ended* questions, rather than yes/no questions: "What happened at school today?" instead of "Did you have a problem at school today?" Remain relaxed and don't appear overly anxious (remember the puppy and reverse psychology). Your child has come to you and revealed herself. She's open, vulnerable. If you want to show her this is a safe thing to do, play it cool, even though the topic may be blazing. Do the opposite from what your emotions tell you. Said one father:

> Rather than amazement, show a matter-of-fact calm interest. Instead of anger, show composure. Don't let on to your kids that you're outraged by what they're telling you or that will be the last time you are—they won't be back. Jackie

told me many a story of her and her buddies that made me fume inside but I knew evaluating it when she came to me for help would have caused her to shut down. I always watched for signs that that might happen and kept gently nudging the conversation to get to the root of what was bugging her. But I didn't push.

Mrs. Cranston's daughter, Terri, was selected as grid queen of her high school, an honor that brought some unwanted pressures with it. The following story shows how well Mrs. Cranston handled a difficult, intimate confession:

I knew the bomb would drop one day. And I knew the attention Terri and her friends were getting by the faster boys was a potential powder keg. Well, the Saturday morning after the grid dance, Terri came downstairs pale as a ghost. And it wasn't from drinking because she didn't drink. After she beat around the bush over I don't know how many cups of decaf, I began asking a few soft questions because I could see she needed a little help. Finally she admitted that several couples had rented motel rooms after the dance. She said, "Things got out of hand once everyone went to their rooms." My stomach did a flip-flop, and I know I turned white too. But I didn't push the conversation. I just kept nodding and let her go on. By then she was staring at her cold cup of coffee without daring to look up. Though I was very concerned about what might have happened, I didn't pry and said, "It's all right, Terri. I'm glad you wanted to talk." She finally volunteered that though things got pretty "far along," as she put it, "nothing happened." With that I slowly let my breath out and told her the exact same thing happened to me when I was her age. You should have seen her color return.

Feedback

To assure your child that you hear her and understand what she is feeling, feed back *in your own words* your interpretation of what she said; you may be surprised to find how far off base you are. She may not articulate how she really feels, or she may just give a hint of what she cannot say outright. Be careful to pick up on clues that help avoid misinterpretation, but always remember that they are just that—*clues,* and nothing more. Don't *guess* at what your child means. If she says, "I'll never finish my essay in time," respond with, "You're feeling pressured and aren't sure you can do a good job on your paper, right?" Give feedback, not advice. *Calm feedback produces a feeling of caring and camaraderie.*

Verify that you understand what you hear by simply asking, "What I think you're saying is such and such. Am I right?" Just ask. At this point, it's not just okay to engage in dialogue, it's necessary.

Younger children especially need to know they have been understood. Avoid just smoothing over problems or offering to "fix" them. The balloon that popped was special to a youngster. Just saying you'll get a new one doesn't acknowledge how he *feels* about his loss. *Acknowledge* those feelings with a confirming statement like, "I know how much you liked that red balloon. You're very unhappy about losing it." This assures him that you understand how he's feeling and, above all, that you care.

COMMUNICATING YOUR MESSAGE

When they needed to get their own messages across, the parents we interviewed did it with something other than attack statements, which usually start with "You." They come in a wide assortment of communication-blocking formats—all negative:

Put-downs: "You look like a slob."
Evaluations: "You did lousy on your homework."
Commands: "You go up to bed this minute!"
Threats: "You'll never go out again if you're home late!"

These statements cause *resistance,* not compliance. And if you are dealing with a toddler, such messages can confuse and scare her. The following example shows how one father's accusatory message instantly turned happiness to hurt:

> Fortunately, my wife was standing right next to me when I tried to stop our four-year-old from splashing in the tub. I started off with a brilliant lack of finesse. I screamed out some hysterical accusation like: "You're getting suds all over the bathroom floor!" And with that, Shannon broke into tears. I felt terrible. She was having a wonderful time until Dad comes in and wrecks it. When I looked at that little pip-squeak with the suds on her head, bawling her head off, I just about started myself. Shirley saved the day when she said just the right thing, as usual: "Shannon, if the soap is all over the floor, there won't be enough to have a fun bath with. Let's play with your boat instead so we can keep all the bubbles." And with that, the crying stopped. I tried to tell Shannon I was sorry for yelling, but she was already too involved with her boat to pay much attention.

If you slip and blurt out one of the above attacks, apologize, as Shirley's husband did, and explain that even though you are a parent, you make mistakes, too. These admissions have a powerful healing effect. *Apologies show a willingness for good relations.*

The problem with accusatory messages is that they tell a child *he* is bad when it is really his *behavior* that is unacceptable. Change your messages from attacks to first-person "concern" messages that tell a child how his actions affect you. This is a *nonpower* method of communicating. Just as lowering yourself puts you on your child's level physically, first-person messages put you on more of an even level intellectually. Good managers rely heavily on this type of equal interaction to *empower* instead of *overpower* their employees.

Make "concern" messages effective by following these tips, which the parents we spoke with used regularly:

- Modify undesirable behavior by using nonvolatile language that *does not accuse* but rather *explains* the rationale behind your directives. Here's an example from one mother:

> I remember once when [seven-year-old] Patty didn't want to take out the trash. All I had to say was something like, "If the garbage isn't taken out, it will overflow all over the kitchen floor and then we'll have to clean it up. I'd rather spend that time making us a yummy dessert." It wasn't a "consequence" thing, it was just a way of changing her behavior without shaming her. Sometimes you've got to give kids the reasoning behind your actions before they get it.

- Make clear what effect your child's behavior has on you. Mrs. Cole, a tax accountant who worked out of her home, gave us an example of a "concern message" that worked beautifully with her six-year-old:

> When Dustin turned six, he became enthralled with the local squirrel population, and felt it was his civic duty to go to the park and feed them on a daily basis. But three o'clock was right in the middle of my workday. He'd always try badgering me the moment he got off the bus, and I'd always respond in kind by telling him, "I'm afraid I won't get my work done if I keep getting interrupted, and then I won't be able to take you to the park. The less interruptions, the sooner I'm done, the sooner we go." I never told him how much of a pest he was, I told him how his behavior affected me, without saying it directly. I think that was what made the difference—telling him how it *affected* me. For the most part he accepted it and went off and played with his toys until I was ready to go.

Mrs. Cole went on to relate an incident that illustrated another aspect of this point. It was about a time when Dustin was an adolescent and had said something particularly upsetting:

> I don't remember the issue now; Dustin had repeated something obnoxious that in the past I would have let go. But for some reason, this time he got my goat, so I confronted him. When I told him how I felt, I was more than a little surprised to hear him respond back, "Gee, Mom, I didn't realize how much I hurt you." It was like a breath of fresh air. I knew then that

I hadn't been communicating very well. I hadn't been telling him how I felt, so of course, he had no clue.

- "Concern" messages show your child *why* she should change her behavior rather than just *ordering* her to change it. If you state clearly that you have a headache, for example, and it won't go away unless you take a nap, it's unlikely your child will ignore you and keep making noise while you suffer.
- The biggest advantage "concern" messages have over attack messages is: *They leave no room for argument.* If you said, "*You* are making my headache worse," you're inviting the defensive response, "No, I'm not!" But no one can rebut the fact that your head hurts and you need a rest.

COMPROMISE AND COLLABORATE

Our parents regularly used two other communication techniques: Compromise and Collaboration.

Compromise

For the most part, the parents we spoke with did not give in to their children's demands. But there are occasions—and very specific ones—when giving in to avoid conflict over minor disagreements is the smarter action to take. It shows you are flexible and willing to see your child's point of view, and when used judiciously, these minor "give-ins" are real treasures to kids, who usually get overruled. Said one lawyer father:

If you and your child have diametrically opposing views, meeting somewhere in the middle is a good compromise. If each of you show some consideration for the other's wishes, you'll most likely reach an amicable resolution to the problem. And if the issue isn't all that earthshaking, who cares? You haven't given up much of importance, and your kid has a great coup since he usually loses his case on everything else.

Another father told us about the time his seventeen-year-old son came to him the evening of a major school dance:

> Carlos came right out with it. He said, "Dad, can we have a drink here before going to the dance?" That meant a lot to me. He and his friends could have gone out with a bottle of Southern Comfort and gotten toasted, but they didn't. Carlos came to me like an adult, so I said yes, they could have a drink. I also said, "Thanks for asking, son."

Collaborate

When you reach an impasse and cannot seem to resolve an issue, collaborate on a win/win solution by using the following format:

- Discuss the issue calmly by letting each other talk for an allotted time without interruptions or negativity.
- Utilize the "Feedback" technique discussed earlier, and in your own words, repeat back to each other what you *thought* you heard. You both may be way off base.
- Then list numerous suggestions for possible solutions, compare notes, and agree on those you think will work. Since you have come up with a *mutual* decision

that is in both of your interests, your child will feel participatory and empowered—and a lot more likely to comply with his own idea!

Here are some concluding tips from the experts that proved to be highly effective for obtaining quality communication:

- Avoid ambiguous or overly lengthy messages; they are confusing and boring. Short messages consisting of a few sentences have greater impact, and your child's attention is better. Again, watch for hair twirling and glazed eyes.
- Just as you would do for an important phone call, plan what you are going to say *before* saying it. Prepare, even rehearse it. And stick to one issue.
- Avoid mixed messages such as, "You're a big girl now, so, yes, you can sleep over at Patty's," followed by, "Call us before you go to bed." Is she a big girl or isn't she?
- Be specific. If your youngster has to guess at what you mean, he's likely to take advantage of your ambiguity, especially if he's an adolescent. To him, vagueness can make a good case for noncompliance. If you want the car back at a "reasonable" hour, you better state *exactly* what hour or you may find yourself watching the sun come up.

How do you know when your communication skills have improved? Well, don't expect a direct, "Thanks, Mom, we're really communicating now!" But do expect better relations with a child you will genuinely like more and whom you will have helped immensely as she prepares to join the adult world.

Perhaps, the best advice of all is found in the words of the late noted educator Bruno Bettelheim of Austria. While directing a school for disturbed children at the University of Chicago in the 1940s, he recognized that the best insights for understanding what your children are going through come from looking back to your own childhood. He said simply, "Think about your own experience. You'll find all the answers there."

CHAPTER 2

ENCOURAGE INTELLECTUAL DEVELOPMENT

May I help you?" asked the woman, eyeing the wild-haired character at her door suspiciously.

"Oh, pardon me, ma'am. I was looking for, ah, one-twenty-eight State Street. I must have made a mistake."

"This is one-twenty-five, sir. One-twenty-eight is over there," she said, pointing across the street.

"Oh, yes, of course it is," said the befuddled man as he turned and trudged off.

It was not the first time the man had ended up at the wrong house; he had a propensity for absentmindedness ever since he was a student in secondary school, where his behavior was so odd, a doctor certified that he had suffered a "nervous breakdown" and threw him out of the school. His teachers said he was "mentally slow, unsociable, and adrift in foolish dreams," and his own father was ashamed of his difficulty in adjusting to school. Who was this day-dreaming, maladjusted wretch? Why, Albert Einstein, of course, the man who didn't fit the mold then and didn't fit the mold later—when he was recognized as the greatest thinker of his time.

THE PROBLEM WITH THE EDUCATIONAL SYSTEM

Many would argue that it is "the mold" itself that is the root of today's educational problems. Brilliant, innovative thinkers like Einstein are not particularly concerned with conventions such as rote memorization of the "three Rs." (In fact, Einstein was notoriously bad at computations.) Their strength lies in their ability to conceptualize and come up with several answers instead of a pat one "from the book." But "the book," rather than creative use of the mind, is what most teachers still emphasize. They rarely appreciate students' ingenuity in seeing numerous ways to solve problems because they are focusing on correct answers and standardized tests. *Subjects should be taught with an emphasis on understanding the process, not just the answers.*

Blindly ingesting, memorizing, and then regurgitating just enough data to pass tests does not make kids smart! Why? Because they are not *thinking,* they are responding. "We fill students full of data," says Richard Paul, director of the Center for Critical Thinking at Sonoma State, California. "But the essence of education is to use information to address new situations and questions. We're neglecting that." *Acquiring information is not a substitute for thinking.*

Another researcher, Professor Richard Askey of the University of Wisconsin, revealed the sad state of American students' math skills when he gave a Japanese college entrance exam to 350 college freshmen math students. The four-step problem required students to solve one step, then apply it to the next step, and so on. The result of the test that most Japanese students passed? Total failure. *None* of the American students could figure out how to proceed because they did not have the analytical and creative reasoning abilities required to solve the problem. They could not get beyond the first step and apply their knowledge to a new situation.

Perhaps if we emulate the Japanese method of teaching as closely as we do their automobile manufacturing, our children's generation will have a fighting chance to compete in the next millennium. But that will be up to you, not the schools. Not only do most lack the wherewithal to teach kids how to think, they fall short in the cultural realm, too.

A few years ago, a National Endowment for the Arts report entitled *Toward Civilization* concluded that "basic arts education does not exist in the United States today." A Music Alliance poll about the same time showed that sixth graders recognized the name Beethoven, but *only 5 percent* knew who he was!

What's the solution to this dismal state of our educational system's affairs? *You.* Because most teachers do not value conceptual thinking as much as they do grades, it is your task to help your child develop it. If she is going to be successful, you—not the schools—must provide the correct stimulation and guidance in an intellectually enriched environment that rewards creative, critical thinking.

In this second key chapter, we will discuss the importance of creative and critical thinking, and define what intelligence really is—and what it is not: a simple IQ test score. You will see how parents can dramatically influence their children's IQ by helping them develop linguistic and mathematical skills, starting with the most important of all skills: reading. You will also see how the parents we spoke with guided their children through school, helping them develop excellent organizational skills that played a critical role in their academic success. Watch, too, how our experts relied on *assistance* rather than *insistence.* See how they avoided pressuring their children to "get smart" through excessive extracurricular activities, classes, and cultural events, which would have caused them to socialize poorly, become rebellious, and resent their parents—and rightly so.

CREATIVE AND CRITICAL THINKING

Unfortunately, we did not have the opportunity to interview Einstein's parents, and don't know what kind of wild ideas he may have come up with as a child. But we suspect he had a great deal of early intellectual stimulation from parents who helped him master the following essential critical thinking skills—skills that are rarely found in school curriculums. These are proficiencies that you, the parent, must impart to your child.

As our interviews proved, it is never too late to do so. Just as people of varying ages can learn to sing, dance, play golf, or fly an airplane, students can learn to change their reading and study habits and improve mental agility. Granted, these skills are best developed in the early years, but as we discovered, children from preschool to high school can improve their cognitive skills. One parent spoke for several we met when she told us how her fourteen-year-old son did a 180-degree about-face upon entering high school and meeting a new group of kids who were motivated to succeed:

> Marty just didn't take school seriously. He had decent enough marks in elementary school, but when he got into junior high and discovered girls and sports and motorcycles, he started palling around with the wrong crowd. Oh, the

kids were innocent enough, but they just didn't have any work ethics; they liked to play. Our position was always: "Come to us when you're ready, we're here to help you. We can't stop you from seeing your friends, but at this rate, your options in life will be next to none." I even wrote something to this effect in a letter to Marty. Oddly enough, two years later, just after he started Claremont High, he brought the letter upstairs to my bedroom one evening and said, "I'm ready." The next day I called his counselor and we set up a meeting to discuss a college prep program. When we left the counselor's office, Marty said to me, "I don't want to be working in a fast-food joint in three years, Mom. I'm going to college."

As your children go through life, they will constantly face new situations that require them to think—*creatively* and *critically*. You will see in this chapter how the experts helped their children prepare for those challenges by providing a home atmosphere that fostered creativity, where free-flowing, unusual, even crazy ideas were not just allowed but encouraged. They helped them tap into their hidden mental powers and move beyond the schools' "three Rs" thinking. They taught them to be junior Einsteins and look at the world in new, innovative, *critical* ways. Effective parents relax controls and preconceived notions of what is right and wrong. They encourage the unusual, value originality and spontaneity, and keep the creative spirit alive.

Here's what one art teacher we interviewed said about developing creativity:

Children express themselves through dancing, singing, drawing, musical instruments—activities that allow them to freely exercise the vast regions of their imagination. The joy of creativity comes from producing something unique, something original—without stipulations or regulations. Kids do better in this department *without* guidance and directions, and certainly without censorship. More teachers ought to pursue some subjects for the mere enjoyment of them and nothing else.

A father we met was a sales trainer for a large corporation. He explained to us the parallel between selling a product to a prospect and raising a child to think creatively. His comments support what the art teacher above said:

> One of the training manuals I use teaches my salespeople not to manipulate or otherwise influence what a customer's needs might be. In one lesson, it shows a little girl standing there with a drawing she did at school, and she's upset. When her mother asks her what's the matter, the girl explains that when she drew her picture, she had a house and sky and that was all. But her teacher said the picture would be more interesting if it had a bird in the sky, so he drew one in. All the girl kept saying over and over to her mother was, "I didn't want a bird in my picture. There wasn't any bird in my picture."

Correcting children when they try to express themselves squelches their creativity and sends the message: "Your thinking is wrong. Better not try anymore."

Here's a tip that will help prevent such messages: *Children learn to think creatively and critically in an environment where new ideas are welcomed, not criticized.*

Creative thinking, though, is only part of the equation. The children we studied learned to combine their creative thinking with *critical* thinking, which enabled them to conceptualize, analyze, question, and when appropriate, reject the validity of information. Rather than merely accept ideas as gospel, they challenged them and drew their own conclusions after looking *critically* at the problem. Then they moved forward to tackle those problems.

A busy CPA and his wife, both of whom had precious little spare time—especially on weekends—still managed to coach the local chapter of an outstanding national program called Odyssey of the Mind, an educational program that fosters children's creative thinking and problem-solving. The not-for-profit program, headquartered in Glassboro, New Jersey, under the title OM Association, Inc., endorses competition between various school teams on projects that only the children are allowed to design and construct.

> The difference between this program and others is, Dad can't get in there with the old hammer and nails and help the kids; it's forbidden. Everything, and I mean *everything*, has to be done by the kids themselves so that the competition is fair and they learn to figure out their own problems. Here's the OM pledge [pulls out booklet]: "Let me be a seeker of knowledge. Let me travel uncharted paths. And let me use my creativity to make the world a better place in which to live." This is great stuff to raise kids on.

The following example of creative/critical thinking probably would not have won the OM competition, but it still showed a good deal of ingenuity. During this student's freshman high school year, when the astronauts were doing their space walks, his science teacher suggested the class do projects related to space flight. But the teacher made the mistake of saying that there is no way to measure the effects of weightlessness on earth. That was all Jason needed to hear. His father explained:

> Jason knew it wasn't true because he read an article about how when you dive off a diving board, you're weightless for a moment at the top of the dive. So he came up with a crazy experiment where he built a space capsule out of an orange juice can, attached a parachute, and then climbed to the top of the redwood tree in our front yard. What does he do? He uses a mouse as an astronaut and throws it out in a big arc that's supposed to simulate space. Then he pulls the poor thing out and puts it through a maze to test its before and after reaction time—and supposedly the effects of weightlessness. I don't think it proved anything, but the teacher still had Jason get up in front of the class and explain the whole thing, which he said showed critical thinking. He got an A, probably more for nuttiness than anything else.

WHAT IS INTELLIGENCE?

Let's dispel the myths about innate intelligence and the ill-gotten notion that "whatever you're born with you're stuck with." For decades, psychologists have debated the relationships of inherited intelligence and environment to IQ, or the "nature vs. nurture" issue. We collected plenty of evidence to show how influential parents can be on the development of their children's cognitive skills.

IQ

The students we studied had IQs all over the board. Some were slow students at first; many had difficulty in several subjects. But in the end, they all were successful because they all had parents who *participated* in their intellectual growth. *Parents directly influence their children's intelligence through visual, auditory, and tactile stimulation.*

Here is what intelligence is *not:* an IQ score. This anxiety-producing term, "IQ," has been bandied about too loosely. In the first place, the test was originally developed by Alfred Binet, who was commissioned by the minister of public education not to measure intelligence, but to find a technique for identifying children needing help in class. It assessed performance scores of academic tasks compared with norms for children in a similar age group. But over time, it has been misconstrued as a way to quantify intelligence with the use of one simple number—a number that *can improve* as a child learns to think better!

Robert J. Sternber, Ph.D., professor of psychology at Yale University, found that the relationship of inherited intelligence to performance in life is more closely related to the *application* of mental abilities and the ability to think in new ways when confronted with new challenges. For example, an American who, on his first trip to England, drives off the French ferry docking at Dover head-on into British traffic going the "wrong" way must immediately modify his thinking to cope with a new situation. In so doing, he expands his intelligence.

In a similar way, our parents helped prepare their children for progressively more difficult cognitive tasks by focusing on the potential they exhibited at all stages of life. Here are some of the things they advised other parents to do:

- Observe your child's personality and the types of intelligence he exhibits. He may be a detail-oriented person who learns best in a quiet, organized environment, or he may favor the big picture or conceptual approach to issues, and may study best with a room full of popcorn-munching cohorts. Avoid intervening with preconceived notions of what his personality *should* be.
- Look for innovative ways to increase your child's interest in dealing with challenges and new learning situations. One teenaged student took on a considerable challenge that worked his brain overtime. Mrs. Newmark explains:

> Gary put together his own stereo—the receiver, amplifier, speakers, everything—from a kit his older brother had pointed out in an electronics magazine. Ernie loved jazz and stereo equipment, and had built his own system, too, so Gary picked up on that. Oh, was it tedious labor, though! Six months or so? But it was worth it, wasn't it, Gary?

Gary, present at the interview, responds:

> All I remember is, when I finally flipped on the switch after soldering thousands of those little colored wires that were all over the place, nothing happened. I got nothing. Then I hunted down the loose wire and tried it again and John Coltrane comes blasting out sweet as anything. It was awesome.

- Provide a stable and stimulating environment that encourages growth. Flip charts and the like have been roundly criticized as "too yuppie" by much of the media, which claims parents are overly concerned with "success" and teaching their children to "be smart." The parents we interviewed, most of whom would not fit into the "yuppie" class anyway, definitely disagreed.

> You've got to get off your butt and *do something* when you're raising kids. You've got to move your body and get involved. You can't simply send your kids off to school and expect they'll come back geniuses. You've got to prepare them in the home, and yes, we used every means available, including Teacher's Helper, a new store designed to help teachers and parents teach kids better. It's full of books, maps, mind games. You've got to find these sorts of things if you want smart kids.

- Maintain ever-increasing but appropriate expectations of your child, whether it involves reading, music, skill games, etc. Once she has mastered one level, move to the next. Here's an important point to remember: *Staying in the comfort zone does not broaden thinking.*

> One Hanukkah we gave Laurie a Labyrinth game, you know, the box with the tilting floor that has all the holes in it. You're supposed to move the little steel ball from one end to the other without letting it drop into the holes. It's pretty tough. Well, Laurie took several weeks to master the game. She was at it all the time. Finally she made it all the way to the end. Then her father says, "How about going back the other way now?" I remember watching her when he said that.

> She looked at the game, looked up at him, looked back at the game, and said, "No problem," and started back the other way! She loved those kinds of challenges—I think because her father always put her up to them when she started to sit back on her laurels. Eventually she got so she could do the game forwards *and* backwards perfectly. Try it sometime; you'll see how hard it is to get past the first hole.

- *Believe* that you can, in fact, improve your child's intellectual power by feeding her the appropriate raw material that puts her brain to work. This means letting go of those misconceptions about inherited intelligence.

You will see in this next section how vital you are to the development of your child's intellectual power. To understand why, let's look briefly at how the brain works. As in chess, if you understand the power of the pieces, you play better and the game becomes infinitely more intriguing.

THE BRAIN

Inside the brain, a system of electrical lines similar to phone lines connects some one hundred billion neurons or cells, allowing them to "talk" to each other. Messages come in along the cells' dendrites, or branches, and then are dispersed to other cells. If you touch something slimy, millions of cells instantaneously telecommunicate between themselves and send you the message, "Yuk!" so you immediately withdraw your hand. If you are playing a difficult violin concerto, millions of other cells go into action to recall the piece from memory and locate the precise spots to press on the fretless fingerboard.

The right side of the brain observes a situation to get a general overview of it, while the left side organizes and calculates the data that the right side observed. You can help your child connect the two hemispheres through intellectual stimulation—the building material for the mental pathways between the two.

Noted brain researcher, Marion Diamon, Ph.D., of the University of California, Berkeley, found through her study of rats that the nerve cells that make up the cortex of the brain can actually be *altered by experience;* their very structure can be changed. "Every part of the nerve cell that we've measured shows a change in response to a stimulating environment," says Diamon. In enriched environments, where rats interacted with other rats and played on swings and treadmills, rats grew bigger, more efficient brains because the stimulation created more new connections between neurons. The key to their brain development was their *active,* rather than passive activities: Reading, for example, is active; television viewing is passive.

The key point to remember is this: Your child's brain grows in size and weight as she actively responds to the new situations and challenges you provide. *It is the process of* thinking *that stretches the mind and exercises problem-solving skills.*

When a baby tries to touch a hanging mobile, or a toddler distinguishes between shapes and discovers that the square peg goes in the square hole, new electrical pathways form to carry the problem-solving transmissions. And the brain grows. On the other hand, if there is no mobile or no peg, there is no new challenge, so the brain remains the same.

Since the brain grows in response to stimulation, an enriched environment is critical to increasing your child's mental capacity. The other critical element is the time at which you offer new stimulation because children go through periods when their receptivity is greater. Growth spurts generally occur around three to ten months, two to four years, six to eight years, ten to twelve years (girls), and fourteen to sixteen (boys). During these periods, more neural networks develop and cortical connections grow. These are prime times to present new material and experiences.

How will you know these times have come? You will see clues that signal your child's readiness for more challenging material. She may start asking new types of questions or have a different, more complex slant on a subject. When she does, take note: New neural connections have formed. She is ready. Feed her curiosity and offer more challenging material. But be cautious. Just as understimulation can thwart kids' learning, *overstimulation* can cause even greater damage.

Problems occur when parents push children to learn difficult material or speak prematurely, before their next growth spurt has occurred, and before the brain and muscles of the throat and mouth have developed sufficiently. If they force kids to try to make sense of information beyond their comprehension, or overstimulate in sessions that become tedious and tiring, a child may lose her zeal to learn, or rebel against *all* incoming information and shut down completely. Some children even develop physiological stress symptoms because they feel pressured to perform instead of learn.

The parents we interviewed found that the best solution to the timetable issue is to watch your child and let *her* guide *you*—not the other way around. No two kids learn the same.

Respect her individuality, and let her needs and abilities determine what activities to introduce her to; she will let you know when she has had enough. A high school counselor told us:

> Parents should introduce their children to new activities such as concerts, museums, exhibitions when the times seem right. Don't be too anxious to expose them to music, art, dance, and everything else. Walking by an art gallery is fine; trying to explain impressionism to a five-year-old is not. These subjects take a certain level of maturity to appreciate. If you're too early, the subjects will bore kids and you may turn them off to the arts forever. Wait until they can respond intelligently. Then, if they show interest in a particular field, offer them classes or lessons or more excursions. You've got to remember that kids have a deep need to be spontaneous and learn at their own pace. Don't deny them that.

Keep in mind that your child may be a prodigy who can play an entire Brahms concerto at five, or she may just want to climb trees until she's seven. Your job is to expose her to both, and then let her decide what she wants to do.

DEVELOPING INTELLIGENCE

Facts make up human intelligence. If someone is not well versed in current affairs, politics, liberal arts, or issues falling within the realm of "common knowledge," he cuts himself off from the more intellectual segment of society and limits his options in all avenues of life. If he applies for a job with a quality company, his job interview won't last very long if all he knows is that company's product or service. *Limited general knowledge means limited opportunities for success.*

People assimilate facts and expand their knowledge through various realms of knowledge such as spatial, interpersonal, and bodily-kinesthetic. For the most part, though, the parents we spoke with discussed two basic areas of intelligence: *linguistic* and *mathematical.* But before we discuss these specific areas, let's see how they prepared their children to acquire knowledge.

Before a child takes the outfield, he has to know how to catch a fly ball. To learn this skill, he must *practice.* Likewise, to get the most out of a field trip, he has to be able to *observe* and *retain* what he sees, or the trip will be nothing more than a bit of short-lived entertainment. Help your child gain a basic level of intellectual competence early in life—*before* the field trips—so that when you present learning opportunities, he will absorb material without frustration. Without question, the first step in this process is early reading.

READING

Since reading is the beginning and arguably most vital part of intellectual development, our parents placed great emphasis on cultivating it early in their children's lives. They knew that during the first few years, children's lifetime reading habits are formed. Certainly, older children can and do improve their comprehension through tutoring and speed-reading classes, but if your child is younger, pay special attention to this section because it is more difficult to break bad (or nonexistent) reading habits than it is to start off right.

Richard Anderson, Director of the Study of Reading at the University of Illinois at Urbana-Champaign, studied the reading habits of fifth graders and found that children who were particularly good readers spent *four times* as much time reading than other kids. The superior students, who reached the ninetieth percentile on tests, read about twenty minutes a day outside the classroom, while students who only reached the fiftieth percentile read a mere six extracurricular minutes per day.

What was the major factor influencing the superior students? Not surprisingly, their parents' reading habits. Here again, you are a role model your child wants to emulate, so let her emulate a bookworm—not a couch potato! (After tallying the television viewing time of the families we met, we came up with an average of 2.2 hours per day, less than a third the national average of seven hours per day.)

Because the parents we met recognized reading as critically important to their children's intellectual development, they had numerous points to make on this topic. Here is how they instilled in their children a deep-rooted love of reading, which, as one mother said, ". . . was the absolute key to Jessica's success in everything."

To assure that reading is an eye-opening, enjoyable experience for toddlers, use a dramatic voice and spirited reading style that stirs excitement. Said one teacher:

> Next to a thrilling mystery or fascinating biography or intrepid voyage story, television can't hold a candle. Kids who learn to read early in life will prefer it to almost any other activity when they grow older.

When children start reading themselves, encourage them to talk about what they read so they come to appreciate the literature more. Ask your child questions about characters, plot, theme, and purpose of the story, then rephrase her ideas in your own language so she can glean the more subtle underlying meanings the author is trying to convey. This is the type of critical thinking her high school teachers and college professors will demand later. One parent, who was a high school teacher herself, went a step further:

> After she read a good story, I'd ask Belinda what she thought was important about it, and then I'd ask her to make up one of her own, one with a purpose. Then we'd work on a simple plot together to make that point. Or she'd make a new point, it didn't matter. When we started these creative writing exercises, she was only about six, so her stories weren't much more than half a page. But she learned what was behind literature, what it meant. I'm sure this early writing is what made her such a good essay writer in high school.

When your child grows adept at one level, continue to develop her analytical skills by keeping new reading material challenging and just beyond her comprehension range. This forces her to think further and ask questions, and makes reading an ever-broadening experience.

Have family reading sessions with a period afterward to discuss how the literature evoked excitement, sadness, or other emotions. Share the best passages with each other; critique writing styles and messages. Point out powerful language. Discuss difficult concepts such as "integrity," "ecology," or "spiritualism." Discuss messages and the symbolism that are hidden in good literature. One parent related his own high school experience with a colorful teacher everyone hoped to get when class assignments were handed out:

> No one ever forgot Mr. Stevens. He was always unpredictable. His was one of the few classes I really loved. I remember once he spent the entire period explaining the meaning behind the short opening line of *Moby-Dick:* "Call me Ishmael." Whoever knew there was an hour's worth of meaning in three words? We did that sort of thing with our kids' reading at home, too. Just reading for the fun of it is okay, I guess, but when we tried to figure out what the author was getting at, or what his purpose was in writing the book in the first place, there was always a lively debate. Literature is fascinating, and we found that by talking about it, we got much more out of the books.

Let your child see you reading all types of material on a variety of topics. When you read newspapers, magazines, and books aloud, your child will find certain subjects more interesting than others. Follow them up. Get more articles and books on those topics, but don't announce, "They're here!" or your child may feel she is being manipulated and quickly loose interest. Nonchalantly leave them lying around; she'll find them.

Next to school, the library is the most important institution in your child's life. To be sure he appreciates it as such, treat the library as a privilege, not an obligation. We interviewed one father, a physician and voracious reader, in his wood-paneled den that was lined with thousands of books twelve rows high. He used an old rolling library ladder to reach the upper stacks. He cautioned that parents have to handle the reading and library issues very gingerly to avoid turning kids off:

> *Bestow* the library gift on your child. Make it a fun, special thing to do. The main idea here is *gift,* not *obligation.* Turn the whole issue around and say, for example, "First I've got to do my shopping, then we *get* to go to the library." This is a long way from "After you do your required hour of reading at the library, we'll go shopping." See the difference? If you handle this right—and you've got to if you have any hopes of producing an academically strong child—you'll find kids will gravitate toward the library instead of being intimidated by it.

When children are very young, get them in the habit of visiting the library. Mrs. Yee started taking her daughter, Carrie, *twice a week* when she was only *eighteen months old!* The result? Valedictorian of her graduating class, dean's list four years running, and just a terrific kid—who was never without a book! Said Carrie:

> I love reading—*everything.* That's all I can tell you. If I'm not into three or four books at a time, I'm not myself. I know it was because I grew up in the library.

Mrs. Yee also told us that she had Carrie take advantage of library reading groups and story times, which increased her love of reading. She highly recommended them to other parents.

Another mother, Mrs. Bellini, told us her daughter, Michelle (whom we interviewed by phone at Robert Wood Johnson Medical School in New Jersey the next day), "read, oh, at least eight or nine books a day when she was seven."

Nine books *a day*. When we asked her if she didn't mean "a month," she said, "Oh, no, Michelle really read that much. They were short books, of course, but the librarian said she always had perfect comprehension and gave her another one."

Allow your child to buy his own used books or suggest he subscribe to a magazine on a topic he's interested in. Like anything else, if he shares in the cost, the material has even greater value to him. Plus, just anticipating the delivery of each new issue is worth the cost alone. Many schools have book fairs. Mrs. Marcus told us that when her son, Daniel, was seven, he still wasn't particularly interested in reading. But when the school book fair came around, she encouraged him to try it since he had never been to one. It turned out to be a turning point for him. Here's what happened:

> Daniel was never really interested in reading, but he *loved* football. When he came home with the book fair list, I told him he could pick out a book he thought he would like to buy. I gave him a dollar to get it, but when he got to the fair, he saw a football book about the two quarterbacks, Troy Aikman and Steve Young, that he went wild about. The problem was, he didn't have enough money because it was a dollar-fifty, so he called me at work to ask if he could have more money. It was the first time I'd seen him excited about books. Since then, I learned to buy him books on subjects—and especially people—he was interested in, and he started reading beautifully.

Mrs. Bellini told us another story about her doctor-to-be daughter that shows either a twist of fate or a direct influence from early exposure to books:

Since we had only small, local bookstores here in our little New Jersey country town, Michelle was amazed when her father took her to a big bookstore in New York when she was four. He allowed her to buy a book, *Teddy Goes to the Doctor.* Well, when she came home on spring break from medical school last month, she pulled out the book and took it back to school with her. Did the book plant a seed? You tell me, but she's on her way to a career in medicine.

Kids have to *want* to read, so build their desire by using a little reverse psychology again. Do not *reward* them for reading. This common mistake sends the message that reading is a job to be completed. Instead, *allow* them to read more when they have completed the other things they are supposed to do. As the doctor advised, make reading a valuable gift, not another chore. Another parent we met did just that:

> When the weekends came around, I'd say to the kids, "Okay, you guys, this is Friday night and there's no school tomorrow. You can stay up an extra half hour to read if you promise to shut the lights at nine." I knew they'd revert to their flashlights after nine. I mean, have you ever read *The Hardy Boys?* It's not that easy to put them down. I know. *Nancy Drew* was no different for me! So, I'd cut them a little slack. And I'd always leave extra batteries in their nightstands. This is one area of discipline we'd look the other way on.

To help your child build an image of herself as a reader, set up a reading environment in her room. Mrs. Daley put up bookshelves and encouraged her daughter to build her own library, which she did—and which she was trying to finally get rid of when we came to interview her. She walked us into the house through a garage full of books she was preparing to sell at her garage sale the next day. Hundreds of paperbacks on all kinds of subjects littered the floor in various stages of organization. When we asked why some were new-looking and others were dog-eared, she explained:

> The newer-looking books are the ones Sandy only read a couple of times. Most of those over there [pointing to a dozen or so boxes] she read over and over again. If she liked a book, she'd read it, then read a few dozen others, then come back and read it again. She even did it with *Shogun* and *Lonesome Dove.*

As Mrs. Daley pointed out later in the interview, it doesn't matter if your child reads the same old mystery or sports book over and over again because eventually her interests will change and her selection will broaden so long as she stays interested in reading. In the meantime, she is cultivating an excellent habit that will profoundly affect her education and her life. And if your child's friends are reading the same types of books, all the better. They will discuss the stories and raise issues that enhance their critical thinking skills.

LEARNING FUNDAMENTALS

Early reading lays the foundation for intellectual growth and the development of the following essential traits. For most people, these are not inborn traits—they must be *learned.* All good creative/critical thinkers have the ability to:

- *Observe* what is going on in any situation.

- *Compare and contrast* ideas to grasp their relationship to one another.
- *Categorize* and store information logically.
- *Sort* through information and *recall* appropriate data.
- *Ask* pertinent questions to *evaluate* problems and *draw inferences* from the facts.
- *Reach* intelligent conclusions.

To help your child develop these traits, several things must be in place. We'll start with some basic "Don'ts," and then move on to our true experts' list of "Dos," after which we will discuss the specifics of linguistic and mathematical intelligence.

- Don't take educational guidelines too literally. Relax your notion of how teaching *should* be and follow your child's lead instead; he will show you what activities and experiences he needs.
- Don't shove fact after fact at your child. Provide time for him to "think about thinking." If parents' goals are to produce superbabies as sources of pride to be shown off at dinner parties, they are doing a great disservice to their children. As we discussed at the beginning of this book, if parents are more concerned with *their* needs to be fulfilled than their children's needs to grow properly, they should reexamine their motivation for having children in the first place.
- Don't "parent" all the time. Don't supply your child with answers the moment he gets stuck, or you risk curtailing his instinctive desire to learn. Help him be an *independent* thinker who does *not* need Mom. Teach

him to "learn to learn" by encouraging him to seek his own answers.

> Shelby was about eighteen months old. We were in the backyard and she was holding her pet stuffed monkey, Murphy. I said, "Let's take Murphy for a ride," and put him in the storage compartment under her tricycle's seat. When we were done with the ride, I watched her try to get him out. She went to work on that latch like a little bulldog, trying every which way to get it open, but she couldn't. Do you think she looked around for help? No. She kept at it while we stood there watching. She didn't *want* any help. Sure enough, after about five minutes of struggling, she got it open and pulled Murphy out.

- Don't protect your child from failing. Welcome mistakes, and assure him that wrong answers and wrong ways are good indications that he is branching out and trying new, more difficult material—the only way to grow smarter.

Remember, kids have an insatiable curiosity to make sense of the world they see. Babies would rather learn than play. Take advantage of their desires! When presented in an exciting, enjoyable way, those one hundred billion neurons can absorb vast amounts of new material.

Here's the list of "Dos" that underlie effective learning:

- Establish a family environment that is conducive to learning. Show an eagerness for new information that your child can emulate. Empower her to be an active participant in her own learning process by setting up her room in an intellectually stimulating fashion. Here's how one parent accomplished this:

> We knew it was our responsibility to help Bonnie develop her mind, so we made her room into sort of a little junior college where she could get lost in her thoughts—and she did. She loved her room. We installed bookshelves and put her desk in front of them like ours was. When we'd sit at our desk and read, she'd go sit at hers. She had an arts and crafts area, a puzzles and games area, and a music corner for her toy piano and saxophone. She went on, as matter of fact, to play sax in the middle school band.

- Watch for readiness. Children acquire learning skills in a natural sequence and cannot learn a higher skill without mastering the one before it. Your child will give you signals indicating the material you presented is either too difficult and she is losing interest or, conversely, she is open for more stimulation. When she is ready for more, be a little aggressive. Kids are like sponges and absorb knowledge best when immersed in a wide assortment of activities and experiences.
- Break tasks down into manageable steps, moving from a comfortable level to a more challenging level. Don't let your child dawdle too long in the "comfort zone" we mentioned earlier; it offers nothing new and is too safe from edifying failures. If you have made learning from mistakes perfectly acceptable, she won't be afraid to move on.

Jack's dad moved him right along with his model building. At about seven or eight, Jack was building simple models pretty regularly—*PT 109,* little sailboats—simple ones. Then his dad bought him a very complex—and large—model of an old sailing ship like the *Pinta* or *Santa Maria* with all the sails and lines. It was quite complicated. But Jack put it together in about three months. Well, I don't know if this is all related or not, but when he was around twelve, he sent away for the plans to build a hydroplane, you know, the kind with an engine that you actually get in and race yourself. He did a beautiful job on it—with a little help from his dad. But I don't remember him ever driving the thing. I think it was more the building of it that was gratifying.

- Discuss intellectual subjects. Even politics can be interesting to a seven-year-old if handled the right way:

When the elections came around, I explained the voting procedure to Colleen. I showed her the sample ballot I had marked up and told her a little about the propositions. Then when I went to vote, I drove her down with me to actually see the polling place. That was what fascinated her, the booths and all. We followed it up by watching the results [of the voting] on television that night. She asked me, "When are we going to see your vote, Daddy?" What do you say to a seven-year-old when she asks you something like that? When one of the digital readouts tallied more votes on the big board I yelled, "There it is! Did you see it?" But she wasn't buying it.

- When on an excursion of any kind, make it a mind-expanding experience. If you are on a nature walk, for example, do more than collect facts; discuss the relevant issues such as natural resources, wildlife, the political implications of pending bills in Congress, the relationship of energy conservation to pollution, or the impact people have on the environment locally and globally.
- During teaching sessions, show new material quickly to maintain interest and excitement, and make the sessions no more than ten or fifteen minutes long for younger children. "Rather than wear kids out or bore them," advised one counselor, "leave them thirsting for more by stopping sessions while enthusiasm levels are still high."
- Appeal to the five senses to build the power of observation. One mother told us:

> I would have Lauren close her eyes and listen to the world around her, and then describe the sounds she heard: people coughing, truck sirens in the distance, rustling leaves, birds chirping in the trees. When I took a bath and put on my Caswell & Massey oils afterward, I'd have her close her eyes and try to guess if I had on lavender, sandalwood, jasmine, or whatever. She loved these games.

- Vary the subjects and teaching methods. Aquariums and museums are essentials, but enlarge the scope of your child's experiences by visiting unusual or culturally diverse places. Visit hospitals, homes for the aged, different places of worship, shipyards, botanical gardens, and cemeteries. Go around the world without leaving your city by going to ethnic restaurants. The list is endless. *Children's intelligence is directly proportional to their opportunities for learning new material.*

With these seven basic elements of intellectual development in mind, let's move on to the two realms of the intellect effective parents concentrate on most: linguistic and mathematical intelligence.

LINGUISTIC INTELLIGENCE

Linguistic intelligence involves the use of language to express spoken and written meanings. Infants and toddlers first begin developing this realm of intelligence when you talk and read to them in slow, short, complete sentences, while enunciating clearly. As their neurons develop, they associate the words you speak with the things you show them while talking. Progressively, they acquire more verbal competence as you elicit more and more language from them. Their brains' "language acquisition devices" are activated by this *social interaction*—the basis of all language development. (See more on social interaction in Chapter 6.)

The following are various methods that parents we interviewed used to help their children improve their linguistic skills:

- Young children's cognitive functions grow by practicing using language, so have your child talk aloud and explain what he sees and what he thinks while engaged in a new activity. If he plays or reads in silence, there is no way to know if the material is too complex or abstract, or if he is grasping new ideas.

- When visiting galleries, museums, concerts, plays, and the like, avoid passive observing. Engage your child in comparative exercises. Point out the differences between woodwinds in an orchestra, or the similarity between finches and flamingos. One parent had an excellent suggestion that he said intrigued his children when the family went on a trip to Italy:

> When visiting art museums, try to find an exhibit showing how a painting was restored; it will often include a photo of an X-ray revealing several earlier versions under the final one. Here's a hidden lesson in perseverance. I explained to my kids that even for the masters, nothing comes easy. And they're not above making mistakes—or covering them up!

- Ask questions that (a) stimulate your child's mind, (b) find your child's interest level, and (c) reflect how well you are communicating. Use mind-opening questions that don't have overly simple answers. In the zoo ask, "How do you think those penguins can live on freezing ice with no clothes? What would you take if you were going to visit them?" At the aquarium ask, "Why do those sharks and dolphins have fins on their backs?" In the planetarium ask, "Where do the stars go during the day?" One mother told us how she turned a visit to a museum into a learning experience:

> When we went to the Peabody Museum in New Haven, I challenged the boys as to what they saw. When

> we came to this big sea turtle on the wall that had a big chunk missing from one flipper, the kids didn't notice it. When they started to walk by it, I said, "Hey, you guys. Look at this!" I asked them, "What's different on one side of this turtle from the other?" When they saw it I asked, "What do you think happened?" It was only then that they really, really looked closely at this turtle and started coming up with ideas like maybe a shark took a bite out of it or it got in a fight with another turtle. They would have missed the whole thing if I hadn't stopped and asked them those questions.

- Have your older child use specific language, not broad, "lazy thinking" generalizations that require little cognitive effort. When you challenge him to talk clearly, you strengthen his linguistic and analytical reasoning powers. Said one parent:

> Try having your kids imagine trading places with other people, and discuss in detail what it would be like to enter a burning building to save someone, or be homeless in the winter, or teach a classroom full of noisy kids. There's no way they can keep saying, "Ya know, ya know." They've got to do the explaining, and make them use specifics.

- In your everyday activities, there are numerous opportunities to stimulate kids' verbal skills. Mrs. Tarkington explains how she took advantage of grocery shopping to teach her five-year-old, Erin, early linguistic skills:

> Usually I would tell Erin to pick up a loaf of bread or carton of milk as we went down the aisles. If you watch parents in the grocery store, you'll see that they're always holding the shopping list, not the kids. Then a friend suggested giving Erin my list and have *her* read the items herself. At first, she couldn't do it very well. But it didn't matter. She liked holding the list herself, and she'd keep running back to me pointing to certain items on the list and asking what they were, then take off to get them. I think it was a terrific way to teach her to read—or show her that she could learn. Kids love using their brains if you make it fun.

Other activities that help develop linguistic intelligence in younger children include creating a family newsletter and sending it to relatives at holiday time, perusing maps, writing to a pen pal, keeping a journal or diary, making up and dramatizing stories, choreographing dances, composing and singing songs, practicing vocabulary words, making up and/or memorizing rhymes, and trying to recall from memory. One mother told us she was surprised when she got a response to an obscure trivia question she threw out during one of the family's regular "memory games."

> One summer we took a trip to Montreal and went on one of those horse and buggy rides around the city. Well, during one of our memory games several years later, I asked the question, "What was the name of the horse that took us around Montreal?" Everyone thought for a moment and then Cheryl came up with it: "It was Mike!" "That's right!" I said. "Good going."

With older children, the successful parents used activities that required more advanced mental reasoning and mind stretching. Many found humor to be an excellent teaching aid because it taught kids there is more than one way of looking at things. Contemplating puns and jokes requires abstract reasoning that gives the brain a workout. Several families we met enjoyed "mind games," with one family in particular making them regular weekend activities. Said one high school senior:

> We looked forward to those weekend games like you wouldn't believe. We did everything, including spelling bees and opposite word games, *Scrabble, Trivial Pursuit,* and *Pictionary.* We hardly ever missed a weekend as long as I can remember.

Other families we talked to played the same games, as well as crossword and jumble puzzles, backgammon, chess, and cards—all of which require associative, logical deduction that develops mental agility.

MATHEMATICAL INTELLIGENCE

Logico-mathematical intelligence is responsible for logical reasoning; it is the basis of all science. It enables people to investigate the abstract relationships in the physical world and the world of logic, and it enables them to think conceptually—the root of Einstein's genius. Computer operations, scientific experimentation and theory, and mathematical calculations all utilize logico-mathematical intelligence. Obviously, it is imperative that your child develop this realm of his intellect, and fully.

An accountant parent we talked to believed logico-mathematical intelligence to be vitally important because it is used in estimating and calculating percentages, two skills he felt were essential to master.

> To survive out there, you've got to see the big picture rather than worrying about methodically dividing or multiplying everything. Percentages are among the most basic elements of math; they're fundamental to everyday life. Take, for example, when you want to sell your house and a realtor tells you he wants 6 percent of the $300,000 selling price—you had better be able to compute quickly whether or not his services are worth $18,000! Knowing how much of the home's equity is going to the realtor is crucial to making an intelligent decision.

Before they understand numbers relationships, children develop this realm of the intellect by observing other patterns in the environment, such as the design patterns in a piece of Scotch plaid wool, or the similarity between two billowy cumulonimbus clouds on the horizon, or the leaves on a tree. Reconstructing torn pieces of paper or comparing and contrasting the subtle differences between cars and trucks takes mental work and builds the power of observation. *Fitting pieces of information together is the basis of intellectual development.*

As they grow older, kids learn about the more abstract or conceptual aspects of patterns, such as the patterns or steps inherent in decision-making. If a youngster learns how to ask the right questions and investigate the variables involved in buying a video game with hard-earned baby-sitting money, she can apply those same principles when buying a bike, and later, an automobile or house. She does not have to relearn how to analyze each purchase because she will have developed logico-mathematical *reasoning* ability.

Learning math is done in a similar way. After learning simple addition and subtraction, kids move on to percentages and then to abstract algebraic or geometric calculations. They need to understand not the numbers themselves, but the *relationship between* the numbers. This, again, is where you come in. If you don't point out the *concept* of multiplication, practicing times tables will be no more than an exercise in passing tests—the problem we mentioned at the beginning of this chapter.

Your child must learn to *think* mathematically and use *reasoning* over *rote.* Here's a problem a business-owner–father explained that exemplifies the problem people have with mathematical reasoning:

> If you return a $10 item to a store and want to apply that amount toward a $20 item, should the clerk first credit you $10 *plus* the tax you paid and subtract that amount from the new total, or just deduct $10 from the $20 and add tax to the difference? Most of my cashiers are stumped by this problem—and so are my customers, who all have their own idea of which way is right.

This type of reasoning problem is simple for some, impossible for others, because there is no mathematical equation to call up to help solve the problem. It takes mathematical *reasoning*—the kind you must teach a child at home because it is rarely taught in school. (The answer is: It doesn't matter; both ways work out the same.)

The following series of vignettes show various ways effective parents taught their children mathematical relationships. Use them as guidelines and be on the lookout for your own teaching opportunities—they are everywhere.

When his children were three and four, Mr. Ramsey started teaching them basic math concepts by pointing out the simple changing relationships between their toy soldiers:

> Had we played army without any strategy and just randomly pushed men around, the boys wouldn't have learned much. The point of the exercise was not just to imagine battles taking place, but teach the kids how to count. When I moved their army men from one row to another, I'd challenge them to regroup and build up their troops again. If I pulled off five men to the flank, I'd have them count out five more men from their reserves—that sort of thing. As they got older, they got bored with soldiers and started building microfarms and keeping track of heads of cattle, horses, and pigs—much more complex.

One Sunday, Mr. Rogers, an avid football fan, realized what an excellent teaching tool watching a game could be for his seven-year-old son, Brad:

> I was watching the Cowboys, of course, our favorite team, and had been yelling at the TV like the football nut I was. When I came back from a snack break, I saw Brad doing what I always did: calculating what it would take for Dallas to win when we're down by so many touchdowns or field goals or whatever. I don't remember the score of that particular game, but, say, if it was seven to fourteen, Brad—at seven, mind you—had figured they would need either a touch-

down and a two-point conversation, giving Dallas the win by one, or a touchdown and a field goal, or three field goals. I stopped eating my sandwich in midbite and stood there in amazement. I realized that when kids are really interested in something, they can learn fairly sophisticated stuff. In our case, game scores were a great start.

Money and math go together, especially when it is money your child earns himself. In the following example, Mrs. Foley's sons (who were a year apart and both recommended for this study), learned not only how dimes and quarters add up to dollars, but how hard work achieves goals:

> Ricky and Jerry both had paper routes when they were about seven and eight. And they did them on their old bikes, the ones with the big balloon tires. When they said they wanted racing bikes for Christmas, we said fine, but they had to save the money from their routes to buy them. We offered to share the expense fifty-fifty. Suddenly, my kids were math wizards. They'd spread out their coins and dollars in piles on their beds after collecting [once a month] and we'd go over them. Four quarters for a dollar, ten dimes, etc., and then they'd keep notes [on their earnings] in notebooks. I'd have them keep subtracting the amount they earned from the price of the bikes, so all in all, the whole thing was a great exercise in math and patience. When they finally got the bikes Christmas day, they were little bankers. They knew *exactly* what a dollar was worth.

Another mother found that the best way to teach her five-year-old a complicated number was by appealing to the musical realm of his intellect. Songs and rhymes sink into the subconscious far easier than random facts:

> When Nathan was five years old and still in nursery school, his teacher had taught the kids in the class to memorize their names, addresses, and phone numbers in case they got lost. Nathan remembered everything okay, except he'd get stuck on the zip code. He couldn't remember 06716, which is a pretty complicated number for a little kid. He'd usually get all the numbers, but they'd be mixed up. So, we made up a little song about the zip code [sings song]. In no time at all—I think it was one afternoon or so—Nat had the zip down cold. He was able to recall it because we put it to a melody.

If kids are having a hard time paying attention to the service, church can be a great place to teach math skills. Here are two techniques a mother used to keep her restless son quiet while stimulating his brain on more secular matters:

> Since he was usually fidgety in church anyway, I was grateful when David [nine years old] started using the hymn board on the altar for math practice. Pretty ingenious, don't you think? The hymns are always large numbers like 358 or 225, so to add four or five of them in your head takes some doing. At first he made mistakes with his long addition, so I'd lean over and whisper something like, "You forgot to carry the one." Then he'd try again and whisper back another answer. I think he liked the fact that he was getting away with something in church, too. Another way I gave him little mental workouts was when it was time to stand. I'd hold his hand and do a Simon Says kind of game where I'd squeeze his hand like this [takes our hands and squeezes three short, two long]. Then, he'd have to repeat it back

and add one squeeze. I'd repeat that and add one, and so on. It wasn't exactly a *religious* lesson, but at least David got *something* out of church. Plus, he didn't mind going so much—and anyway, I'm sure we've been forgiven!

SCHOOL AND STUDY

After twenty years of studying Japanese culture, University of California anthropologist George DeVos found that the key to the Japanese children's extraordinary academic competence was—not unexpectedly—their *mothers.* This is good news for American parents (mothers *or* fathers). They too, can follow the example set by the Japanese mother who, as DeVos says, "takes it upon herself to be the responsible agent, reinforcing the educational process instituted in the schools." This statement captures the crux of the educational issue so perfectly: *Parents must reinforce the educational process.*

To help your child excel in school, do what successful Japanese mothers—and effective parents do: *Get involved.* Here's how:

- Become active in the PTA and local politics. This means doing a lot more than just going to a few parent-teacher conferences. Join education political action groups, community health agencies, or after-school activities programs. Said one father:

> Ask your local congressperson for her views regarding educational issues like busing, prayer in school, sex education, and condom distribution. My neighbor was quite vocal about school funding and the community

library programs that were getting cut. She went nuts every time she went to the library and it was closed because the hours had been cut again. Anyone can listen passively to those in a position of authority, but parents who want a better life for their kids have to let their voices be heard on the pertinent issues.

- Talk over with teachers and principals your concerns about curriculum and school policies. If the policies are not progressive, suggest that they expand their views. If they are, take advantage of the programs like this mother did:

> Our district has the best—and only—summer school program of its type that I've ever heard of. It's so popular, there's a waiting list to go. When I was in school we hated summer school because we wanted to be out playing. In this school, kids *are* playing—and learning. They take nonacademic, fun classes that teach them [new skills] and keep them occupied them for eight weeks of the summer vacation. Craig took the cartooning and computer discovery classes last summer. Melody took animal care and training. They both loved it and they're going again this summer. If parents get together, they can get programs like this started. That's what we did.

- Another mother, who had just changed careers to become a lawyer and had precious little extra time to spend away from her law books, told us how she singlehandedly changed her local school system's policy when it conflicted with what she knew was best for her son:

When Tommy was in Cook Junior High, he was at the top of his class. His classes were too easy, so I asked Cook to send him down to Burlington High to get into their freshman math and science classes. But Cook said no, they didn't have any way to do it, it wasn't policy, it had never been done before, blah, blah, blah, excuse after excuse. So I made arrangements myself to pick Tom up in the middle of the day, take him the six miles to Burlington, go back home to study for a couple of hours, and then pick him up again after the two classes and take him back to Cook. When they saw it could be done and saw how it benefited kids who were ready to move ahead, they instituted an achievement program—just like the one I spearheaded.

- Get to know your child's instructors. Determine their teaching styles and what is expected of your child. Is he getting the attention he needs? What are his weaknesses, his strengths? How can he do better? Before tests, papers, and other projects, spend a few minutes talking to the teacher about what is expected and how your child can best prepare. Like the true experts, you will be one of the few parents who do.

Bill's fourth-grade teacher said me and a couple of other parents were the only ones who seemed to care very much about our kids' assignments. "You parents stand out from the crowd, I've got to tell you," she said once. I knew the teacher respected our concern.

- Another counselor we spoke with said something similar:

> It is the children whose parents are involved who tend to get teachers' extra attention when time is limited, and it is *always* limited.

- Mrs. Ponti discovered how true that counselor's views were when her daughter, Denise, found out that teachers really do remember the families who get involved, as the Pontis did.

> We had these two rocking chairs at our house, but the kids liked this one rocker in particular, so they had to take turns sitting in it each night. Somehow their Spanish teacher—all the kids had the same teacher—heard about this chair and when they came to school in a good mood, he'd say, "What's with you? Did you get to sit in the chair last night?" He was a wonderful teacher. The amazing thing was, four years after Brian had him, Denise got him. The first thing he asked her when she walked into his class was, "Who's sitting in the rocking chair these days?"

- Get help for your child the moment she needs it. If you wait, or she is reluctant to admit she has a problem, you will exacerbate the problem and she will quickly fall behind. The parents we spoke with proceeded very carefully when it came to class difficulties. They did not try to coach their children themselves because, for one thing, they were not qualified, but more important, they knew their children were embarrassed enough without spotlighting the problem further.

When your kids need help—and all of them do at some time or another—get professional tutors—and quickly. Don't pretend everything will work itself out—it won't. Susan didn't want us to see she was having trouble, so we didn't look. We helped her arrange for a biology tutor after school. It took the pressure off and she recovered right away. Sitting at the dining table harping on a kid to "do better, do better," is useless—and frustrating! The whole idea is to make her feel better so she can pull out of the nosedive, not be ashamed of herself.

- Help your child *balance* his life. School is not the only job he has; *living* is the other. Academic endeavors should be balanced with extracurricular activities. There is a time to study, and there is a time to relax and enjoy sports, drama, journalism, dance, or collecting. One counselor explained:

> Compulsive study is no more compatible with a well-rounded lifestyle than rote memorization is with building thinking skills. Undue concern over grades—usually from anxious parents—gives students their own angst. It stresses them out and gives them a lopsided view of what the educational process is all about.

GOALS AND ORGANIZATION

Hundreds of books have been written on the subject of time management, and here's why: It is impossible to succeed without a high degree of *organization.* If you were to study the Japanese model, you would find that Japanese parents teach their children how to get things done, and done quickly and accurately. To succeed in school, children need a *systematic approach* to assignments. When he was a child, one father's father used to say to him in a heavy Russian accent, "Plan yer verk and verk yer plan!"

Here's what the successful parents recommended for teaching children the organizational skills necessary to make it to the top of their classes:

- Help your child establish goals. Without a clear destination, there is no way to select a route to get there. Discuss your child's dreams and aspirations, and lend support to those that are *realistic.* Some may be immediate, such as making the wrestling team; others may be long-term, such as deciding what college to attend. Such discussions make goals come alive and build desire—the single most important component to achieving them. But heed this warning from one parent who had to temper her son's aspirations:

  > Openly discuss your child's limitations, too. This is the real world and not everybody is a star at everything. If he's having a tough time in geometry, as Sean was, calculus might not be the best choice. If he is only an average reader, a book report on *War and Peace* may sound good, but he'll never get it done. Help kids set goals they know are within their reach; if they're too far out, their desire fizzles and they burn out.

- Ask your child mind-opening questions about her goals. Find out what she wants to achieve, and what is motivating her—including the most basic question: "Why?" "Why do you want to do that project?" "Has anyone influenced your decision?" "Have you talked to your teacher about it?" "Have you determined the number of hours it will require?"

- To stay on track, have your student use the most basic of time management tools: a calendar. Most of the students we met used large, desk blotter–type or oversized wall calendars with plenty of room to write in details. School projects, however, were not the only entries on the weekly grid.

> For Cindy, what worked best was filling in literally every hour of her day. Oh, she had plenty of free time slots when she could do what she wanted. I mean, *she* was the one filling them in. But she liked to have very specific times for everything: sleeping, bath time, ironing, church activities—even telephone time. *We* added that! She didn't just pick up the phone whenever she felt like it. We tried that and she never got anything done because she was bouncing to the phone every two minutes. She logged her two hours of TV time, but she could save it up and watch more on the weekend if she wanted. We went over that calendar together at least two or three times a month from the time she was thirteen to the time she graduated high school. Cindy was the type of kid who wasn't that organized. She relied on that calendar as much as I did on my appointment book.

Assisting your child in organizing her schedule is one thing, doing it *for* her is another. Give her all the help she needs, but let *her* make the final decisions so she can experience the results of not following the plan that *she* drew up. (See the section on Contracts in the next chapter.)

- Guard against the greatest hazard of all: wasting time. Your child may set out with the best intentions, but distractions, loss of interest, and lack of stick-to-itiveness may derail him midway to his goal, whether it is simple assignments or a major project. This means checking in regularly to see how he's doing—assuming he's "doing" at all. Said one highly successful mother:

  > I always wanted those kids where I could see them. It was unbelievable how much time they'd waste when I wasn't around! And these were bright kids, mind you. All of them were A and B students. But they weren't exempt from procrastination. Their biggest problem always was getting started. I remember so many times I had to push and remind and then *demand* that they get going on the darn report or whatever! I figured that if the homework was going to take, say, two hours, start harping about 7:30. I didn't want them staying up late because they'd been goofing off. They knew that unless it was a life-threatening project, the lights were going out at ten."

- Check the amount of time your child has slated for school projects before he starts. Be sure he is being realistic, and advise him to add another 25 percent to be on the safe side. He can relax if he finishes early, but not the other way around: When he's out of time, he's out of time—and the project is still due. One parent recalled advice she read: "Start studying for finals the first day of class." Another parent spoke for several when he said:

> Have kids leave at least a day's buffer between completion and due date of long-term assignments. Two days is even better because last-minute ideas always come up and you don't want them to run out of time to add them. The other thing is, you know kids sometimes get sidetracked and aren't going to stay on their schedules. That's what we had to watch for the most: keeping them on track and having them *stay* on track so there wasn't a crunch at the end.

Another parent gave similar advice:

> Plan what is to be done day by day, not just that the whole thing is to be completed by a certain date. The project has to be done no matter what, so plan for completion a day ahead so there's time for apple polishing. The other thing is to break projects into segments. Have a beginning, a middle, and an end. If the work is going to take a week, day three better be looking pretty good.

It didn't work that way for Tom, the student whose lawyer mother drove him to Burlington High for advanced classes. When he was a senior and had already clinched admission to Harvard, he thought he could cruise through his last few projects without much effort. But his overconfidence was his undoing, as his mother's story reveals:

> Well, I guess it happens to everyone sometime. But I never thought Tommy would sluff off *this* bad. He knew he was a brainy kid, but who waits until the night before a major science paper is due to *start* it!

Tom was present at the interview and interjected here: "It wasn't actually the *night* before, Mom. I mean, I had been *thinking* about it all day," which got laughs all around.

> Oh, great, Tom. Thanks so much for that. So anyway, here he is at midnight, and I hear a horrendous screech: "Aaaggg! I did it WRONG!" We all came running in and there he was holding his head in his hands. He had done twenty-five pages of his forty-page report wrong—and he realized it at *midnight!* Well, to make a long story short, we all—his brother, me, him—we started all over, stayed up all night, and after I threatened to kill him about a hundred times, got the thing typed and handed in by nine. God I'm glad he's going away to college!

One student we interviewed along with his mother told us a humorous story about how, when he was in sixth grade, he failed to complete an assignment, and out of sheer terror, came up with what he thought was an ingenious way out of the predicament. It wasn't.

> I thought I was so smart, but I've never seen anything so dumb! I guess I was a lousy liar. I still can't believe I actually thought I could get away with this. What happened was, my teacher sent me home with a note to be signed because of something I hadn't turned in. So, I took a stack of papers—trying to look casual—and told my Mom I was doing a *handwriting analysis!* [Paul and his mother explode into

> laughter.] I put the teacher's form on the bottom, and after having Mom sign the top few pages—to get her warmed up—I tried to slip out the bottom part of the teacher's note to get a signature! Real dumb. Pathetic. I mean, it was pink and all the other papers were white! [more laughs] It was *obvious,* plus I was shaking like a leaf. She knew what I was up to and busted me.

One final story helps put all of what we have discussed in this chapter into perspective:

> I used to tell Gerald: "Don't do what I did." I goofed off in school, never learned much until now, when I'm finally getting my Ph.D. at forty-five. It's too late and it's too hard. I should have put forth the effort when I was his age, and I told him that all the time. But he never listened, and so, at the last minute, he had to break his back to make his grades. But he made them. I'll never forget when he graduated with honors. [Starts to Cry] He looked out from that stage into a crowded auditorium of a thousand people and looked right at me. He smiled at me and mouthed the words "Thanks, Mom." God, I just fell apart.

CHAPTER 3

DISCIPLINE

Your preschooler goes on strike and defiantly refuses to cooperate with a reasonable request. How would you resolve the situation? Would you put Chapter 1's communication skills into action? Maybe so. But what if you weren't getting anywhere—including to work? When would you forgo the delicate techniques and resort to threats like no dessert after dinner? No more Ninja turtles? A spanking, perhaps? How about a bloodcurdling primal scream? The following example shows how Mrs. Andretti found a better way to handle her two-year-old's obstinacy:

> Billy went through a period when he refused to get dressed to go to day care. I'd put his clothes on him, and he would take them off. I'd put them on, he'd take them off again. On, off, on, off. I had no idea where his behavior stemmed from. Nothing seemed to work. He was controlling me, and it was always when I was in a rush to drop him off and get to my office. Then it dawned on me. "Well, if he won't get dressed, don't get into a tug-of-war with him," I said to myself. "Take him to day care naked." And that's exactly what I did. The next time Billy tried his stalling trick, I outsmarted him and simply walked him by the hand to the

> car and drove him to day care—stark naked! I said, "Goodbye, Billy, I'll see you when I come to pick you up. You've got to get out of the car now. Have a nice time in day care." No response. No car door opening. "I've got to be running along. You better get out now or you'll be late, too, Billy." The next thing I know, Billy's taking a headlong dive into the bag of clothes in the back seat.

Problem solved. Point made. No more naked car rides. By using a discipline technique called logical consequences, Mrs. Andretti claims another victory while teaching her child another lesson. Later in this chapter, we will see some examples of natural consequences that occur without parental intervention.

Contrast Mrs. Andretti's modern discipline style with the rigid, uncreative style of the early 1900s, when evening meals in many American homes found children with well-worn-but-clean clothes, slicked-back hair, and freshly scrubbed faces sitting upright at the dinner table, obediently waiting to be served. They answered smartly, "Yes, sir," when their fathers addressed them. No elbows on the table, no chitchat. If they dared reach rudely across the table for the bowl of potatoes, their knuckles paid the price with the smart whack of a wooden-handled spoon. And if children really got out of line—a rarity—there was, indeed, a stinging willow switch kept always at the ready above the icebox.

What's happened since then? Good and bad. For one thing, parents have lightened up. It's now okay to be a person—even if you *are* only a kid. But some families have plunged off the other end of the discipline scale. Life's a party! Most parents have turned 180 degrees from their predecessors and now give their children too much—too much freedom, too much money, too much of everything—while ignoring the traditions that once bonded family members.

So, which is harder on kids, the strict disciplinarian style of the 1920s or the permissiveness of the 1990s? As we discovered, neither style was acceptable to the true experts. They found, instead, a middle ground that permitted considerable *freedom* within very specific *guidelines*—two critical ingredients for teaching children the self-reliance they will need in their adult lives.

An equine veterinarian father we spoke with pointed out that a good example of this healthful balance can be seen at updated city zoos, where facilities have been modernized:

> Primates are rarely imprisoned in tiny cages, as they once were. Now, zoologists open large areas so animals can swing freely from tree limbs, climb to simulated mountain hideaways, and socialize with one another. But because they are not cognizant of their need for barriers or their inability to survive beyond their small worlds, they still need the outer boundary of a perimeter moat. Though they become neurotic and sick when sequestered in loveless cages, conversely, they cannot live without nourishment and care. Kids are really no different.

In this chapter we will see how effective parents replaced the "C" words of earlier generations—*constriction* and *conformity*—and those of more recent vintage—*competitive* and *compulsive*—with new, healthy ones: *creative, confident, competent,* and most important, *content.* They emphasized *self-reliance* over *servility* by carefully avoiding both permissive and restrictive parenting styles. Their main tool was sensible, no-nonsense discipline—employed *consistently* and *courageously,* two more valuable "C" words.

Why "courageously"? We answer that question in the first section of this chapter, which begins with a brief but vitally important look at parents' motives for having children in the first place and how it affects their ability to discipline. Next, we discuss the discipline style our experts selected, and why. You will see that they established rules and set limits, and then let their children *live* within those limits without constant assistance, harping, advising, overprotecting, indeed, *parenting*! But when kids violated those limits and their parents' trust, they suffered swift and certain consequences with no hesitation, debate, or bargaining.

One of the most common behavioral issues, especially among younger children, was attention-getting behavior. Our discussion of how parents handled it will give you a sense of how they handled similar problems. We conclude this chapter by highlighting the one aspect of child rearing that is perhaps parents' greatest downfall: *overprotection.* Watch in the following vignettes how, when disciplinary measures were necessary, they were employed in a loving rather than a domineering way.

Underlying parents' successful disciplinary measures were always two important elements: (1) a sense of justice and fairness, and (2) an undeniable logic that even the youngest children could understand. One mother explained part of that logic and what child rearing meant to her:

> My overriding philosophy in raising my kids was: The relationship is more important than the behavior. What I

> mean by that is, it's not worth it to get excited about every little, crazy, irrational thing your kid does. Don't assume he's doing things on purpose or to make you mad or show he doesn't have to listen to you. That behavior comes when parents think they have to be right all the time. You've got to let things slide, let the water roll off your back a little, and remember that the most important thing is the love you share in your family, the relationships—not the police state you create!

With those sound words of advice, let's begin with parents' motives and briefly examine what is possibly the greatest single obstacle to quality child rearing: *fear.*

PARENTS' MOTIVES

Many parents fear losing their children's love. The very reason people choose to have children in the first place often prevents them from disciplining them appropriately. And if parents have a deeply rooted need to capture the love they never had from their own parents, to save a failing marriage, or to keep their spouse from leaving them, their will to discipline will be perilously weak. If they fear making necessary but unpopular decisions because they may upset or offend their children, parents usually ignore their own halfhearted rules and give up control. This fearfulness increases the likelihood of *poor* relationships—precisely what they wanted to avoid!

Giving up when disagreements arise is not the easy way out—it's the hard way. Giving in to the whims and demands of disobedient children is like planting mines in your own harbor. And when you hit one and begin to sink, guess who's circling your ship in the water below? *Kids,* like little sharks, sense your insecurity and instinctively move in to take advantage of it, knowing there will be no rebuke for misbehavior. Of all the parenting mistakes, this is one of the most common—and most destructive. A father we interviewed saw one such manipulator in action. He described a two-year-old he knew who, like any shark, feared nothing—including abandonment:

> One morning I got in the elevator with my next-door neighbor and her little girl, Mary. She was a moody child; we often heard her screaming her head off through the apartment wall and now I saw why: She controlled her mother and she knew it. When the elevator door opened, everyone got out except Mary, who leaned against the back wall and refused to move. Her mother said, "Come on, Honey, we're going to be late." I tried to coax her out too by saying, "Let's go, Mary, let's go, door's gonna close." Nothing. She could have been wearing one of those T-shirts that says, NO FEAR. She laid back and glared at us with no intention of doing anything. Sure enough, her mother immediately moves in and picks her up—just like the kid wanted her to do! I would have *at least* let the door start to close to give her a dose of reality.

What would the true experts do in such a situation? We were lucky enough to get a very similar story—but one with a different response from a parent who was as fearless as her daughter. Here's how Mrs. Lopez explained her highly effective disciplinary action:

> I got sick of telling Florencia to stay next to me in the department store. She was about three then, and she was always exploring, not listening, so I finally tried something else. I let her do what she wanted instead of keep telling her, "Stay here. Stay near me, Florencia." I figured it was the only way to teach her *why* I wanted her near me. What I did was, I let her get lost! That's right. And I recommend it to all parents because it was the only thing that worked. After telling her one last time, I let her wander off. It didn't take long. All of a sudden, she realized she was lost. I could see her, but she couldn't see me. No mama anywhere. Oh, the scream! You should have heard it! But I didn't run and save her right away. I let it sink in for a few moments, and then I went over to her. All I had to say was, "See?"

If you think you might have some fears that are keeping you from taking proper measures when they are called for, post the following rule on your mirror; it's one of the most important in the book: *Giving in to children's every demand is* not *an act of love.*

As writer and motivational speaker Zig Ziglar said, "If you're out to win a popularity contest with your child, you're in trouble."

DISCIPLINE STYLES

Let's clarify one issue immediately: *Firmness* does not equate with *meanness* and it does not result in loss of love—the great, debilitating fear so many parents harbor. Quite to the contrary, fair and judicious leadership is more closely aligned with respect because even though they will rarely express it, deep down, youngsters want *more,* not less, reassuring guidance. Parents in our study found that if they remained firm in their discipline and did not cave into children's demands, their kids were more relaxed and better behaved.

Of the three basic discipline styles—permissive, authoritarian (strict), and authoritative (reasonable and respectful)—the most pervasive is the permissive one. Why is this? Perhaps because it takes the least effort, perhaps because it gives parents a false sense of security that their children will always love them. Whatever the reason, avoid it at all costs. The following anecdote describes a situation that was clearly on a collision course with disaster:

> I attended a self-esteem for infants seminar and had struck up a conversation with the father sitting next to me. He had quite a philosophy about disciplining his son, which was basically this ingenious theory that parents should *never* use discipline at all, just *distraction*! When I asked him for clarification, he explained to me that he didn't believe in saying "No" to his child because it might cause him *frustration*! He said distracting kids with other subjects would prevent them from becoming pent-up little neurotics! I couldn't believe what I was hearing—and I didn't hear anything like it from the lecturer, either.

What this father failed to understand was that the real world is not so accommodating. Here's a tip we gleaned from the experts that directly refutes his assertions: *The less quality disciplining a child receives, the more likely he is to grow up unloving and disrespectful.*

Are children really happier and better adjusted when their parents are afraid to discipline them?

Is it any wonder that when one father, Mr. Phillips, heard a neighborhood girl of three say "darn," and told her it was a bad word, she responded, "That's not a bad word. 'F_ _ _' is!"

On the other side of the negative parenting coin lies the strict, authoritarian style. Compared to the permissive style, it's a toss-up as to which is worse. But if you have ever witnessed a domineering parent in action, you know how enervating and humiliating it can be—especially to a young child who has no one to turn to except the fire-breathing monster he is trying desperately to love.

The parent in the supermarket who, when asked by his child, "Why can't I have the candy?" snarls back, "Because I *said* so, that's why!" is applying *authoritarian* discipline and it doesn't work. It is dictatorial and offers a totally inadequate answer. A child may well reason to herself, "Well, if *that's* the only reason, I'm not going along with it—it doesn't make any sense." And it doesn't.

Unfair, illogical bullying can drive kids to question authority as they grow up, leading to all kinds of trouble down the road. Militaristic, caustic discipline leaves children not only emotionally and intellectually impoverished, but also pathetically unprepared for life. Kids are deeply scarred by this type of irrational discipline, and though they may be very young, they will always remember how unfairly they were treated. Remember this: *Children develop an ability to make decisions only if they are allowed to interact with their parents.*

Here is what Mrs. Donaldson, a wise, *authoritative* parent, did when her five-year-old kept harping about candy: She said with a funny Gabby Hayes–type toothless grin, "You can't have candy because it will rot your teeth. Want to see?" When he nodded his head, they jumped into the car and drove to the library where they thumbed through a book on dentistry and took a long look at photos of cavities and other dental problems. This is how she explained the incident:

> When Darren tried to close the book, I said, "Oh, no you don't, buddy. You wanted to come down here. Take a look at what candy does. Do you want rotten teeth?" I knew something registered when, on the way home, he broke a long silence with, "Well, what about ice cream?"

Two other parents gave us their "pet" stories, both of which were quite similar and demonstrated excellent authoritative skills. The first one involved a thirteen-year-old girl who was given the choice of meeting her responsibilities to her pet or suffering the same fate he (Tiger the cat) did. Said Mrs. Popovich:

> I didn't think much about it, but I knew I was getting sick and tired of feeding Tiger when he was Pamela's responsibility. One night I told her I wasn't going to do it anymore. "This is your last warning. The next time you think it's OK for Tiger to starve, we'll let you starve right along with him so you can see what it's like." This, of course, went in one ear and out the other. So, when Pam sat down to dinner the next evening without having fed the cat, I "forgot" to serve her. I served everyone else, but I passed her by. No discussion—and no food. So, she rolls her eyes like it's *my* fault, gets up and dumps some dried food in the cat's bowl—

> which he hates—and comes back to the table. "Sorry, Pam," I said. "Tiger's dinnertime was two hours ago, so I think you've missed yours too. Oh, and no snacks tonight either."

Mrs. Popovich went on to explain that her impromptu method was effective because she did not "lay a guilt trip" [her words] on her daughter and had given her fair warning. She added that if Pamela still had not met her responsibilities, she would not have hesitated in giving the cat away. Could anything have been more reasonable to all parties (including the skinny cat)?

A father we spoke with told us a similar "dog" story involving his seven-year-old son, who had begged and pleaded with his father to let him have a dog. The father believed his boy was old enough to take care of an animal, so he allowed him to select one from the local pound. He had only one stipulation for the boy, which he reiterated over and over for several weeks before adopting the pet: "You must walk that dog every day without fail, even when you don't feel like it. Are you sure you can handle that?" The boy concurred (of course), but soon began to slack off from his responsibilities. As in Mrs. Popovich's case, after several reminders, the talking stopped and the action started. Here is what Mr. Shansby told us:

> Scotty was looking forward to going fishing off the Coyote Point pier with me on Sunday. But when that Sunday came and I put Lucky [the dog] in the car instead of Scott, he asked in disbelief, "Hey, Dad, what about me?" "I'd love to take you, son, but I've got to spend the day exercising Lucky since you haven't done it all week. He needs someone to play with, as we've discussed many, many times." When we

returned, Scott was in a sullen mood. But I decided I might as well put the icing on the cake. "You know, Scott," I said, "Lucky and I had a pretty good time today, but he wasn't the same. He seemed to be whining a little and looking around, I think for you. Whenever I mentioned Scott, though, he'd start wagging his tail and making that dog smile of his. I really think he missed you."

RULES AND FREEDOM

Now that we have seen what discipline style works, let's look at the structure of the entire system in which it is applied. Like any organization, there must be clearly defined rules that outline the limits of acceptable behavior. To be fair and effective, these rules must be clearly laid out and agreed to by the members of the organization. The successful parents accomplished this by (1) anticipating what was likely to occur, (2) planning *in advance* how to handle it, (3) holding meetings to discuss those rules, limits, and consequences for noncompliance, and (4) obtaining their children's concurrence on everything.

Keep this parent's comment in mind as we look at rules and freedom:

> Our long-term goal was not to *maintain* control over our children forever, it was to gradually *relinquish* it as they grew up and became more and more capable of fending for themselves.

When their children made inevitable slips, our parents reinstated restrictions until their kids again felt comfortable with new freedoms. Such restrictions are most effective when they are clear, concise, simple, and few. When infractions occurred, the clearly outlined consequences left no room for discussion. One couple, for instance, simply followed through on what they had promised: They took away leisure time, ten minutes at a whack.

> When someone did something wrong, they had to go to bed ten minutes earlier every night for a week. If they did something else against the rules, we lopped off another ten minutes. For young kids, staying up is a big privilege. If they're going to bed a half hour before everybody else, they're definitely not happy campers.

Successful parents did not spring such corrective measures on their children, they prearranged them and openly discussed them at family meetings—a vital component of any parenting program, but one that in most families is usually reserved for crisis management.

FAMILY MEETINGS

If parents bicker over discipline and are uncertain about what to do in a given situation, their child may easily rationalize that his misdeed may not have been so bad after all. If his parents finally do agree on a directive (which they often don't), it will have far less impact than intended because the child has witnessed his parents' ambivalence. If they're unsure, he's unsure. Avoid this problem by *preplanning* your courses of action and then laying them on the table for discussion at family meetings.

Though you may not accept your children's protestations

over the rules and regulations you outline, they should be a welcomed part of these sessions. It is here that debate, discussion, reasoning, perhaps even a little bargaining on the small items is acceptable—*not* at the time of an infraction!

Get kids involved in the discussion and let them vent their feelings and ideas. This is the essence of fair, authoritative discipline, which is founded on respect and interaction—not militaristic commands. The side benefit of kids' involvement is, they go on record as having clearly *understood* and *agreed* with the rules, leaving no room to hedge later if they step over the line *they* helped draw.

Regularly scheduled family meetings are similar to the "special times for talking" we discussed in Chapter 1 in that they give children time to prepare for what they want to say, and they offer them reliable, preset forums to freely air frustrations and joys. Meetings also give both you and your kids opportunities to slow down the pace of everyday life and take "breaks in the action," which is especially important for younger children, who are constantly flying around on whirlwinds of exploration and adventure. They long to tell you about the gopher that popped his head out of a hole, or the secret hideaway they found down by the creek. Preplanned meetings give them something to look forward to—and they give all of you time to relate to one another in a way that isn't possible on a day-to-day basis.

The meetings we heard about took several forms, but there was a general consensus on the following basics:

- Family meetings are not to be used for damage control after a crisis erupts; they are designed to *prevent* crises.

- Hold meetings at least once a month, unless there are specific or recurring issues that need more attention.
- Make meetings no longer than thirty minutes for younger kids, one hour for older ones.
- Allow the children to begin the meetings and air problems, grievances, or suggestions.
- Discuss past issues before bringing up new ones.
- Don't censor any subjects.
- Take turns speaking and don't interrupt one another.
- Get children's concurrence with all rules.

As one couple discovered, family meetings have another major benefit: The mere fact that they are going to take place tends to head off trouble.

> We found that friendly reminders during the week like "the meeting is coming up" were quite a deterrent to misbehavior. Invisible kids can't be so invisible when they're sitting at the table explaining why they broke such and such a rule, or whatever might have slipped through the cracks had there been no meetings. When Pauline came home late or hadn't done her chores, all I had to say was, "We'll discuss this at the meeting." That's what she worried about because she knew we were going to bring it up all over again and *talk* about it, *dissect* it. Kids hope these things go away—and they do if you don't sit down and confront them. We cleared up a lot of problems at our regular sessions. I highly recommend them to all parents, but the secret is sticking to them.

Family meetings aren't seen as cure-alls that bring instant compliance with rules. But parents found that when they adhered to the following six basics, their discipline was absolutely fair and highly effective:

- Impose a few key rules, not a lot of general ones.
- Explicitly state rules and write them down so that if they are violated, there will be no debate as to what you meant.
- Eliminate the phrase "one more chance."
- Institute the phrase "take responsibility for your actions."
- Enforce rules *consistently* and *confidently.* Follow through with the consequences of a broken rule without fail.
- Discipline silently through actions—not warnings, threats, or discussions.

Mr. Schultz followed through perfectly with these rules when he applied the Five O'Clock Rule, to which each family member had previously agreed at their meeting. Mrs. Schultz explained the incident to us:

> Michael was about five and had been in the midst of an epic battle between Ninja turtles and army men. Then he went outside to play with a neighbor, leaving everything scattered around the playroom. That was fine. But when his father called out to him around 4:45 to remind him it was time to clean up his toys, Michael ignored him. So, according to the rule, at precisely five o'clock, Jim took out a shopping bag and began collecting the toys. When Michael arrived on the scene, it was no longer the battleground it was, nor was it going to become another one between those two. As Jim headed toward the attic to stow the toys, Michael

went into hysterics. He cried and pleaded but it was no use. There was total silence from his father and everything was concluded without any more discussion.

Mr. Schultz did not fear losing Michael's love or hurting his son. He knew character-building measures like this had to be taken no matter how much fuss his child put up. Another parent echoed Mr. Schultz:

> Children who aren't disciplined when they are young, by their parents, will be disciplined much less lovingly later, when they are out in the world—looking for jobs or forming social circles.

Here's another tip our parents felt was instrumental to successful family meetings and parenting in general: *Offer to consider your children's point of view so they feel* empowered *rather than* dominated.

One mother called this philosophy "participatory democracy," which she felt was appropriate not only because children have a fundamental right to voice their opinions at the proper time, but also because they are supposed to be gaining a sense of self-reliance. Giving them a say in how they lead their lives is an integral part of that growth.

Another mother, Ms. Riley, found that when she broached a new subject with the line, "I don't know if you're old enough to discuss this, but . . . ," it never failed to get her daughter, Donna's, undivided attention. Donna, who was present during our interview, told us why this worked:

First of all, Mom piqued my curiosity when she'd start a sentence like that. But really, I think it was because I felt respected and trusted to handle whatever the issue was. I felt mature when Mom used that line with me. She treated me as a grown-up and it really meant a lot to me. What she said hit home because I knew it was important when she started like that, and she put me sort of on her level. It all came down to trust.

Rules have another key function that often goes unrecognized: They actually *increase* children's freedom and peace of mind because they act as signposts in an unfolding, complex world. Without these paradoxically liberating restrictions, children feel no more certain of where they stand than do travelers entering foreign cities at rush hour without road maps. One parent described the reaction of his two children, who not only didn't have road maps in dangerous territory but didn't have any way to escape from it. Here's what happened when his two young sons violated the Rule of the Yard—and quickly gained a whole new respect for restrictions:

The boys were told never to go through the rear gate into the field that adjoined our backyard. It was off limits at all times, which, I guess, was the enticement. As I happened to look out my upstairs window, I saw them heading toward the gate. Apparently Steven, the five-year-old, had discovered how to open the latch, but never ventured further without the moral support of Paul, the three-year-old. As I headed downstairs, they slipped into forbidden territory and I guess the gate latched behind them without their knowing it. By the time I arrived three minutes later, they were bonkers—shrieking and crying, clawing at the gate, and going on about monsters and all. They knew they were in trouble, but they didn't care; they were never so happy to see their dad.

SETTING LIMITS

Even though kids know they will have to face the music at the family meetings, they can still test limits to the breaking point. Your job: Don't break! The true experts never did, and it was one of the secrets to their success.

When kids argue, pout, defend their position and deride yours, acknowledge their feelings but don't play their game. Hang on tenaciously to those limits! Remember, kids want what they want and often act like puppies: No matter what you've done to keep them safely within the backyard, they find ways to burrow under the fence and defiantly turn up at the front door, tails wagging and thoroughly delighted with themselves.

Mr. Peterson explains how he prevented such a victory when his seventeen-year-old daughter, Robin, suspiciously placed a call to him at work—something she rarely did. Knowing he was busy and unable to talk long, she quickly rattled off a barrage of unconnected, confusing details about a trip she wanted to take from San Francisco to Los Angeles the following month. In obtaining his consent, she intoned an unusual urgency, which, it turned out, was a ploy to avoid the grisly details.

> By the time I had returned home and eaten dinner, I had forgotten about the conversation, and Robin never mentioned it again. It apparently was a dead issue—until later

the following month when she was ready to walk out the door with her suitcase! "Where are you going?" I asked. "Oh, you know, to L.A.," she responded. "Remember the trip I told you about?" "No, not really," I said. "Would you mind explaining?" Well, it turned out she wanted to drive over eight hundred miles with a friend who had just received her driver's license in order to go to some *party*! Oh, that was a swell idea. She planned to leave on Saturday night and return Monday morning in time to make it to class. She conveniently left out these "minor" details. "Good try, Rob, but you're not going," I told her. Needless to say, she tested our limits and lost, big time.

Here is an additional list of tips our successful parents used to assure reason over rebellion:

- Avoid excessive or unnecessary discipline. One parent told us about a ten-year-old neighborhood boy who was restricted from playing with his next door neighbors for the *entire summer* because he had accidentally thrown a baseball through a small windowpane in the neighbors' breakfast room (the victims made no fuss over the incident). This type of excessive punitive measure can breed hostility.
- Take measures that are appropriate to the crime, that are thoroughly justified, and that can be enforced. When you say, "You're grounded for a month," you and the jailbird both know you'll never make it that long. Ms. Bentley, a highly experienced manager for a major HMO, knew exactly how to curtail her then two-year-old's delight in spreading his peanut butter sandwiches on her light gray living room carpet. She

simply stopped cleaning up after him and let him do the dirty work himself. Not only did he have to put in hard labor for his crime, he also went without another sandwich.

> I used to clean up Alex's mess without thinking about it. I'd just do it. Then I stopped "just doing it" and made *him* do it. I guess it dawned on me one day: He's two! He's not six months old anymore. So I stopped—and he stopped. Apparently it wasn't so much fun when he didn't get a rise out of me.

- Be certain measures have a distinct beginning and end. Whether it was a simple "time out" or a "you're grounded" (both of which our parents used regularly), they immediately stated the *exact* duration of the restriction period. One parent used weeding as "therapeutic behavior modification" [her words] for her fourteen-year-old daughter.

> Pulling weeds for an hour every Saturday morning for a month gave Jessica something more productive to do than talk over her telephone time limit every night for a week—hoping I wouldn't notice. Since she obviously assumed I made rules for my own good and not hers, I decided to take her up on it. Now I've got a beautiful garden to prove she was right.

- Insure that measures teach a lesson. The girl who went without dinner when she forgot to feed the cat is a good example.

- Stick to your guns! Give clout to your measures by following through with the actions you promised. As one parent said, "You want to hear your kids say to one another, 'Better do it, Mom *means* it!' "

These measures and the others we have discussed carried weight because the expert parents did not forgive too readily or renew privileges too quickly. And above all, they did not negotiate or argue with their children. One parent said, "Don't *ask* your younger children if they are ready for dinner, *tell* them it is time for dinner." There is a big difference between the two postures.

CONTRACTS

So, you have preplanned your disciplinary measures, discussed them during the family meetings, and set fair and equitable limits to which everyone has agreed. Everything is working relatively smoothly, but then something happens: Kids grow up. As our parents discovered, when little kids become big kids, the complexion of the game changes considerably. Adolescents begin their quest for independence and have a greater tendency to question their parents' judgment. Many measures are not as earthshaking as they once were, so you will need to employ a more sophisticated, interactive tool: written contracts.

In a court of law, the first thing a judge asks disputing parties is, "Did you have a *written* contract or just a verbal one?" Kids, like everyone else, are more likely to abide by the terms of written versus verbal contracts because if they are simple, unambiguous, and visible, they leave little room for teenagers to squirm out of them—and kids will try.

Visibility is one key to effective contracts. They don't do much good stuffed in the back of a messy drawer. Post them and refer to them. When conflicts arise, you have binding contracts on your side. Like a good lawyer, you can enter the "courtroom" prepared with contract and penal code in hand, and signed in indelible ink. (One father said he had his kids sign in red ink and told them they were signing in blood!)

On the following page is the simple, no-nonsense contract that Mrs. Chandler used with her teenaged daughter, who was having difficulty coming home on time. When Patty Chandler willfully defied the clearly written terms of this contract and came home at eleven instead of ten o'clock, she instantly established her own new nine o'clock curfew. When she foolishly tried to argue the merits of her case—when the terms *she had agreed to* were clearly posted on her closet door—Mrs. Chandler refused to discuss it. "Look inside your closet," she told her with a laugh. "There's nothing to discuss."

Another parent found there was indeed something to discuss, but not with her daughter—with the police. Mrs. Griffith had stated in her sixteen-year-old daughter's contract that she would "call the authorities" if Lucy was ever more than thirty minutes late. So, when the gallivanting girl tested the policy one night, she found the kitchen transformed into a bustling missing-persons headquarters.

> When Lucy strolled in over an hour late that night, I was sitting at my command post surrounded with telephone books, her little red address book, and a yellow notepad full

CONTRACT

I, Patty Chandler, agree to the terms and conditions set forth in this contract. I agree to abide by all of these rules and regulations and acknowledge that I have discussed them with my mother and we have mutually agreed that they are reasonable, sensible, and in my best interest. I understand them perfectly and agree that if I violate any terms of these rules or regulations, I will be penalized with the prescribed restrictions, which I agree are fair and justified. I will not argue or complain in any way if I violate the following terms of this agreement.

1. My curfew for Friday and Saturday nights is 10 P.M. sharp.

2. I understand that if I am home after 10:05 I have violated curfew, unless I have first called Mom and told her why I will be late.

3. I will not call Mom to ask if I can stay out later than curfew unless I have some kind of emergency and can't possibly get home on time.

4. I understand that my penalty for coming home after curfew will be grounding for the next two weekend nights and a new curfew of 9 P.M. for the next month.

Signed______________________________Date__________

of checked-off phone numbers and other child-hunting hieroglyphics. She walked in to hear, "Oh, wait a minute, officer, I think that's her now." It was my latest call—after having contacted the highway patrol, several of Lucy's friends' parents, and the local pizza hangout. But I didn't restrict her. I came up with a better idea. "Next time I'll start calling twenty minutes after curfew. And guess what? *You* get to call everyone back and apologize for the hassle, because I'm not." Needless to say, curfew immediately ceased to be a point of contention.

A student we interviewed who had gone to a Montessori school as a youngster explained that his teacher also believed in contracts and found them useful for instilling self-discipline and self-reliance:

> Our teacher would have us individually write out a contract about an assignment, usually on Mondays for assignments due on Friday. Then he wouldn't bring it up again. We signed them and gave them to him—and everyone turned everything in on time. It really worked! I think it was because none of us wanted to let him down since he trusted us to hold to our end of the deal—and he didn't hassle us about it.

PUNISHMENT VS. CONSEQUENCES

Certainly, leniency can result in unruly, disrespectful children, but slapping, hitting, publicly scolding, screaming, and other verbal abuse can cause long-lasting, deeply felt wounds that fester into resentment, humiliation, shame, and anger. It is *never* acceptable. One father told us how even a casual remark can be detrimental when it is disparaging and disrespectful:

> Rachel was about seven years old then. It was remarkable how much she was affected by this comment I made in a fit of anger. She did something that made me mad and I blurted out, "Rachel, sometimes you've just got no brains! You don't have the brains God gave a goose!" What a mistake that was. For weeks afterward, she tried to compensate and prove herself by doing something and then saying, "See, I'm smart. I've got *lots* of brains, Daddy."

Another mother, a florist, said that when she lost her temper and was about to insult her son, at least she had the wherewithal to call him a botanical name. "My favorite was *podocarpus gracilior!*"

But when the tables are turned and it's the kids who are spitting out epithets of a less creative variety, try Mrs. Hamilton's behavior modification method:

> I know teachers make kids write bad words a hundred times, but I don't think that's enough of a lesson. I made Eric *say* his favorite filthy word five hundred times, over and over so he got sick of hearing it. Oh, I didn't stand there and listen to him, I gave him the cassette recorder and told him to fill the tape with the sound of his own voice.

Neither Mrs. Hamilton nor any of the other parents we interviewed resorted to humiliation or harsh punishment to correct their children's misbehavior. Rather, they relied on very specific *consequences* related directly to misdeeds.

They discovered that two, in particular, were very persuasive: *isolation* and *withholding affection.*

Perhaps more than anything else, children crave their parents' affection and approval, especially when they are younger. When they have misbehaved, nothing makes a bigger impact than removing that approval to demonstrate your disappointment. This is not shaming and should not be confused as such; it is highly effective *teaching*—when done without disgust or disdain. Said one father:

> Isolation was a big one for Tom. When he did something wrong, all we had to do was send him to his room. He hated it more than anything else I can remember.

Banishment to the bedroom does not always work, however. This mother said that, for her kids, it wasn't nearly enough of a consequence:

> We tried sending the kids to their rooms, but when we stopped getting arguments, we realized, "Hey, they don't mind going to their rooms because there's lots of stuff they can do there: Play with their toys, read, listen to music. It's like sending them to a resort!" So, when they were really disturbing the rest of the family—usually at dinnertime—we gave them ten-minute jail sentences to Siberia: the bathroom—with no Walkman. *That* we heard about.

One parent told us that he, like several other parents we met, found telephone restriction to be an exceptionally effective consequence for misbehaving teenagers because it is so central to their lives; it is their vital link to the outside world. When sequestered away in their self-made prisons, there is no way to keep in touch with the gang, to let everyone know they are still around. The result? They start getting worried—and presumably start thinking about what brought on the restriction in the first place.

> Pulling the telephone cord was torture for Nancy. When she stepped over the line, her social life was on hold for a week. No incoming calls, no outgoing calls. We'd gladly take messages for her when her friends called, which probably rubbed salt in the wound, but that's the way the cookie crumbles. We'd tell her friends, "Nancy's not taking calls this week, but we'll relay a message." She couldn't stand it!

Another father explained how powerful withholding affection can be in a family where affection is usually free-flowing. One day he received a call from a local department store security manager who had caught his twelve-year-old daughter and her friends shoplifting bottles of nail polish.

> We picked Erica up and drove her home without saying a word. There were no words to say. She knew what a blow this was to us and how she had let us down. Cutting her off emotionally was more devastating to her than getting caught. Since we had always had an open, communicative relationship where she could come to us anytime she wanted, suddenly reversing the whole thing really blew her away.

As we saw at the beginning of this chapter, Billy faced the *logical* consequence of embarrassment when he refused to get dressed for day care. The following anecdote demonstrates a *natural* consequence, which is the direct result of violating a law of nature or society—or in this case, school.

Effective parents know, as Mr. Davis did, not to interfere with this type of natural training. It has its own way of teaching a valuable lesson—*if* parents don't get in the way.

Mr. Davis related the time he received a call from the dean of men after his son, John, who had never been in any trouble at school before, was sent to the dean's office for a minor infraction. John chimed in while his father was explaining the story and gave this account of what happened:

> When Dean Mancini got off the phone with Dad, he turned to me and said, "If all parents were like that, I'd have fewer problems down here." "What do you mean?" I asked. Dean Mancini responded, "He said I should take whatever disciplinary action I felt was necessary; he left the matter entirely up to me. That's the kind of parent I like! Too many parents deny their kids did anything wrong and try to protect them." Then he handed me one of his infamous Vic sticks with the nail in the end (his name was Victor Mancini) and a box and made me pick up papers during lunch hour. Usually you only saw the troublemakers with the Vic sticks. Of course he assigns me to the commons area where everyone was eating. You feel like a criminal out there. All your friends see you and the worst part is, your teachers and coaches see you, too. It's totally embarrassing.

When an adolescent makes a serious error in judgment, the best thing a parent can do is not threaten disciplinary action, but explain that such misjudgment carries a high price—or natural consequence—that he cannot mitigate. There comes a time when parents can no longer bail out their offspring even if they want to. The real world awaits, and it awaits with the expectation that young adults will have made the switch from *parental* discipline to *self*-discipline.

To help your child make this transition to responsible behavior, explain the natural consequences of unwise actions. Mr. Delaney related such an incident regarding his son, Chris, who had been a top-ranked varsity football player the better colleges were now looking at with interest. But to be accepted to the schools, he needed to do particularly well in the last semester of his senior year. When the midterm examinations came around and Chris was under a lot of pressure to prepare, he did something quite uncharacteristic.

> Instead of studying, Chris went out drinking with his friends on a school night. Even the most straitlaced senior may be tempted to have a beer on a Friday night, but for Chris, shirking his responsibility—and his last chance to shape his college career—was unusual. When he got home at 11:30 P.M. on that Sunday night, I met him at the door. What do you do, take a 225-pound linebacker over your knee? I sat down with him and said, "What's the *deal?* You're a few credits away from getting into a decent school, you've got to get the grades now or it will be too late, and you go out and drink *beer?* God knows, we've all had a few beers before we were twenty-one, but not before walking into a midterm!"

Mr. Delaney explained that their ensuing discussion focused on priorities and the fact that only Chris would be able to pull himself out of the fire. He told his son that it was his college career and his future. "You, not me, are responsible for making it or blowing your last chance to start off in the right direction. I hope you make the right decision."

This example brings home the important point: *Trusting deserving children breeds trustworthiness instead of the deceitfulness that comes from suspicion.* When kids occasionally falter, as Chris did, having a nonjudgmental, loving parent there to point out the consequences and guide them back on course is what parenting is all about.

SPANKING

Though a 1988 Harris poll found that 86 percent of adults felt it was acceptable to spank or physically discipline their children, the parents we met generally disagreed. They had various reasons for avoiding spanking: "It shames kids." "It's humiliating." "We gave up flogging along with debtors' prisons, didn't we?" "Hitting builds resentment and anger." "Violence breeds violence." "I don't want to *hurt* my kids." "Spanking doesn't work." But as our interviews progressed, we found a large percentage of our parents, around 75 percent, who believed there was one condition when a spank was not only appropriate but *required:* when children are in danger.

Virtually all of these parents found that when nothing else was effective in modifying behavior and their children urgently needed to learn something that wasn't coming across intellectually, a physical jolt was the only thing that worked. The following father put it very simply and echoed the feelings of the majority of parents we met:

> We lived near a creek where the winding street made it impossible to see kids. What were the consequences of my

> three-year-old daughter running into that street? A dead kid. After I'd told her several times and she still didn't get it, hell, yes, she got a spank! Sometimes a flat hand on the butt is the only thing a three-year-old understands. What's the alternative? A dead kid.

What became of this girl whose father was not afraid to spank her when it was necessary? When we interviewed her father, she had just completed her second year at Princeton University, where she had advanced to first seat on the women's crew team. Her proud father was heading to New Jersey the following month to watch her compete in the national championships, which, we found out later, her team won. If you know anything about sports, you know that the main difference between the winners and the losers when all else is equal is *discipline.*

A mother related another spanking story, this one a comical tale about her adventuresome four-year-old who strode next door to the neighbor's house one morning to lob two dozen of their freshly delivered eggs off their porch because, as he put it, "I like watching them explode." The light spank he got wasn't nearly as painful as the trip to the grocery where he had to pick out two dozen more eggs, pay for them with his own savings, and deliver them to the scene of the crime.

Another mother said this about spanking:

> Let's get over all this mumbo jumbo about beating kids. We're not talking about beating kids. We're talking about when little Ricky has been told over and over again not to play with matches, but still wants to light little Susie's hair on fire and has the lit match poised inches away from her

> golden locks. Yes, a spank is in order, and *immediately*! What would you suggest someone do with a wild five-year-old like this? Sit him down and have an intellectual conversation about pyromania? Ask him if it wouldn't be too much trouble, could he please stop setting the neighborhood girls on fire—pretty please? Try a quick spank and see what happens! You'll be amazed how effective it is when it's used sparingly and in the right situation.

Most parents concurred that an attention-provoking (not pain-provoking) spank at times like these makes an important point better than anything else. The child understands, he is forgiven, his parent still loves him, he still loves his parent, and his life goes on. It's quick, fair, and highly effective. Even a mother bear instinctively knows very well that a quick and harmless swipe of the paw will stop a mischievous cub's antics on the spot. Normally quite tolerant, she will allow her cub to gnaw her hind leg or lag behind on a foraging trip, but the moment he nears danger or steps too far out of line, *whack!* and he quickly learns another survival lesson.

One final spanking story demonstrates just how effective a simple spank can be and how Mr. Johnson quickly taught his son, Ron, to find a better solution to his problem:

> Just after school started and Ron was about six, he came home covered with mud. He was covered from head to toe and had ruined his new school clothes. When I asked him what had happened, he said he was chasing a frog in the creek. I told him he couldn't do that in his school clothes. But next day, the same thing: covered with mud, still no frog. I warned him one more time, but the next day, mud

again. So I gave him a spank to make the point. Wouldn't you know, the next day he came home clean—but with the frog! It wasn't until weeks later, when I dropped by Mr. McNulty's pet shop, that I solved the puzzle. "How's your boy Ron doing with that frog I sold him, Mr. Johnson?" asked Mr. McNulty. Suddenly, it all came together. "Oh, he's doing fine," I said. "And my wife's a lot happier, too."

ATTENTION-GETTING BEHAVIOR

The parents we met believed a key ingredient of their parenting success was their ability to look beneath a particular behavior and understand what it *meant.* Rather than just *reacting* to problems, they tried to determine what underlying issues might be causing them. Negative attention-getting behavior was one they dealt with quite often, so we have included two vignettes about how one mother handled it.

In both cases, she proved the following to be true: *Finding the* cause *of behavioral problems, rather than treating the* symptoms, *will change behavior.*

Kids often misbehave out of frustration or a sense of helplessness. Sometimes they are unhappy about their performance at school or they may be angry and insecure about a new baby who suddenly steals all the attention they used to get. To compensate, they may behave in a way that refocuses parental attention on them, where it used to be. They may also be painfully honest, as the following example demonstrates.

Mrs. Cortney told us how, out of the blue, her son, Wayne, made a shocking statement about his eight-month-old brother. "I hate Brian," he said one day as they were riding in the car. Then, to make matters worse, her other child, Reggie, chimed in, "Yeah, and I wish he would die!" Out of nowhere came feelings she never knew her children were harboring.

What did she do? Well, what she did *not* do was yell, scream, reprimand, demand apologies, show outrage, and exclaim, "How could you say such a thing!" Instead, she took a mental note of their feelings and simply did not respond. She did not make an issue out of something as natural as sibling rivalry. After all, her two children had always received all of her attention until *he* came along. Now the monopoly was broken by culprit Brian. What kid would want *less* attention than he was used to and who wouldn't lay the blame squarely on the cause of the breakup?

Mrs. Cortney was, however, perceptive enough to realize that in order for her two children to feel secure, they needed more attention and more interaction with the affairs of the new baby. Her shift of attention had been too severe, but without this eye-opening incident, she never would have known it.

On another occasion, Mrs. Cortney mitigated Reggie's misbehavior with logic. Again, he was silently harboring resentment over the loss of the maternal attention he once had, but he was asking for it through unacceptable, attention-getting antics. While she was changing Brian, she called for Reggie to come inside for lunch. After a few moments, she called again but still received no answer. Finally, as she grew more irritated, she went outside to see why he wasn't responding. To her amazement, she saw him standing in the middle of the yard, violently tearing out the pages of a book. She felt her own anger rise immediately, but as she took a step toward the agitated boy, she stopped.

> Suddenly, I saw something through the fog in my mind. A lightbulb clicked on just as I was about to make the wrong reaction. I saw that he was really upset. He wasn't ripping the book up to be malicious or to entertain himself. My first reaction was to spank him, but then I realized something was terribly wrong. Instead, I hugged him and said, "Reggie, you're angry. Say it! Say you're angry!" But he couldn't. He could only say, "I can't." "You have to!" I said. "Now tell me you're angry. It's OK to be angry." Then he let loose. "I'm angry! I'm angry! I'm angry!" As he was venting, it came out that he was still upset about Brian. I explained that he would have to get used to a newcomer to the family. I told him that Brian wasn't going to be leaving for a long time, that I didn't love him any less, and that he only had a limited supply of books! He laughed about that, and pretty soon all was well and we walked back into the house hand in hand.

OVERPROTECTING

By the time we had finished our interviews, there seemed to be a consensus of opinion that rose to the surface in regard to discipline. One mother summed it up this way:

> Once you have fulfilled your obligations and the systems and boundaries are in place, the only thing left to do is get out of the way. Kids don't need to be under your wing every moment of the day. Give them the widest possible latitude and let them solve their own problems. There's nothing more stifling to a kid than a parent yelling down the

street every ten minutes, making sure he hasn't fallen out of—or even climbed—the neighborhood oak tree. Think back to when you were a child. Kids are *built* to climb trees! They love them and they need them and, yes, sometimes they fall out of 'em. That's the way it goes. Don't project your own fear of trees, spiders, lizards, dirt, germs—and all the rest of the things that make childhood worth living—on to children whom you want to be happy, healthy adults one day.

"And avoid stereotyping kids," said one mother. She told us how her family couldn't wait until Friday nights when their ten-year-old son would put on an apron and create fabulous homemade pizzas from scratch. Another family's fourteen-year-old daughter was bigger and better on the basketball court than her older brothers—and most of the high school varsity squad! The whole family went to the games and cheered her on.

Said Mrs. Spitzer:

> If kids are stifled, they can't grow—emotionally or spiritually. Sometimes parenting is nothing more than getting out of the way at the right times and letting kids breathe—without worrying about how polluted the air is!

Overprotecting and overattending children does nothing positive for them and, as Mrs. Robbins believed, only temporarily reduced her husband's fear that "something will happen" to their son. She walked us out onto her sunny back porch after our interview. Along one side was a long, wooden bench that stretched the length of the yard.

> You see that bench? That's what Steven used to jump off when he was three. But only when his father wasn't around. He would run through the yard, climb on that brick wall over there, then come running and jump off this bench. I wouldn't stop him, but his father said it was dangerous. It wasn't dangerous and I knew he needed to do it. Now, at fifteen, he wants to jump off a thirty-foot bridge into a river somewhere. Even though his friend's Dad said it was safe, Steven's the only one of the kids who isn't afraid to do it.

Kids are much tougher than they are given credit for. When two siblings are squabbling, for example, sometimes it's better to just let them work out their differences themselves (provided there's no physical fighting). And if they can't, simply apply Mrs. Garcia's proven method:

> When the two girls were fighting and couldn't resolve their dispute, I'd take one girl outside on one side of the plate glass window, put the other one inside at the same spot, and make them stand there and clean the window while looking directly at each other! Pretty soon, they were both laughing and giggling at each other through the window and forgot what they were arguing about.

Another parent related a story that demonstrated how effectively one mother she knew also avoided the overattending problem:

> I was leaving a sporting goods store one afternoon with a couple I knew. Their eighteen-month-old boy, David, had recently begun walking and was about ten feet down the sidewalk. All of a sudden he tripped rather hard and went right

down on his hands and face. What David's mother did next was really remarkable. She was very aware of the purpose of parenting. She did *not* run hysterically to her child, yank him off the pavement, and begin making a fuss over him. Instead, she walked calmly to his side, kneeled down, placed her head on the concrete next to his, smiled warmly, and said in a peaceful, reassuring voice, "You're OK, David." Then she let him lift *himself* up, observed that he had not hurt himself, and then turned around and walked back to her husband. Little David toddled on down the block without a peep. It was beautiful to watch.

This is another example of excellent, skillful work by a tuned-in, intelligent parent.

In conclusion, remember, the purpose of discipline is to impel children to think about *their* misbehavior, not yours! If you are frazzled and ready to explode like a volcano at any moment, your discipline will be nothing more than a way of relieving your own stress. Follow the examples of the true experts who, as we have seen, disciplined their children without anger in a calm, loving manner. When you do, you send your child the message: "*You* are not bad, your *actions* are."

To be sure you are on the right disciplinary track, ask yourself these questions: Are you open and tolerant enough with kids who want to be part of the decision-making process? Are you sure you are not *too* tolerant? Have you established clearly defined rules and explained them at family meetings so everyone knows where they stand? Do you have an agreement from your children that your limits will be respected? Are you willing to follow through with immediate and inevitable consequences for misdeeds?

If your answers to these questions are predominantly "Yes," your children will, in the long run, understand that you discipline them because you love them. They will understand intuitively that if you did not believe they were worth the sacrifice of many years or that they were not excellent material with which to work, you would never put forth the effort. They know that it is because you believe in their potential that you are willing to help them realize it. When you respectfully, intelligently, and affectionately correct your children, their independence and self-esteem flourish.

CHAPTER 4

INSTILL SELF-ESTEEM

When we arrived in San Francisco to interview parents for this book, we stayed with a professor from San Francisco State University who lived in the colorful Haight-Ashbury district, once famous for its "flower children," "free love," and later, crime, drugs, and decay. Strolling through the somewhat revitalized area one day, we happened upon a young person randomly panhandling passersby. He showed little enthusiasm as he approached people and said blankly, "Spare change," and then seemed to lose his concentration and just stand there, gazing off. He seemed deflated and disheartened, and not particularly interested in raising cash.

We watched him from a distance until he walked into a donut shop. We decided to follow him in. As he stood in front of the display case with his back to us, unable to decide what he wanted, we asked from behind, "Want a donut?" When he turned around, we were shocked to see not a boy, but a stunningly beautiful young blond girl whose fair skin was blackened with street grime. Her oily hair had been haphazardly tucked into a ragged, black, turbanlike hat that had a green rubber lizard pinned to the front. She stood barefoot, wearing a torn gray tunic over dirty army fatigue pants.

Without hesitation she replied, "Uh-huh. Can I get two?" as if responding to her mother, who was noticeably absent.

"Sure. How about a carton of milk?" we asked, feeling indeed like parents.

"Um, okay," she said.

We explained that we were doing a book on kids and asked if we could join her at a table. "Sure, I guess so," she said vaguely, as she took her bag of donuts and milk to a nearby table. But she didn't sit down. She stood looking at us, waiting for directions.

"This will be fine," we said.

She sat down and began picking the frosting off her donut, then nibbling at the inside, leaving a sort of crust ring, which she eventually ate, too. The most obvious thing about her, besides the dog leash chain around her throat and her nose ring, eyebrow ring, and lip ring (all on the right side of her face, for some reason), was the black grime under her fingernails. They looked like an auto mechanic's, but she took no notice of them as she picked slowly at her donut.

Since we did not have time to interview her that day, we spoke for just a few minutes and made a date to meet the following day. But at eleven o'clock the next morning, no street kid. So, what follows is only a quick glimpse into the life of a lost little street urchin. Even so, in the short time we spent with her, one message came through loud and clear. See if you can spot it as you read our short conversation.

"What's your name?"

"Widget."

"Widget, like Bridget with a W?"

"Yeah."

"Sounds like a nickname. What's your real name?"

"I don't have to tell you," she said sharply.

"No, you don't have to tell us," we agreed. "We weren't trying to be nosey." We then tried another risky question: "How old are you?"

"Fifteen. I'll be sixteen in a month," she said through a mouthful of donut.

"Don't you worry about snagging something and ripping out your lip with that ring right there in front?" we asked as she ate.

"I like piercing."

"Are you making enough money panhandling? Are you getting enough food?"

"I'm hungry a lot. Yeah, I'm pretty hungry. A lot."

"What do you eat?"

"I'm a vegetarian. I eat mostly starch," she said as she licked at the sugar frosting.

"Where do you sleep?"

"In the park. Or we squat."

"You mean, you take over abandoned buildings?"

"Yeah."

"Isn't that illegal? Don't the police hassle you?"

"They can't do nothin'. I don't have any ID or nothin'."

"Isn't there some curfew or rules for young kids like you?"

"I don't know. They don't do anything to me."

"Isn't it dangerous just sleeping in the park? And you're a young girl."

"Yeah, it is. But I usually sleep with other people."

"What's your story? Why are you up here? What are you doing here on the streets?"

"I'm up here from Hollywood. Well, I'm really from here, but then we moved to Hollywood. But I left seven months ago and now I'm up here."

"Where's your mom? What's she think of all this?"

"She's down there. She don't care."

"What do you mean, she doesn't care? You're only fifteen. Does she think it's okay for you to be out here by yourself?"

"I don't know. She didn't say nothin'. I just said I was goin' and she didn't say nothin'."

"Does she send you money?"

"No."

"Do you talk to her on the phone?"

"No. Why should I? She don't want to talk to me."

"What about your dad?"

"He's a bastard!" she snapped. "In the end, before I left, he was abusing me. Well, not like that, really. Just beatin' on me a lot. So I left. Then I was put in a mental institution, but I just walked out 'cause it wasn't a lock-down. It was easy. I was in a lock-down before and you can't get out no way."

"Why were you in a hospital?"

"Drug abuse."

"You don't look like you're on drugs now. Do you still do them?"

"I still do 'em. Yeah, sometimes when I can get stuff."

"What do you do?"

"I shoot heroin, mostly. But there's some bad smack goin' around. I got some and the s—— made me sick."

"You're shooting?" we asked incredulously. "What about AIDS?"

Widget rolled her eyes, as if we were just too boring worrying about that kind of straight-world media hype. Then she threw us with the response:

"I have my own needles."

"Your own needles. Guess that's a good idea. Do you clean them with bleach?" we asked, to which there was no response. She had faded off and was starting to pack up her tattered gray blanket and an army knapsack that had obscenities and punk slogans written on it in black marker.

"Can I bring my friends tomorrow?" she asked.

"Yeah, you can bring your friends," we answered, feeling like parents again. She then turned without saying "thank you" or "good-bye," and shuffled out the door like an old woman, already hunched over by the load of her pack and her situation. We never saw the five-foot, hundred-pound, beautiful child again.

Widget's is not an isolated case. Though they may not go to the extremes she did, the vast majority of today's children suffer from poor self-image. They lack the will to reach out to life, to make friends, or to try new things because their parents have convinced them that they will fail if they do. So, what do these "defective" children do? They hide and they hate. The real danger is, if they don't improve their self-images, they will indeed fulfill their parents' low expectations and fail at everything they try—a kind of self-defeating prophecy. Thousands of kids like Widget already have.

Because low self-esteem is so prevalent among today's youth, we will discuss it first, and then move on to how the successful parents instilled in their children a sense of high self-esteem by reassuring them they were capable of handling new challenges. Note how that growing confidence developed into courage and then perseverance, because these no-nonsense parents stalwartly refused to pamper their children or accept halfhearted efforts. At the end of the chapter, you will see perhaps the best esteem-builder of all: praise—but praise doled out only at the right time for the right reasons. One father explained that the real reward for achievement was achievement itself. He said, "You can wear a ribbon on your chest, but the real reward is way deeper down—in your heart."

DEFINING SELF-ESTEEM

Self-esteem is the mental picture people have of themselves, the sense of self that comes from feeling capable and competent, the inner feeling of "okayness" and adequacy that lies deep in the psyche. Indeed, self-esteem is at the very core of mental health. The strength or weakness of one's self-esteem becomes quite evident during failures or when frustrations and pressures mount. How does a person respond when rejected? How does he face adversity and uncertainty? For too many children, the answer is: not very well. Like Widget, they run away and fall prey to drug abuse, prostitution, or hard crime—if they don't kill themselves first.

Consider this powerful assertion: "The lack of self-esteem is central to most personal and social ills plaguing our state and nation as we approach the end of the twentieth century." Such was the conclusion of the California Task Force to Promote Self-Esteem and Personal and Social Responsibility, spearheaded by Assemblyman John Vasconcellos. Self-esteem is so singularly impressive that his report, *Toward a State of Esteem,* referred to it as "a social vaccine." His statement said, "[Self-esteem is] something that empowers us to live responsibly and that inoculates us against the lures of crime, violence, and substance abuse, teen pregnancy, child abuse, chronic welfare dependency, and educational failure." Referring to these ills, New Hampshire educator James Weiss said, "If youngsters feel good about themselves, those temptations won't be so strong."

LOW SELF-ESTEEM

If parents lack the ability or desire to build self-confidence in their children, those children are at high risk from the moment they are born. Dysfunctional individuals, whether they be excessively shy toddlers or hardened criminals, almost always suffer from huge personality deficits stemming from poor self-image. Their worlds are lonely, sad, angry. They feel the pangs of worthlessness and fear that eventually disintegrate into bitter negativity, frustration, hostility, and finally rage—against property, parents, spouses, and other innocent people. What other result could there be for children who have asked, all their lives, the unanswerable questions, "Why doesn't anybody love me?" "Why can't I do anything right?" "What did I do to deserve this?" The only conclusion they can possibly reach is: "I must be bad."

Let's begin with this immutable fact: *Children, parents, indeed, all people need to be approved of.* Even the most confident people have difficulty maintaining a good self-image without some type of validation. This need to feel loved and admired begins in infancy and is met almost entirely by parents' words of encouragement. Because children have not had time to develop the personal incentive and *internal* motivation that come with maturity, parents must bridge the gap until kids are older by providing an *external* source of approval. This is the critical missing element in most children's development.

All animals nudge their offspring out of their nests, into rushing streams, or over steep terrain to teach them they are capable of surviving on their own—all except us. Only humans leave their kin to figure this out on their own—if they are so lucky. How can kids know they are doing okay if they do not hear it from their parents? How do they know where they stand? When they are not *validated,* they remain unsure of themselves. And when left in this vulnerable state, they are susceptible to the fears that insidiously take over and cripple them emotionally and intellectually. *Without parental reinforcement, self-worth simply cannot develop.*

Kids who feel defeated before they begin usually don't begin at all. Understandably, they resist trying different tasks because they fear the humiliation that comes with failure. Quitting (or never starting) is less painful than the gut-wrenching feelings of worthlessness that come from losing. One mother remembered her fourth-grade classmate's embarrassment about reading:

> I'll never forget poor Doug Hardman. He was so shy and afraid of everything. And he couldn't read very well. I don't even think it was the reading itself, because he seemed bright enough. It was that he couldn't stand reading aloud in front of the class. When Mrs. Jaten would go around the room and have students read, I'd watch Doug. As it got closer and closer to his turn, he'd get visibly nervous; he'd start shaking. Most kids are a little shy at first, but he never got over it. It was like he was convinced he couldn't do it. Mrs. Jaten saw what she was putting the poor kid through and finally changed to picking kids randomly, and she always passed over Doug to save him the agony.

Not all teachers are as perceptive as Mrs. Jaten, nor are they immune from criticizing children in whom they are supposed to be building character. Researcher Hill Walker found in one study that teachers—who are trained to know better—averaged 182 disapproving comments a day, compared with a mere *twelve* approving ones! They focused more on what kids did wrong than what they did right—the exact opposite of what is needed to build self-esteem and the opposite of one mother's favorite slogan: "Never deflate, always inflate."

Children with a poor self-image are in a constant state of deflation. They typically have the following characteristics:

- *shy* and apprehensive about new activities or people
- *dependent* on their parents for simple decisions
- *humiliated* by criticism
- *incapacitated* by fear of failure
- *crushed* by minor failures
- *overly concerned* about excelling

- *needing* constant approval
- *worried* about image. "What do they think of *me?*" rather than the healthier "What do I think of *them?*"

These self-defeating traits are heavy baggage to drag along into adolescence, when new, more complex problems inherent in that stage can blow even minor setbacks up into massive failures. Even the most stable adolescents find it difficult to cope with rapidly changing bodies and the enormous rush of hormones that suddenly make relationships outside the family—especially those with the opposite sex—more important than ever.

In the teen years the pressure is on. Competition stiffens. Being popular is vital to self-conscious teenagers, who obsess over looks. (Only 29 percent of young girls say they are happy with their appearance, according to a nationwide survey commissioned by the American Association of University Women and released in 1991.) Pile these new social pressures on top of increasingly tough academic expectations, add some parental indifference along with a hefty amount of criticism, and the shaky braces supporting self-esteem quiver and collapse.

Failing to encourage children is bad enough, but parents do further damage when they use the following put-downs, all of which seriously undermine children's self-esteem. Kids learn to doubt and even hate themselves when their parents use (1) punitive discipline and physical abuse, (2) critical evaluation and harsh judgment, (3) unfavorable comparison, (4) lack of trust, (5) lack of respect, (6) lack of consideration, and (7) guilt. Attacking children who are already uncertain about their self-worth is like pouring gas on a fire—with emotionally disturbed parents as the arsonists. In his best-selling book, *The Road Less Traveled,* M. Scott Peck, M.D., refers to this arbitrary, irrational parenting when he writes about "undisciplined discipline," stating some children are "punished frequently and severely throughout their childhood—slapped, punched, kicked, beaten, and whipped by their parents for even minor infractions."

Back in 1967, psychologist Stanley Coopersmith conducted a landmark study that found mothers who raised boys with a high sense of personal worth used "verbal reasoning and discussion" rather than the "arbitrary, punitive discipline" of the boys who suffered from a poor self-image. There is a big difference between "Gerald, do you really think it's a good idea to go driving in this weather?" and "Ask for the keys one more time and you'll never get behind that wheel again!" The first statement is logical and asks for calm reasoning; the second is curt, demeaning, and unreasonable.

What goes on in the minds and hearts of these victims of verbal or physical abuse? First, *confusion,* especially for younger kids: "What did I do wrong?" Next, *shame:* "I must be very bad to deserve this." And third, *terror:* "I'm going to get killed." How can self-esteem develop in this insane environment where kids are hoping just to stay alive? For younger children, the horror is worse because they are trapped; they have no escape from the rage. At least adolescents can get out of the house and find comfort among accepting peers, like Widget did. But that is not much of a solution because, as we will discuss in Chapter 6, those peers usually come from similar backgrounds, so they become partners in crime, drugs, and the rest.

While not as vicious as physical abuse or as deeply scarring as sardonic criticism, unfavorably comparing a child to siblings or other children is another common but debilitating mistake parents make. "Your brother can do it, why can't you?" "Your sister got A's in algebra and all you can get is a C?" "You might be prettier if you fixed your hair like the Taylor girl." Though some parents mistake this for encouragement, such comments are nothing more than criticism—and do nothing to motivate change. After all, would you risk tarnishing your burgeoning new image by trying to match up to someone who has already proven his competency? What if you fail? Kids aren't dopes. It is a lot safer to retreat than risk losing the battle in full view of the commanding general.

A couple we spoke with recalled the time they made an unfair comparison of one sibling to the others, and though they laughed about it when we talked, they realized how desperate their child was to take the action he did.

> We were always telling Pat he was too skinny, which translated to, "All the other kids are fine, you're puny." Beth and I were constantly on him to eat more, put on weight. We didn't realize that he saw this as a real dig, no different from calling chubby kids fat. Being a calm, sort of shy kid, he really shocked us with what was for him a radical act or maybe an act of desperation. I said casually one day in the kitchen, "You've got to put some meat on your bones." With that, he walked over to the refrigerator and said, "OK, Dad, I will." He took out the leftover roast beef and started rubbing it all over his arms! "I'm putting meat on my bones, Dad," he said, but he wasn't smiling. I really think he was just so damn frustrated and tired of us harping on him that he sort of

> snapped. What seemed funny at the time sank in later in the day, when Beth and I talked about it and realized we had been hurting Pat by comparing him to his brothers and sisters.

Turning the tables and telling a child she is the best at something may seem like a better motivation, but it isn't. It is just another form of comparison and no better for building self-esteem than the unfavorable variety. What could load on more pressure? And what happens when a youngster hears her parent's proclamation, "You're the best!"—and comes in third?

Children also feel deficient when their parents neglect to take an interest in those things that mean the most to them, as the following anecdote demonstrates:

> When I was bringing up my kids, I wasn't going to make the same mistake my mother did. I'll never forget—and I'm still hurt even to this day—when I was in 4H [agriculture/farm club], my mother never came to see my sheep. I loved that sheep so much. I wanted my mother to love him, too. I was so proud of taking care of him and feeding him and keeping him groomed. My mother had no interest. She never once came to see him. I'll never forget how terrible that was.

Another parent confessed that he had neglected his son, but in a completely different way:

> Buddy wanted me to help him make a box car like all the other kids, so we started in. The problem was, I took over the project because I was getting a kick out of it. I com-

> pletely forgot about Buddy, that it was his project, that *he* wanted to make the car. He only wanted my help, not for me to hog the whole thing and forget about him. But that's exactly what I did. I remember that after an hour or so, when I hadn't let Bud participate or help at all, he gave up hope and wandered off by himself. It didn't register, though. I figured he lost interest in the project. It wasn't until three months later, when I was lying in bed one morning, that it dawned on me: I totally neglected that kid! Later, I sat him down and tried to explain the whole thing, but the damage had been done long before that. All I could do was apologize and hope he took that to heart, too.

As you have seen, the parents we came to know were not immune from making mistakes, nor were they reluctant to talk about them. They knew that by highlighting these common pitfalls, you would be better able to recognize your own children's needs and quickly make course corrections, as they did. *The essence of good parenting is not in doing everything perfectly, but in perfecting what you are doing.*

BUILDING SELF-ESTEEM

While most people neither possess nor instill in their offspring a high degree of self-esteem, the results of a nationwide January 1992 Gallup poll show they at least recognize it as fundamental to success in life. When respondents were asked, "How important are the following in motivating a person to work hard and succeed?" the percentage saying "very important" was as follows:

35 percent	Status in eyes of others
44 percent	Fear of failure
49 percent	Responsibility to community
77 percent	Family duty or honor
89 percent	*Self-esteem,* the way people think about themselves

This 89-percent figure is an interesting one when juxtaposed with the 29 percent of girls (and 46 percent of boys) who don't feel good about themselves. What's the missing link between the adults who know self-esteem is important and their children who lack it? *Skill.*

The parents we interviewed took specific measures to foster self-love and confidence in their children. Those children told us they always had a sense that their parents loved and approved of them, even when it was not openly verbalized. This leads to one of the key tenets of self-esteem: *For children to feel good about themselves, parents must feel good about them first.*

But just "feeling good" about kids does not automatically make *them* feel good, too. This is where skill comes in. By following our experts' lead, you can help your children feel competent enough to trust their own judgment, stand firm on their own decisions, accept life's challenges—and meet them with courage when the outcome is uncertain. By helping them build an internal sense of self-worth, they will see inevitable defeats as learning experiences, not confirmation of inadequacy. Here are some of the initial steps to take:

- Prove to your child she is *worthy* and *deserving* of love by loving her *openly* and *unconditionally*—when she succeeds *and* when she fails. One mother occasionally put "love notes" in her son's lunch box that simply said, "I love you"—nice way to start a lunch break. Another mother said she didn't wait for birthdays or holidays; she gave her children "for no reason presents" whenever she felt like it.
- Remind your child that regardless of the outcome of her endeavors, what she does matters—to you, her teachers, her friends, and most of all, herself. It is not the *result* but the *effort* she puts forth that shows her character and makes everyone feel proud. When a child brings home a drawing from school and tosses it to the side, saying, "It's not very good," pick it up and show her just how good it really is. Her perspective may have been a little off, with the farmer ending up bigger than the horse, but point out that she started with a blank page, conceived her subject, and created something new and unique that tells a story. It doesn't have to be perfect.
- Encourage your child to participate in all aspects of life—school, religious worship, sports, clubs, hobbies, work, and friendships. Such participation helps kids become more assertive and learn leadership and speaking skills as they share experiences with an ever-widening circle of friends. One father reminded his child, who came home despondent, that team sports take a team effort—not only to win, but to lose:

> Just because you were the [soccer] goalie, doesn't mean you're solely responsible for losing. Remember, the ball had to get by all the other kids before it got by you.

- Teach *self-reliance,* which leads to *self-fulfillment,* by refusing to pamper your child with handouts every time he demands them. Let him develop the *resourcefulness* to do the most with bare minimums. With a little scrap lumber and determination, kids can build a tree fort, doghouse, or bridge across the creek that they will appreciate much more than the store-bought variety. Or, as in the case of one student we met, kids can take on more imaginative projects:

> When I was about eight, I wanted to build a duck pond so, as I said, "The ducks will come." Sounds kinda like Holden Caulfield. Well, instead of hiring a bulldozer and concrete truck like I wanted to do, my father suggested we start on a smaller scale with a minipond of a few feet across, and line it with old chicken wire and cement to see how it looked. So that's what we did and it looked fine. I was impressed with myself. After we finished it, I didn't care much about a big pond anymore. I was so proud of myself, I didn't care about the ducks anymore either.

Another student described how she and her mother and sister created Halloween masks out of papier-mâché:

> You asked about self-esteem. I think Mom taught us we could do a lot more than go out and buy everything. Even though all the other kids were buying their Halloween masks down at Toyland, Mom knew we'd get a lot more out of our masks if we made them ourselves, and she was right. We had a ball! It took us hours with the newspaper strips and hair dryer, but we made great masks, and when everybody saw them, they wished they had made their own, too.

Here is one absolute *law* of child rearing that every parent should memorize; it may be the most misunderstood notion of all: *Saying "No" a hundred times more often than "Yes" makes for happier, more self-reliant kids.*

Hearing "No" does not frustrate kids. Though kids *seem* happier with a "Yes," it is the "No"—the delayed gratification—that builds character. What kids need more than acquiescence is reassurance that they will do all right.

REASSURANCE

Many children today fear that the big world beyond the home is too difficult to tackle and definitely not much fun. Their fear stems from the people they see around them who are supposed to *reassure* them that they can "make it." But kids have been double-crossed. Idolized rock stars are embroiled in child molestation suits; adored sports figures are charged with drug abuse, gambling, and most recently, a heinous double murder crime so gruesome and so bizarre that it was beyond the scope of even the most imaginative mystery writers. The world does indeed look threatening.

Fortunately, you have a good deal of control over which

role models your children are influenced by. One way is to monitor what your children watch on TV. But even more importantly, kids need to see that *you* are self-assertive and action-oriented. They need to see *you* making it in the big world, tackling tough challenges, and holding up under the pressure. Just a simple thing like standing up for your rights, as Mrs. Conway did, can teach valuable lessons. Her daughter explains the impact of one such incident:

> My mom and I were in a department store one time and when she went to pay for something with a check, the cashier said she needed to show her a credit card. I remember so distinctly how my mother took control of the situation. She said, "I'd be happy to show you a credit card if I had one, but I don't *use* credit cards. I use checks. And this check is what I'd like to use to buy this sweater. If you'd like, I'll discuss this with the manager." She wasn't intimidated and she didn't back down; she stood her ground. I think what I learned from her was that she was sure of herself and wasn't going to be pushed around. That day has always stuck with me.

When your child sees you handle yourself with confidence, she learns a critical lesson in self-esteem: "Believe in yourself and succeed." If, on the other hand, you throw your arm over your eyes and collapse onto the couch with every headache, or you're so tense about upcoming business meetings that everyone has to creep around the house speaking in whispers, you send the message—and not in a whisper, but a roar—"I CAN'T DO IT!"

The parents we met reassured their children that problems are not insurmountable if you possess one key ingredient: *willingness* to face them and do the best you can. Two different parents from different families had this motto tacked on their children's walls: "I'll find a way." They and the other parents we met regularly told their children that they, too, had shortcomings when they were growing up but searched for ways to overcome them. The following three vignettes are examples of these admissions, which were instrumental in reassuring kids that no one is perfect:

> To parents I would say: Recount your own stories about the trouble you had making friends or the fact that you weren't such a hot athlete. For my kids, it alleviated a lot of pressure to perform. I told them I was anything but perfect as a kid in a big high school from a big midwestern city. I told them I wasn't good enough to make varsity basketball. In fact, most of my high school career was spent on junior varsity—and second string at that. But I kept practicing and playing on the team. I still was having a good time. Then one day the varsity coach stopped me in the hall and said, "I saw you make that jump shot at yesterday's game. I think we can use you on our team. Come on by after class." I did and I made the team. From second-string junior varsity to third-string varsity! Hey, it was a step up—even if I was a bench-warmer most of the time! So what? I still had a good time.

Dissolve your child's misplaced notion that she must perform flawlessly. State unequivocally that such perfection is not expected, not desirable, and not possible.

> I explained to Candy [when she was having trouble in math] that I wasn't an ace with numbers either. In fact, even with a tutor, I barely pulled C's in geometry. But you plow

ahead anyway and you do your best. Sounds basic, but Candy needed to hear this all the time.

Mrs. Friedman went on to discuss how she handled her daughter's chronic concern about her looks:

> Candy, like all her friends, was obsessed with looks. The thing I found most helpful was to explain my own apprehension about fitting in when I was her age. I used to pull out pictures of myself in my absurd beehive hairdo that Candy called "totally nerdly." And those black horn-rims! I just can't believe we thought we looked *good* in those things! "And look what I ended up with, Honey, *your father!* Not exactly bachelor of the year, but to me, another Paul Newman." I'd openly admit my own anxieties about looking beautiful when I wasn't, and pointed out that in the end, it wasn't the looks at all that made the difference—especially in attracting her father. [Laughs.] I told Candy that a lot of times, the kids who were popular as freshmen because they were the cutest kind of fell out of favor when the other kids realized that was all they had.

By relating your own hardships you show that (1) you were not defeated by your lack of perfection, and (2) you did not change your opinion of yourself just because you did not excel in everything. Reassure your child that though it may not seem like it at times, her talents and abilities are perfectly adequate, and she is a highly capable kid—just not at everything.

> Eventually, when our kids verified what we had been telling them for eons, and they saw we were right, that they

really were great kids, their determination to succeed at things really snowballed. Neither of them were devastated by setbacks—and there were plenty. Ricky ran for two class offices and never made it. Jimmy couldn't make the swim team because he was a lousy swimmer. Sure they were disappointed. What did they do, cry? No. We suggested Rick look into journalism because he was always a good writer and had a knack for it. He took our advice and helped publish the school paper. Eventually he became editor. Jimmy went out for wrestling and took all-league honors in his junior year. The boys learned to look at difficulties as challenges. And they knew they could handle them because we *told* them they could.

A high school counselor recommended Steve Howe for our book, claiming the student had the most amazing mind he had ever seen. Mr. Mills told us Steve had received a rare perfect score on the SAT test, a fact we couldn't resist bringing up during our interview.

"Oh, that's a big myth," said Steve. "Everyone thought I got a perfect score, but the truth is, I missed a question."

"How could you mess up so bad?" we teased.

"I guess I wasn't concentrating," he said, as quick-witted as we expected. As we laughed over the comment, his mother told us that even a brilliant child like Steve needed reassurance when he was younger:

Steve wasn't perfect at everything. When he was small, he couldn't learn to tie his shoelaces. He kept trying, but he just couldn't manage to get them tied. One day he said, "I'll never learn to tie my shoes." Well, I could see he was getting frustrated and that we needed to take the pressure off. I

> calmed him down and told him he would learn in time, there was no rush. Then I went out and bought him a pair of sneakers with Velcro instead of laces. I said it was a lot easier to practice when the shoes were off his feet.

AUTONOMY

Independence is a sign of healthy self-esteem. To achieve that independence, children must first gain a sense of autonomy. One mother explained how she helped her children move toward that goal with the help of an old tradition she had learned from her own mother in Mexico:

> When babies are very tiny, we bundle them tightly, like a papoose. This gives them a feeling of security, that they are loved and taken care of. Then we roll the babies on the bed twenty or thirty times, from one side to the other, back and forth. They are not scared. They learn trust and they learn risk. You must start teaching risk-taking from the very beginning.

As their children grew, the successful parents we met continued to inculcate in them a sense of self-reliance by slowly but surely pulling back the protective veil of familiarity. Trying new things such as new foods, new activities, and new people is of primary importance in building character. One mother explained her philosophy about picky eating:

> There was no "I don't like it" in our house. My mother used to say, "How do you know you don't like it if you don't try it?" But I didn't use that line. It's the worst possible way to get kids to try new things. I used what I call the Tom

> Sawyer approach, which was basically, make it a privilege, not an obligation. When I fixed something new, I used to say, "There might not be enough to go around," or "You've got to finish what's on your plate before you can have any spinach." Believe it or not, my kids thought spinach and squash were treats! What you *don't* want to say—and I've seen many a mother do this—is, "Please, please just *try* it!" or "Will you try one bite for Mommy?" Let me tell all new parents: This will never work.

As your child approaches adolescence, the need for autonomy heightens dramatically and the balancing act begins. She may very much want to break out of the secure, protective bubble she once lived in, but she still needs to know you approve of her. Your child may test your love by complaining about physical imperfections to see what your reaction is. This is the perfect time to give her a lesson in autonomy. Mrs. Rondale was painfully honest when her fourteen-year-old daughter, Cynthia, started questioning her looks:

> I could see Cynthia was getting ready to take that big step. She had just started high school, she was starting to wear some makeup, talk about dating. But she wasn't quite sure of herself with all the prettier girls she found at Scofield. I told her, "You're not ever going to be Miss America, assuming you really want to waste your time trying. So face it and do something else a little more important with your life. Being a cover girl is certainly not something we feel is worthwhile and we don't love you any less because you're a normal-looking kid. If you're liked or not liked because of your

looks, whoever is doing the judging has her own problems to deal with. Don't make them yours."

Another mother suggested that parents stop referring to their children as "beautiful" all the time:

> External beauty has nothing to do with anything real. We're not bodies, although it's hard not to believe that in our boobs-and-butts, cosmetic-surgery-crazy society! We're minds and intelligence and love and spirit. Why all the emphasis on the body? Why are thirteen-year-olds going under the knife? What a mistake it is to tell a child she is worthwhile and valuable because of what's in her head and her heart, and then go back on your word by saying, "Oh, you're such a beautiful girl," or to another parent, "What a beautiful baby you have." A bit hypocritical, isn't it? And confusing, to say the least. People are not possessions! You don't shine them up like you shine up your car.

To help kids feel autonomous and get a realistic perspective on how they fit into the world, try following the experts' advice:

- Self-esteem cannot be given to anyone, or bestowed upon them—it must be *earned.* Teach your child to take responsibility for his own happiness by stepping out and putting his abilities into action, by trying things. One parent's favorite quote was: "Never be sorry you did it, only be sorry you didn't." Another parent told us how she was her daughter's advocate in making a tough decision:

Freddie didn't know what to do. She wanted to run for student body president, and her friends told her she would win. But she wasn't so sure, and the real dilemma was, she would be running against her best friend. What if she *did* win? It might not be all that pleasant. I told her she had to be prepared for somebody to lose, but if it were me, I'd go for the gold. Well, after much talk, I came up with an idea: "We'll have a winner's cake and a loser's cake! You and Darlene can both celebrate!" I think with that, Freddie saw that it [running] could be lighthearted and not earth-shattering if she lost. She'd gain lots of experience doing something like this, and it would be good for her. She said she was prepared to take the loser's cake, too. As it turned out, she did run and she won.

- Help younger children achieve small successes they are capable of. "Find out what they can succeed at," said one mother. "Set up challenges that are well within their reach." These opportunities allow them to earn the recognition that *convinces* them they are good—something your verbal accolades cannot do. One father from a rural community told us how he progressively graduated his son to more difficult tasks:

In the summer, Jack was usually right beside me in the fields. When he was a tyke, I got him his first play tractor. Then I moved him up to the small gasoline tractor, then the backhoe. Finally he was riding the full-sized diesel—all by the time he was ten. As soon as Jack was competent on one machine, I'd move him

> up to the bigger one. You should have seen that little buster up there on the John Deere a hundred times bigger than he was. But he manhandled it. It got so that I could go in to take lunch and leave him out by himself. He knew what he was doing.

- Be cautious when selecting activities for your child. You don't want to sabotage her opportunities for success by offering activities that are beyond her skill level. Likewise, watch what she selects for herself. If she sets goals that are too difficult, she may find she cannot complete them and become discouraged and quit.
- Watch for signs of interest in particular activities. Some things will be of no real interest to your child, while others may spur increased attention that may be a sign of hidden talent for that field. If a child takes to an activity and becomes proficient at it, her sense of autonomy grows immensely.
- As kids grow, compliment them on the attributes they have developed and back it up by asking for their opinion on things. One mother explained how much her son helped her when she bought her first computer:

> I didn't take to it very well, but Kevin was a computer whiz. I sure felt the shoe was on the other foot when Kev said, "OK, Mom. Let's go over RAM again, and this time we'll take it a little slower."

- Encourage kids to make decisions. Get in the habit of saying, "What do *you* think?" or "You decide" when they ask questions. Many parents automatically make even the simplest decisions for children who are perfectly qualified to make them themselves. Also, use "How do you feel about . . ." questions; they show that you value your child's opinion and want to hear what she has to say. If you really do value her opinion, be careful to avoid the attacking phrase "You're wrong" when she makes an obvious mistake in thinking or judgment. A mother we met advised parents to try a nonvolatile phrase that worked well for her. "When you disagree with your kids, say 'That seems wrong,' " she said. "It's softer, and it encourages kids to think a little further rather than defend themselves."

COURAGE AND PERSEVERANCE

Einstein underscored the value of perseverance when he said it was not special talent that made him succeed, but "obsession and dogged endurance." Edison, too, attributed his great triumphs to perseverance. If you were down in the basement toying with a filament and bell jar, trying every conceivable idea you'd heard about, read about, or dreamt about to keep that filament glowing—all to no avail—how many different experiments would you laboriously pursue before calling it quits? Ten? Fifty? How about a thousand? What person in his right mind would keep trying—and failing—over *ten thousand times* until he was successful? Answer: only someone with a massive amount of confidence and *perseverance.*

Self-esteem and perseverance are closely intertwined, so much so that it's a bit of a chicken-and-egg question: Which comes first, the self-esteem it takes to persevere, or the perseverance that builds self-esteem? Regardless of which comes first, concentrate on developing perseverance in your child and he will develop self-esteem naturally. Whether it is entering a toddler's play group, zooming down a giant water slide, trying out for cheerleader, learning to play the piano, or confronting the school bully, encourage your child to *face the challenge* and *persist* until he has done his best. And don't worry about the outcome. Kids are resilient. Sure, your child may not make the team or become a professional musician. So what? The pride and satisfaction that come from taking action—and sticking with it—far outweigh these consequences. *Admiring children's courageous* actions, *not* outcomes, *inspires them to act again.*

Here are some of the things you can do to foster courage and perseverance:

- Remind impetuous youngsters that Rome wasn't built in a day. Michael Jordan shot thousands of baskets (thousands more than other players) before he achieved stardom. Jet pilots log thousands of hours in prop planes before taking the controls of a 747. Kids tend to see only the end result, the glory of a polished performance, but don't see the years of discipline and hard work that went into it.
- Relate stories of others who endured hardships and huge challenges to achieve their goals through perseverance and confidence. Helen Keller was deaf and blind, but made more contributions to society than

most hearing/seeing people. Alan Shepard trained arduously to become the world's best pilot so he could sit atop a volatile, smoldering rocket and blast into space—with no guarantee of coming back! Perseverance to get the job, courage to carry it through: Those are the qualities necessary for greatness.

A couple we interviewed told of a less glamorous hero, but one whose valiance was no less than those with greater accomplishments. Every child who complains he does not have enough toys, clothes, good looks, or money would benefit from this story:

> We lived at the top of a steep hill, so steep we never walked it ourselves, and way too steep for the school bus to climb. So, the kids had to be let off at the bottom and walk up. The only kid who lived up here at the top was Raymond Valesquez. Every day around 3:30 the bus would stop, a few kids would get off and run off on the side streets, and then little Raymond, who was around nine, would get off last and start the terrible climb by himself. Only he couldn't walk. He had polio or multiple sclerosis and had absolutely no use of his legs. To get anywhere he'd have to get himself centered, then move his upper body ahead a foot or so with his two arm crutches, then lift himself up and slide his feet across the pavement until they were under him again. Then he'd start the whole process over. It was heartbreaking to watch, especially when he got to a curb. He'd have to reach down and lift one leg onto the sidewalk, and then the other. And then start up the block. I don't know where Raymond's

mother was—if she was working, or didn't have a car, or thought it was best not to make him feel like he needed special attention. All I know is, he was a courageous little boy and a lovely boy. The one time I passed him on the street, he was cringing from the effort, but when he saw me he looked up and smiled the biggest, warmest smile you've ever seen.

- Avoid lecturing or threatening punishment when your child shies away from activities. What she needs when she is uncertain of her abilities is gentle coaxing, not reprimands or reminders that she is inadequate. Have her keep a distant eye on the outcome, but concentrate more on the *process,* which is what will get her to the top of her own hill.
- *Perseverance* and *procrastination* begin with the same letter but have almost directly opposing meanings. One means the ability to keep going, while the other means the inability to get started. Define these words clearly for your child and put the definitions on the wall, as one parent did. "If you embrace one and avoid the other," she said about the two words, "you can't lose—assuming you pick the right one!"
- As we discussed in Chapter 2, the human brain has ways of figuring things out and finding ways to succeed. Teach your child to rely on it and not worry about having everything in place before starting (procrastination). If she is incapacitated by a fear of making mistakes—as unsuccessful people usually are—she will not take the risks necessary to move ahead (courage).

- Remind your child that it takes courage to start journeys when the outcome is uncertain, whether that means going down a slide by herself or trying for admission to the best university. Forewarn her that she will occasionally go astray or may not arrive at the destination she had envisioned. Teach her to take the next corrective step: Stop and analyze the situation. Have her ask, "Where was I heading?" "Where did I go wrong?" and "How can I correct my mistake?" One teacher we spoke with explained this point as follows:

> I like mistakes. They mean more to me than correct, safe answers because they show students are branching out and trying new things they are unfamiliar with. If all the Ts are crossed perfectly, I worry that the student lacks courage and is not confident that his creative abilities will hold up to scrutiny. This tells me that, to some degree, he lacks self-esteem.

- Help your child visualize success before starting by painting a picture of her successfully completing her mission. Charles Lindbergh saw himself landing in Europe before he ever left the ground in America. Babe Ruth came to the plate during one World Series game and pointed to a center field wall. When the next pitch arrived, he proceeded to hit the ball over that very wall!
- Point out that nobody is good at everything. Quarterback Joe Montana may not have been great in science and Albert Einstein probably couldn't throw a football, but they both made tremendous contribu-

tions in their chosen fields. They did not lament over what they could not change but instead concentrated on what they *could* do—and then persevered until they excelled.

- Make clear what you expect, based on your child's proven ability, and then *relax.* If you are nervous, you are really saying, "I *think* you can do it, but I'm not so sure." Remind your child that what matters is trying your best, finishing what you start, and learning from mistakes.

Your child wants nothing more than to live up to your expectations. If you have made them realistic and taught her she can meet them through courage and perseverance, she will have the formula for success. When she does succeed, as inevitably she must, reward her with the praise she deserves.

PRAISE

Certainly praise is critical to a child's sense of self-esteem, but when lavished too liberally for too little, it kills the impact of real praise when it is called for. Everyone needs to know they are valued and appreciated, and praise is one way of expressing such feelings—but only after something *praiseworthy* has been accomplished. One counselor told us of a school in the Midwest that gave stars for *just showing up!* Another gave *trophies* to all members of the athletic teams, whether they excelled or not. Awards are supposed to be *re*wards—*re*actions to actions, honors for *doing something!* The ever-present danger in bestowing such honors too lightly is, children may come to depend on them and select only those things they know will produce prizes. If they are not sure they can do well enough to earn merit badges, or if gifts are not guaranteed, they will avoid the activities.

Too-easily-earned praise fosters just the opposite of what parents are trying to accomplish: *low* self-esteem from egotism and dependency on praise, and *low* actual achievement. Psychologist Harold Stevenson of the University of Michigan studied the consequences of unwarranted praise. American children, he discovered, ranked ahead of Japanese, Taiwanese, and Chinese students in self-confidence about their abilities in math, but *behind in actual performance! Thinking* they were great did not *make* them great. Asian kids, on the other hand, did not receive unfettered praise. They had to work hard to get applause, and even then, it was meted out sparingly from parents who were cautious not to spoil them. This just demonstrates that *praise must be earned.*

Spoiled kids who are pampered, protected, and praised for menial tasks and never forced to look at their imperfections will soon enough pay the price. Teachers, peers, and coworkers will be much less tolerant of mediocre performance and they'll take every opportunity to blast kids' misconceptions about themselves with, "Big deal, that's nothing special!"

Here is what you can do to instill self-confidence and avoid false praise—and teach your child there are more important things to value than external rewards (a subject we will cover more thoroughly in the next chapter):

- The only way to feel better is to *be* better. Teach your child to improve his intellectual, physical, and social skills so he can face challenges without constant rewards and reassurances that he is all right. One father told us how his ten-year-old, who was shorter and thinner than his classmates, only needed a casual suggestion to improve his self-image:

  > As a little boy, Mark always admired my biceps, which I guess to him looked big. He'd always ask me to make a muscle and then feel my arm. When he was in fifth grade, I told him he could build himself up quite a bit just by doing push-ups and sit-ups every day, like the marines did. That's all I said and I never mentioned it again. To make a long story short, he worked on himself for three years and completely transformed his body. No weights or anything, just push-ups and sit-ups. He started with ten push-ups, then added one every week or so until he was up to around sixty. When he graduated junior high, he won the push-up competition and took the school's all-time record of eighty-three push-ups!

- Do not commend your child arbitrarily in an effort to spur him into action—your efforts will fail. He will never learn where he needs improvement because *everything* gets praise. Parents who make no demand for excellence mislead their kids into thinking even feeble efforts are just fine.
- It is fine to look for things to praise in your child, but be sure they are meaningful to *her. You* may think she did something terrific, but to her, it may have been

second nature. If the easy tasks get the same raves as the difficult ones, your child will feel cheated—and she'll be right. Tougher tasks should reap greater rewards.

- Don't be fooled by kids' clever ploys for praise. Watch for real efforts, not just appeals for approval. When you see your child's efforts are only halfhearted, the worst thing to do is cave in and give her unwarranted gifts to make her "feel good"—she won't. *She* knows her efforts are disingenuous, so the only thing she'll feel good about is her ability to deceive you. One such clever ten-year-old was called on the mat by his no-nonsense uncle when he tried for some unearned accolades:

> Jeffrey said he wanted to show me the "book" he was writing. It was called *My Life.* I thought, "Well, that's an ambitious writing project." Then I opened it up. Three pages about nothing—and a first draft at that! No effort, no imagination—he just liked the idea of writing a book. "Let me see it when you've *done* something, Jeff. Anybody can buy a little red notebook. You've got to fill it with something interesting if you want people to read it."

- Make your kudos specific rather than the general "good girl" variety. If your child solves a jigsaw puzzle rapidly, commend her on her speed. If it took her a long time, commend her on her perseverance. If she quits, don't commend her.

With all these cautions to avoid insincere, unearned praise, don't lose sight of the flip side of the coin: *under-praising*. It can damage self-confidence as much, if not more, than overpraising. If you do not acknowledge genuinely difficult accomplishments, where your child works hard but doesn't seem to please anyone, what motivation does she have to continue? "I can't do anything right, so what's the use in trying?" Remember, as we said at the beginning of this chapter, everyone needs approval, so praise generously when it is truly warranted; it is then that it has impact. Even more meaningful, though, is the inner satisfaction that comes with genuine achievement. That's the real reward.

REAL REWARDS

Winning isn't everything. As we state many times throughout this book, what matters is the doing, the participation, the trying. If you love getting up to bat but your batting average is only .150, who cares? It's taking the swings that gives you the kicks! Conversely, if hitting home runs is the sole purpose of all your endeavors and you participate only in those in which you can excel, you miss the fun of the activities themselves—and leave by the wayside those others you might really enjoy!

Activities must be inherently rewarding, or there is no point in doing them. Competitive parents often encourage their children to just whack the ball and sprint around the bases like madmen. Don't stop. Don't look. Don't enjoy. Just make it home, score runs, and above all, beat the other guy! Such competitiveness undermines children's motivation because what may have been pleasurable suddenly becomes an obligation. What happens to childhood when everything is laden with high-pressure adult expectations? How can self-esteem incubate when kids are constantly being pushed to their limits?

This misplaced drive to succeed usually comes from parents whose own self-images need bolstering. Unfairly, they rely on their alter ego kids to do the repair work. Some parents get so involved in their children's activities that when the kids win, they take credit for it, and when they lose, they feel guilty for not having prepared them sufficiently.

Here's the problem with such external standards, set by competitive parents: *Kids cannot internalize their own sense of achievement when it is their parents' victory.*

The following are tips successful parents relied on to help their children experience the real rewards of personal effort:

- When tempted to get too involved in your child's activities or academic endeavors, step back and look at the situation: Your own needs may be taking priority. Instead of living vicariously through your kids, *observe,* don't participate; *encourage,* don't demand. And most important, applaud the *effort,* not the *ribbon.* A father we interviewed told us how he did this:

> I never missed Karen's soccer practice. I missed a few games, but never a practice. Those kids worked their tails off preparing for their games and it was that work—the drills and passes and defense—that I wanted her to know I saw. I'd take my sand wedge down to the soccer field and chip orange peels while

she practiced. She said I looked like a geek, but we both got some practice in.

- Since it is the *intrinsic* rewards, the ones that are felt emotionally and intellectually, that are lasting and valuable, they are the ones you should emphasize. One mother's motto was: "Compliment the act, not the award." When *extrinsic* rewards such as grades become students' only focus, kids miss the whole point of the scholastic process, which is more than accumulating brownie points. "We don't give dollars for As," said another father. "The grade itself is the reward, one the whole family can look at and be proud of."
- When a child feels anxious about an activity or just loses interest, be the first to spot it and assure him it is okay to let it go. Sometimes kids feel too much pressure to compete, pressure that can be overwhelming if they are not as competent as the other members of the team. Such was the case with Mrs. Sonnenberg's eight-year-old daughter, Teri, the youngest player on her baseball team:

Teri thought she had to do everything her older brother did. He was good at baseball, she had to be good at baseball. But she wasn't good and she wasn't enjoying herself. Part of the problem was, she had a coach who thought they were playing in the major leagues. During one game—her last—she was upset because she didn't know the signs. There she was, standing in the infield shaking, and I see a trickle of urine going down her leg. I ran out there and asked

> her if she wanted to go home. She looked at me with tears in her eyes and nodded. I took her out of the game right then and there, and you've never seen such a relieved little girl. I told her that it was okay not to be a good baseball player, that it didn't matter. She never played again and she never missed it.

Mrs. Sonnenberg made it clear to Teri that she still loved her and still valued her even though she didn't perform. Had Mrs. Sonnenberg insisted she not only stay in the game but excel, you can imagine the pressure Teri would have suffered. Kids have rights, too, and parents must honor them.

- Move your kids beyond the cushy comfort zone. Encourage your children to take on more difficult tasks for which they are qualified. Only in meeting tough challenges and making their own decisions can they feel personal satisfaction.

  A father told us about the time his fourth-grade son had to deliver his first oral book report in front of the class. Speaking in front of a group is one of man's innate fears, a fear Mr. Sullivan had experienced himself:

> I knew exactly what Jay was feeling and I also knew how important it was for him to carry through with this assignment. I told him learning to speak was invaluable later in life. I also told him that I used to be afraid of public speaking, too, when I first went into my line of work. He said, "You *did*?" with these big wide eyes. I think it gave him some measure of com-

fort to know his dad felt the same as he was feeling. "Everyone's a little scared they're going to make a mistake and get laughed at," I said. "And you know what? They make mistakes—all of them—and they *don't* get laughed at. Don't worry about it. Just get up there and do it." Presenting in front of people takes courage—and what a terrific way to build confidence!

Another father explained how, when his daughter had saved enough money and wanted to buy a car, he visited car lots with her, advised her what to look for and which questions to ask, but would not help her with the final buying decision. "It was her money, her car, and her responsibility. Who was I to make her decision for her?"

- Trying to do well is commendable, but knowing when to step down graciously shows class—the class that comes from not worrying about proving oneself over and over again. When children want to back out of an activity such as sports, for example, it may be because they prefer solitary tasks to team-oriented ones or they are quiet nonconformists who are perfectly happy without uniforms. As in Teri Sonnenberg's case, it may be that they simply cannot do well enough at the activity to enjoy it. Fine. Praise their independence and support their decision; it shows an increasing sense of self—and a *decreasing* need for trophies.

We have discussed a variety of self-esteem issues, all of which are important. But it may be that the best way for kids to experience a deep sense of self-worth is by taking responsibility for someone else's welfare. When your child does something genuinely worthwhile and concentrates on people other than herself, two things happen. One, she relaxes because she worries less about how *she* is doing and two, she learns valuable lessons in giving and generosity—two subjects we will cover in the next chapter. When kids undertake significant jobs where they feel needed, their self-esteem blossoms—and their own fears diminish. Such was the case with the student in our final story, who learned a valuable lesson from a smart parent:

> I was about seven and I was scared to death to go off to summer camp. I'd never been away from home and I didn't know the other kids [boarding the bus]. My dad saw me standing there all tense, so he pulled me out of line and took me to the side. "See that little kid over there?" he said. The boy was a year or so younger and a lot smaller than most of us. "He looks pretty scared, Phil. I think you'd be a lot of help to him if you made friends and sort of helped him through this, maybe sat with him on the bus, you know." It was like I took some kind of tranquilizer. I remember clearly not being afraid any more, and going over and trying to help relax the kid. What really happened was, *he* relaxed *me.*

CHAPTER 5

TEACH VALUES

The smell of freshly baked apple pie wafts out to the front porch on a warm Sunday evening after church. A kitchen full of giggling, flour-covered kids and knowing grandmothers greet uncles, neighbors, and puppies as they follow the scent in, anxious to join in the good food, friendly conversation, and camaraderie that have kept their vibrant community alive.

A scene from modern America? Not likely. Probably turn of the century. Today the porches are empty, as writer Amy Saltzman discovered when she set out to determine how people's values have changed in our modern competitive society. In the first pages of her book, *Downshifting,* she describes neighborhoods as if they were ghost towns: lots of nice houses, pretty elm-lined streets, comfortable porches—but no people.

Where have all the people gone? To the mall? To the office for yet another meeting? Or are they huddled together in the dark recesses of family rooms, glued to a made-for-TV miniseries? Wherever they are, they are not on the front porches, and they are not sharing time with family and friends like they once did.

In this chapter, we will examine first what is behind our lack of values as a nation and a culture. Then we will define values and see how the true experts imparted them to their growing children. Next, we list those values these parents believed were the most important, citing numerous examples of teaching opportunities that you can follow. Finally, we devote an entire section to the issue of money—the one "value" that seems to have replaced all others.

WHERE HAVE ALL THE VALUES GONE?

Why are the porches empty? For one thing, because our *values* are empty. America has changed. Close-knit communities are now bedroom communities. Churches are losing parishioners. Marriages are failing at a phenomenal rate, with the divorce rate *doubling* since 1965. We no longer cherish the heartfelt warmth and sense of togetherness that came from the communities we once depended on to help shape our children's values. Now where do we look? Where do the wide-eyed kids, who once soaked up every word of old folks' adventurous tales, now learn values? Answer: Television viewing, the single most pernicious influence on modern society, and one that has almost single-handedly decimated our common values as a nation.

TELEVISION

Television itself is not evil; our twisted dependence on it is. We mentioned at the beginning of this book how our gross overdependence on television distorts our view of reality, of what is important—or what ought to be—and how we have turned our value system over to a group of people whose sole mission in life is to sell commercial time to advertisers. We would be remiss if we did not again address in this chapter on values the issue of television and its too-central role in our lives.

According to a National Opinion Research poll of 2200 parents done a few years ago, the values that once defined our society have fallen miserably by the wayside. In response to the question, "What values would you like your children to have later in life?" a mere 10 percent answered: "Learn to work hard." Only 14 percent thought "Help others when they need help" was of prime importance!

In January 1995, a Bill Moyers PBS documentary examined at length the ill effects of excessive television viewing. One particularly poignant and infuriating clip showed a room full of young children, ranging from only a few months to about ten years of age, watching television early one morning before their parents were up. They had found a horror video depicting a knife-wielding villain slashing away at helpless victims. As they watched the terrifying, bloody scenes, they, too, were helpless victims, both mesmerized and petrified at the gruesome carnage they witnessed, but unable to turn off the television. Interestingly, the children who appeared to be around five or six were handling the material without too much difficulty. The young girl of about ten was holding and rocking the baby, who was screaming in horror, adding to the overall hysteria of the scene.

Numerous other studies have shown a direct correlation between excessive television viewing and today's lack of values. One problem with television is that, as it takes up more and more of our leisure time, we become desensitized to the insanity portrayed on the screen. So, like any other addicts, we require higher and higher doses to get high. But what about the kids? Studies have shown over and over that when children repeatedly view shootings, gang violence, or a particularly popular theme—the lurid depiction of sadistic brutality against women, just for the thrill of it—even young children eventually lose their sensitivity and can quite comfortably view such material without becoming disturbed, as we saw in the Moyers special. Is it any wonder violent crime continues to skyrocket when it is *glamorized* on television?

Said one mother:

> In the eighteenth century, values were communicated to the masses through literature and the Scriptures. Now it's television, which wouldn't be so bad if the message wasn't always consume, compete, be beautiful, and hurt each other to get what you want. Isn't this lovely? More shows ought to be scrutinized by Congress or *someone,* like they did with that cartoon with those two delinquent characters [Beavis and Butthead]. I'm trying to teach my kids to grow up to be decent adults, and I've got this junk to contend with. It doesn't help.

Commercials are no spiritual boon either. Who do we see pitching products? Social workers, scientists, therapists, volunteers, soldiers, or others who personify courage, generosity, sacrifice, and loyalty to nation? No, we see basketball players! Michael Blonsky, professor at New York University and analyst of cultural trends, was interviewed in Nike Town, a modern store on Michigan Avenue in Chicago. He looked around and exclaimed, "This is a church!" He turned to a life-sized figure of Michael Jordan and pointed. "Look! There's God!"

Blonsky sees a new culture of glamour, fitness, power, and eroticism moving in to take the place of old-fashioned values like modesty, virtue, and humility. But kids are not quite so easily beguiled. They instinctively know there is more to life than this, but what? If they rely solely on television to provide the answer, they cannot help but feel confused and hopeless. Here is an unpleasant statistic that bears this out: Teenage suicide has *tripled* in the past twenty years. That's a 200-percent increase in desperation and it is, in large part, related to what children see as unattainable ideals on television.

By the time they are adolescents, television-raised kids suddenly realize they have no belief system, no value system around which to model their lives. But just because most kids don't hang themselves to end their hopelessness doesn't mean they are feeling all that great.

With all the mixed messages from television, school, teachers, peers, and parents—all flying in different directions—how can today's children feel secure in their beliefs and comfortable with themselves? How do they know deep inside what they truly value? How many are at peace and how many are struggling to make sense of the madness that surrounds them? Unfortunately, the answers are no more forthcoming from their peers than they are from television.

PEERS

The other reason children fail to procure a decent set of values is peer pressure—a potent force that takes over values orientation for absent parents. As we saw in the last chapter, when parents are not committed to child rearing, kids look to peers for love and approval. And what better way to be accepted than to adopt the group's ideas and values? The problem is that what kids adopt today is a far cry from what it used to be in the front-porch days. As recently as thirty years ago, we had an entirely different view of things, as one father recalls:

> To us, the biggest thrill was taking my father's keys to the Thunderbird convertible when he was out with my mother. I remember picking up Bobby Thompson and Dennis Brush and screeching off to South Main Street for the big cruise. Top down, someone got a pack of cigs somewhere. Let me tell ya, this was a *big deal*. Today, kids don't joyride in cars, they *steal* 'em and strip 'em for coke money.

Without an internalized code of ethics from which to draw rational, sensible decisions, malleable children are open to all kinds of sinister suggestions. What the group says goes, and unfortunately, it often goes the wrong way unless kids have a true, inner commitment to religious or social values.

We will discuss peer pressure in greater detail in the next chapter, but as a preview, keep this in mind: As kids face adult issues at an earlier age than ever before—sex, pregnancy, drug experimentation, and violence—there is a pressing need to return to an old-fashioned value system that has proven its worth. Help prevent problems by devising a working plan with the aid of these suggestions from successful parents:

- Whatever the issues are, be sure to be up on them. Know the street lingo, the "in" drugs and their effects, the sexual activity and expectations of your child's peers.

- Discuss with your child peer pressure itself. Talk about why some kids try to tempt others into things because they lack values, have poor self-esteem, and are looking for approval.
- Remind your child in a nonjudgmental, nondiscriminating way that not all of his peers' families share the same moral or religious values as yours. Explain that it is important to believe in something, and to have ideals rooted in goodwill and decency.

COMPETITIVENESS

In our confused, overrevved society, many of us define our success in life strictly by our earning power, our trappings of success, our *automobile.* Excessive competitiveness and the desire to "get ahead" by racing at breakneck speed to a nonexistent pot of gold cost us dearly. When we are so intent on winning the status game, we find out too late that we have lost the parenting game. Then come the midlife regrets, the longings to relive those lost years spent at the office instead of at home where the real meaning in our lives comes from sharing and loving. If we could remove our Italian sunglasses for a moment, we would see the real colors of our rainbows are our *values,* and the pots of gold are our happy, well-adjusted children.

Amy Saltzman discovered during her research for *Downshifting* that many midlife professionals had misplaced their goals and were suddenly faced with a dilemma: Continue the relentless search for "success," as they had once defined it, or at long last put meaning in their harried lives. Many reinvented their idea of success, and decided to slow down and move laterally instead of upward in their companies or change careers altogether in order to have more time with their families. It seemed they had come full circle: They had left home and parents to educate themselves and get a job, they had joined the race to prosperity, and then they returned home again, this time as parents themselves, to the things that meant the most to them, to those things they *valued.*

WHAT ARE VALUES?

Richard McCormick, professor of Christian ethics at the University of Notre Dame, said about values: "A value is something we find fulfilling, rewarding, and important to us. Therefore we treasure it, protect it, seek it, and structure our lives around it." A value, then, is something of tremendous significance, a foundation upon which our very lives are built. Marian Wright Edelman, writer and founder of the Children's Defense Fund, said, "Family values and family traditions are an old tradition that we have to rediscover." To get a better understanding of the concept of values and what they mean, let's look at a variety of definitions.

Values are:

- Criteria by which we determine if something is good or bad, right or wrong, important or insignificant.
- Beliefs we hold that determine how we feel about specific issues.

- Beliefs that define who we are.
- An internalized code of ethics.
- Beliefs that form a union between us and society.
- Concepts by which societies define themselves.
- Beliefs that stem from religion, law, or convention.
- Ideals, standards, or traditions that shape our behavior.
- Things that are important, that control our lives, and that affect how we live.
- Attributes such as independence, ambition, courage, industriousness, optimism, education, respect, honesty, integrity, tolerance, self-discipline, civility, justice, honor, generosity, faith, humility, patriotism, spirituality, friendship, kindness, and love.

Where do these ideals that control our lives come from? They are the consensus of all the beliefs in our society, transmitted through family, the media, schools, religious institutions, friends, and associations. And they have differing degrees of importance to different people. For example, someone from a big metropolis may value independence or civility more than someone from a farming community, who may find friendship or faith of greater importance. A business owner may value courage and industriousness, while a teacher may find education and self-discipline highest on her list. But the most important thing about these deep-seated beliefs that shape who we are is that *we learn them from our parents.*

The successful parents found that, like all the other key elements we have discussed this far, values are transmitted best in a family where parents treat each other and their children with respect, love, and admiration—at all ages and in all situations, including those in which there is only one parent. Conservative religious and political factions, led most recently by Dan Quayle and Rush Limbaugh, have laid claim to the notion of "family values," appropriating the term as their own while espousing the importance of two-parent families. But they don't have a monopoly on morality, and perhaps their views are not all that moral anyway if they don't include *tolerance* as a virtue.

Old-fashioned values are sorely lacking today, but that's not to say they exist only in traditional family structures, as the Quayle/Limbaugh contingent might suggest. Those family structures have changed considerably from the idyllic days of Ozzie and Harriet, who exemplified the "perfect" '50s' parents with the squeaky-clean, straitlaced, trouble-free kids. Today, many families are headed by single parents or mixed-race and mixed-faith parents—all of whom we met in our study. But even though structures have changed, three things still have *not* changed: the *way* values are transmitted, the *values* themselves, and the *purpose* of values, which is to create moral, law-abiding, generous, respectful, genuinely nice people who are independent, self-expressive, and most important of all, able to make a *contribution to society*. No one could have put it better than Marian Wright Edelman, who said her parents taught her that life is about serving others and that service is "the rent you pay for living, not something you do in your spare time." Another mother put it this way:

> I'm not a New Age person, but I do believe in karma and that you get back what you give out. It's the most valid principle in the universe; it's the one we should live by. I'm not concerned with life after death; I'm concerned with life *before*

death and what we can do to make other people's lives better. That's why we're here, and that's what I've taught my three kids, who have turned out to be wonderful, generous people.

TEACHING VALUES

If your child has the opportunity to cheat on a test without getting caught, will he? What if he can impress his peers by telling a lie that hurts someone's reputation and elevates his? Will he have the character to resist violating his own morals? The answers to these questions depend on his view of right and wrong—a view only you can teach and only by *years* of modeling the values you wish to impart.

The true experts' goals were to progressively instill in their children a code of ethics both by example and by direct moral instruction. By "instill," they did not mean "refer to occasionally when convenient"; they meant *genuinely believe* internally. To accomplish this, you will need to draw on some of the other key elements we have discussed.

First, communication. Remember, *lectures don't work,* especially when teaching moral behavior. Some direct instruction, yes, but asking the right questions in the right way is the most effective way to make your point.

Second, intellect. Make your questions eye-openers that force kids to think. Ask questions that stimulate the mind, such as "What if you found a wallet loaded with money on the street? What do you think you should do with it?" "What if you saw another kid stealing in the market? What would be the right thing to do?"

Third, discipline. As we saw, criticizing misbehavior is

never a good idea, but it is a particularly *bad* idea when it involves poor moral judgment. Such shortcomings should be viewed as moral slips and treated no differently from how you would treat a skier who takes a fall while schussing down a slope. The best help is to point out where he made his mistakes and then lead the way down the hill so he can follow in your tracks. One insightful mother put it this way:

> Kids are *in the process* of learning good judgment. They're *getting* it, but there's no reason to expect they *have* it yet—because they're still *kids!* It's amazing how many parents tell their little children, "Act like an adult!"

Another mother told us just how far off the mark kids' judgment can be:

> Here's why kids need parents: They don't have poor judgment, they have *no* judgment sometimes! Willie calls us long distance from school [his freshman year in college] to ask if he and his friends can go win a hundred-dollar prize for eating some pizza—four states away! "Oh, good idea, Will," I said. "Drive halfway across the country (it was about twelve hundred miles), don't get any sleep, don't study, and spend the hundred bucks you win on gas anyway. Just a minute, your father's gonna want to talk to you on this one! Biiiiiill, pick up the phone."

Remember the self-esteem issues in the last chapter. When it comes to moral judgments and the concept of right and wrong, you are dealing with particularly sensitive areas that tie in directly to self-worth. Be certain to deliver any message of morality in an understanding, calm manner where you hold your child fully responsible for misdeeds, but at the same time forgive him for his mistakes.

INDEPENDENT VALUES

Imparting values does not mean molding moral clones. It means modeling and teaching the beliefs you hold dear, and then accepting your child's individuality and tendency to modify those beliefs. One parent cautioned:

> Make it clear in your book that we do not expect our children to become our robots. If they don't believe in their own morals and can't distinguish right from wrong without us being there every minute, they won't be much good at withstanding the peer pressure to try things they shouldn't.

Another parent put it this way:

> As kids grow toward adolescence, there's a big change. A parent has to adapt. He may still be king, but his kid is no longer a serf; she wants to be a knight of the round table.

Here is the danger in raising overly compliant children who merely *adopt* your value system and then passively act the way they think they are *supposed* to: When temptations to violate that system arise, kids cannot draw on their own internal beliefs because they don't have any! Taking a wild guess and randomly selecting a response to a particular situation is entirely different from *consciously choosing* a response from a personal set of beliefs. *Responsibility for one's thoughts and actions cannot be imposed.*

Parents who try to dictate moral behavior are in for a surprise: Their children may rebel with even *looser* morals! Responsibility must grow internally from seeds of independence planted by parents who are willing to let their children feel their own feelings and form their own identities. Successful parents we met believed that manipulating their children's moral decisions or preaching specific gospels was a big mistake. This does not mean you cannot explain your views; you should. Direct moral teaching has its place, but it is usually not enough. As we have seen before, kids need to be *shown* how to live morally.

ROLE MODELING

Most of the time, values cannot be explained any more than you can explain how to ski down that black diamond slope. You may be an expert at both, but both skills are difficult to pass on with mere verbal explanation. Just as you would ski down the hill with your child following, model the behavior that exemplifies your values and the basic concepts you believe in. Your child will *absorb* them naturally.

The true experts we studied saw themselves in many roles: friend, educator, psychologist, minister, police officer, and moral teacher. But teacher was hardest to define in relation to values. After all, how do you teach someone to be "moral"? It's nothing like algebra, where equations are cut and dry. The concepts of "morals," "values," and "ideals" are too abstract, too intangible to simply explain on a chalkboard.

One parent said, "To grasp internally what a clear, starry night is like, you have to walk outside and actually *observe* it, because it defies description." Similarly, children must *see* their parents acting (not just talking) in moral ways. Later in this chapter, we list what our parents believed were the most important values, but first let's start with some underlying fundamentals they felt had to be demonstrated on a daily basis:

- Treat others with consideration.

  As trite as it may sound, follow the Golden Rule: Do unto others as you would have them do unto you. Kids need to witness their parents being kind to others, so demonstrate your kindness on a daily basis, whether it is simply holding open a door for someone, letting another driver into your lane, or calling a restaurant to let them know you will be a little late for a reservation. Remember, kids learn how to treat others by the way their parents treat others.

- Offer assistance and empathy to those in need.

  Every day there are opportunities to demonstrate empathy, too. One student told us how he drove up to an intersection one day and spotted an elderly man with a cane stuck in the middle as the light changed to green. As cars whizzed by, a woman screeched to a halt, leapt out of her car, stopped traffic like a policeman, and led the man to safety.

- Be patient and tolerant of other's views.

  Respect people of various backgrounds. One parent said:

  > Accept everyone unconditionally. Be willing to form friendships with those whose religious or political views differ from yours. Remember, your children

are watching! If you expect them to be open and respect other people's thoughts and needs, you better not respond to bigotry with bigotry.

The mother in this following story kept a cool head and showed her daughter the quality of tolerance in the face of intolerance:

> I bumped into an old high school friend one day, and we had no sooner started talking than he began preaching that Jesus loved me and that I *had* to come to his church that Sunday. I told him, "Jim, I'm Jewish, remember? Jesus wasn't around five thousand years ago. We don't see Him as our Lord the way you do." "Sarah," he said, "there is nothing wrong with Jews; they just haven't seen the way yet." As we walked away, I told [my daughter] Rebecca that everyone has the right to their own beliefs; ours happen to be different from Jim's family.

- Obey the law.

  If you expect your children to obey the law, you had better not speed or finesse your tax return.

BE PROACTIVE

Be proactive rather than *reactive.* Toughen your kids' abdominals if you expect they'll be taking a punch one day. That is, don't wait until something happens to discuss the issues related to a misdeed. Head off trouble at the pass by fortifying your children with information and activities that foster morality. As we discussed in Chapter 3, the successful families we met held semimonthly or monthly meetings to discuss various issues, some of which related to discipline and behavior, others of which related to political and social issues, as this father explains:

> Before our family night, my wife and I would plan the meeting like we would any business meeting. We prepared the agenda beforehand so the time would be well spent and we'd be sure to make the session stimulating for the kids. Our topics varied, but they were usually on current affairs or social issues we thought were important. We would start [the meetings] with any suggestions from the kids and then be sure to bring up our own issues before adjourning.

When children are younger and unable to sit in a family meeting, take another proactive step to impart important values: Tell stories. Read to children, *carefully selecting* the literature based on its ability to edify and inspire. Old-fashioned storytelling drives home valued messages that appeal to young children's emotions and imaginations—the two most powerful areas of their minds. One teacher we spoke with said:

> Once learned, kids never forget the significance of the lion, the scarecrow, or tin man in *The Wizard of Oz*. Many new stores have popped up recently that cater to children's education. The books are better than ever with beautiful graphics and illustrations. If you peruse the shelves carefully, you can find loads of literature that teach morals and values, and it's a good thing. We need them now more than ever.

When passion, humor, fear, and joy are interwoven with moral messages, abstract terms like "loyalty" or "courage" take on profound meaning. "It is the emotional impact of the stories that gets ideas across without children even knowing it," the teacher continued. Since kids look up to heroes with an undying loyalty parents rarely enjoy, stories can be an impressive way to teach important concepts that would never come across in lecture format.

In addition to reading and family meetings, don't overlook the old tried-and-true institutions such as Boy Scouts and Girl Scouts; Little League baseball, Pop Warner football and other team sports; after-school activities such as stamp collecting, dance, music lessons, and horseback riding; clubs such as 4H and YMCA; and religious training.

Get your children involved in these established organizations whose purpose is to inspire good citizenship and sportsmanship. One parent we met noticed his daughter's early interest in politics, so he had her contact Girls' State, an organization that brought together students from different cities to meet at the state capitol and hold mock elections.

Such involvement should not be left to chance or to the hope that one of your child's friends might invite him to join some group. A former scoutmaster father put it this way:

> Make the suggestion [to join a club] in an appealing way. Come up with something enticing. You've got to excite kids' imaginations by describing what they're going to do and the kind of fun they'll have. Sometimes you've got to present new activities as a privilege they'll be fortunate to be part of "*if* you can get him in."

If you were to just make a drab, ho-hum suggestion like, "Any interest in joining the Cub Scouts?" your child may very well respond with, "No, I like watching cartoons all day, but thanks for asking."

Because the concepts of values and morals are abstract and hard to grasp, take an "unparentlike" stance and share your own difficulties learning good moral behavior. Tell about the times in your past when you made moral missteps—it relieves the guilt kids feel when they make their own and it relieves the pressure to perform flawlessly. You don't want your kids to feel they have to tiptoe gingerly through a moral minefield everyday.

One father had an excellent way of strengthening his relationships with his children on a friend-to-friend basis:

> They weren't teenagers yet, but at ten to twelve, I felt the boys were ready for a close personal relationship. So I'd take each one away on a solo trip, just the two of us. We'd go away for a long weekend and usually visit historical places or look into our family heritage. I wanted the time away to be educational, but the other reason was for us to form a better bond between us. I think the kids grew up on those weekends, and I think we became a lot closer.

THE MOST IMPORTANT VALUES

In a study of the world's major religions, researchers found a number of universally accepted values. Of those that have stood the test of time, the following, in no particular order, were selected by effective parents as the most important to teach their children.

Courage

Moral courage is a youngster's strongest weapon against peer pressure; it is the one thing on which he must rely when tempted to do something he knows is wrong. Drug and alcohol use, sexual misconduct, even suicide, can stem from the frustration a child feels with his lack of courage, his absence of internal fortitude to resist illicit temptations.

Courage helps kids see beyond the immediate enticement of an illicit opportunity. Having courage also means being able to see the light at the end of a dark tunnel, to face difficulties and believe in yourself enough to push on, knowing you will make it through all right.

How is courage developed? We have already discussed several ways parents instilled self-esteem and self-confidence in their children, both of which are key components of courage: Encourage your child to take risks without worrying about the outcome; let him make his own decisions without criticizing them if they are wrong; let her openly express her feelings and ideas without censorship or disapproval.

The virtue of courage is also strengthened when unexpected change occurs. Events like moving to a new neighborhood, the death of a pet or relative, changing schools, or experiencing divorce all require heart-to-heart talks that assure children these difficult times will pass if only they maintain the determination and guts it takes to see the matters through. Remind children that crises are part of life and getting through crises now helps handle those that will inevitably occur later.

One father recalled a scene from his childhood that demonstrates what life is like when a child is incapacitated by lack of courage:

> There was a good-sized pond down this country road where all of us kids would go ice skating starting around Christmastime. For years I watched my dad go out with a long stick and check the ice. When I was about ten I started doing it. But there was one kid, who actually looked older than us, around twelve or so, who stood on the bank with his skates and never could get up the courage to step out there with the rest of us. I felt sorry for him. He'd watch for a while, sometimes he'd put one foot out there to check it out, then he'd get on his bike and slowly ride away. I never saw him come on the ice, but I saw him standing there a lot of times wanting to.

Another father helped his son develop courage when he literally led the boy off the beaten track as they were backpacking in Yellowstone National Park, an area known for grizzly bear:

> Now, mind you, Gerald was only fifteen when we took this trip into bear country. We were hiking along lockstep with everyone else when I finally said, "There are too many people on this trail. There's an old, unused trail on my topo [map] up ahead. If you're game, we can take it and see where it leads." Gerald said, "Great," but then I reminded him, "The only thing about this kind of trail is, it's unused and quiet, so if there are any grizzlies in the area, they haven't been scared off by hikers. They might be around." "I don't care, Dad," he said. "If you're not scared, I'm ready to go. We just make noise and scare them away, right?"

"Right," I said. "We'll sing songs along the way so they know we're coming." "OK," said Gerald. "Let's go."

Ambition

Ambition, by one definition, means "vigorously pursuing an aim." Another says, "an earnest desire for achievement." Have you ever seen a small child hiding behind his mother's skirt? He doesn't look particularly ambitious, does he? That's fine for a three-year-old, but some kids stay there forever. No courage, no ambition. It is only when the mother slowly pulls her child out from behind the protective barrier that he develops the willingness to step out into other uncertain territory. Such willingness is *ambition.*

Ambitious people embrace life. They possess a spirit of curiosity and a bright optimism that fuels every conquest. Where does this spirit come from? From the seeds planted by parents who spur their children to seek out new experiences and untried paths, paths that lead to uncertain destinations.

One father suggested his fifteen-year-old son take on an ambitious project that would teach him to appreciate his own abilities to accomplish the unusual:

> When Lee decided he wanted to be a surfer, I wholeheartedly supported him since I was a surfer of sorts when I was his age. Except I lived in Hawaii then; now we lived in Maine—big difference, but anyway. I told him how I built my own surfboard when I was fourteen. Started from scratch. Got a foam blank, read up on fiberglass and resins, how to place the skeg [fin]. It came out great. He had never thought about something like that before, but it hit a nerve, so he built his own, too. He loved it. You should have seen the attention to detail. Fine-sanding every seam, buffing the

bright yellow pigment when he was done. He even let his pop get in on it and mix the catalyst with the resin. But he drew the line when it came to taking the board out!

Another student, who was encouraged to put forth his own effort as a young child, recalled how much more he enjoyed a purchase after doing the legwork to research it.

> Dad wasn't the type to do things for me. When I was seven and wanted a gasoline-engine airplane, he told me to call all the stores myself and find out what they cost and what they could do. I wanted one that could do loops and stunt flying. By the time I was done, I was pretty much an expert on what was on the market and which one to buy. When I got my plane, I knew it was the best one around. I think it meant a lot more to me than if I had just gone with Dad to any store and let him buy me the first one I saw.

Spirituality

God is back. People are returning to church after a long hiatus in the '70s and '80s (theirs, not God's). Why this is, and the controversial issues surrounding spirituality, God, atheism, and the rest, can be debated until doomsday. We're not going to. Suffice it to say that belief in a Higher Power of some sort provides children with another kind of courage—one that does more than insulate them from drugs, sex, and the like. Religious faith debunks the media's hedonistic notion that all that really matters in life is wealth and pleasure—right now! It empowers people to see beyond the ephemeral and the superficial, and strengthens their resolve to resist material temptations.

Several parents told us that to them, the real importance

of religion and faith was the concept of love, and it did not matter whether the message came through the Gospel, Torah, Koran, or modern doctrines such as those in *A Course in Miracles.* Said one father:

> We learn to serve God by treating one another with the love and respect and dignity we ourselves want, and by forgiving everyone—including ourselves—when we think we have made a mistake. The most powerful thing a young person can learn is to give thanks for God's gifts. Kids need to spend prayer time thanking God for His help—not asking for more possessions they don't need.

One mother frequently reminded her children to stop now and then, and just look at themselves in the mirror:

> "Look at your eyes. They are the lamps to your soul; they let the light in. Your ears, your nose, your mouth—they're all perfect. Be thankful for what you have and take care of it. Extend your love to everyone." I often recited to my children the old saying "Love in your heart wasn't put there to stay; love isn't love 'til you give it away." If kids really learn to believe this one, simple idea, they will be happy. They'll forget about trying to *get* and learn that life is about *giving* to others. It's really not about anything else, in my book.

Though most of our parents were members of an organized religious institution, they felt "spiritual" did not necessarily mean being affiliated with one. To them, what was important was the internal, highly personal feelings of contact with a Higher Power who is here to guide us through our difficulties and our relationships. Several religions and spiritual pathways were represented in our study, but whether families lived strictly by the Scriptures (which many did) or took a less orthodox view of spirituality, they all valued the family closeness mutual worship afforded.

Here are some of the ways parents taught their children the concept of a Supreme Being, Creator, Higher Power, Eternal Love, or God:

- Avoid "serious" talks about God or a supreme being that may make the concept of religion unpleasant, if not frightening, to a young child. Likewise, if you introduce a concept that is too difficult to comprehend, your child will become bored and retreat to his own fantasy world.
- When your child is very young, ask her to draw a picture of God without any help. Keep this exercise lighthearted as you have her explain her view of a Supreme Being. Said one mother:

  > The main idea I tried to plant is that there is someone watching over her, a benevolent God she can depend on who is full of love and forgiveness and who is there in times of need.

- Watch for opportunities to discuss religion and God, and stay alert to your child's receptiveness. If he asks a cursory question and your simple answer suffices, stop there; don't belabor the point. Philosophical discussions are a guaranteed turnoff and will make religion into a noxious subject your child will avoid in the future.

Honesty

Mr. Williams, a successful trial lawyer who is used to thinking on his feet, admitted he was not prepared when his six-year-old daughter, Susie, came to him one day and exclaimed, "Lynn Powers said there's no Santa Claus!" He had to quickly assess the situation. At six, Susie was awfully young to have the Santa Claus fantasy ruined, along with the years of gift-giving from the North Pole. On the other hand, if he tried to preserve the Santa story by outright lying to his young daughter who had now put the issue before him, he knew the day would come when this trusting child would find out he had lied to her. Here's how he expressed his dilemma:

> I've always felt that you have to teach the things you believe are important and sacrifice the things that aren't. In this case, honesty was the most important issue at hand. My daughter had come to me in good faith and wanted the matter resolved. Was there a Santa or wasn't there? I wasn't about to blatantly lie to her when it was convenient, and then turn around and try to teach her the merits of honesty as she grew up.

Mr. Williams went on to explain how he used this opportunity to explain his belief in God:

> Since I wanted to be perfectly honest with Susie, there was no better time than this to explain my view of God. I told her that no, there wasn't a Santa, but there was a God. "Just because something's invisible doesn't mean it's not there," I told her. "Electricity is everywhere, but you don't have to get hit by a lightning bolt to know it." Since I was lev-

> eling with her about mysterious things you can't see, I think my honesty about a God, who is as invisible as Santa Claus, really made an impression on her.

Mr. Williams understood that honesty is about being able to be trusted. From lessons like this, children learn to recognize their responsibility to be honest with others. Only in that way can they enjoy a genuine sense of personal integrity.

Another parent, Mrs. Moretti, explained how she learned her most important lesson about honesty, which, unfortunately, was the result of dishonesty on her mother's part. Her story drives home what we have been saying throughout this book: You are constantly being watched and looked up to by your children, so if you let them down, the consequences can be devastating.

> I can tell you why I've never lied to my children and have taught them that honesty is so important. I grew up as a child in Italy. One day when I was five, my mother said she was going to the store and never came back. I waited for her day after day, but she didn't come back for five years—and I remember every one of those torturous, lonely years. She had gone to America to try and make a place for us, but she never told me. She wasn't honest with me because she thought it would be too painful, I guess. But the dishonesty is what hurt the most. I didn't trust her for years after that, and I'm still not sure I've completely forgiven her.

Our parents helped their children develop their own concepts of honesty by asking them questions that involved trust. This was not an occasional thing but a regular exercise that you, too, will find is a great asset for teaching your children to think conscientiously. Here are some of the questions they asked, progressing from those for younger to those for older children:

"Why is lying wrong?" "What difference does it make if you cheat on a test at school?" "What's wrong with stealing candy from the store?" "If you have to mow the lawn every weekend to save up for a bike, how would you feel if someone stole it?" "If someone offered you a lot of money to give them information you were sworn to keep private—and no one really got hurt from it—would you do it?" "If you asked a rich man for a donation for a good cause and he turned you down, what would you do if you saw a ten-dollar bill fall out of his pocket as he walked away?"

In each case, parents explained whose trust was violated by the infractions. Cheating violated the teacher's trust, stealing, the store owner's, and so on. One parent told us her nine-year-old son was having a hard time with the concept of trust violation:

> Barry couldn't get the idea of a victim—including himself—when it came to the consequences of dishonesty. So I explained that more than anyone else, *he* was the victim because when he cheated someone in some way, he violated a kind of bond they had. Since he was the one doing the breaking, he was the one who would feel the guilt. Half the time the store clerk or whoever doesn't even know when something is stolen. But the thief does and he has to live with himself, knowing he can't be trusted. It's a terrible burden to carry around.

Lying

Youthful untruths are often nothing more than wishes. Young children live in fantasy worlds where things come true just because they say they are true—one of the great benefits of childhood! They are incapable of distorting the truth intentionally because their sense of ethics is not yet developed. Remember, kids will fib because they don't want to say what really happened and be thought of as "bad." Don't punish such childhood foibles and don't accuse young children of lying or insist they confess to their crimes. Instead, relate your own stories. Tell about the times you made similar mistakes; it relieves pressure and lessens guilt.

The picture changes considerably, though, when kids hit adolescence. They may go to great, if not preposterous, lengths to avoid the truth, as one mother told us: "Here's a little advice for parents of adolescents: Beware, if the story they tell you is so outrageous that you know it couldn't be made up, it usually is!" With a laugh, her daughter then took over to relate the incident her mother was referring to:

> You asked about honesty. Well, I never really lied to Mom, but this one night I knew I would really be in trouble big time because I was super-late. And we were having such a good time, I *couldn't* go home! I didn't even want to take the time to go to the phone, but about twelve o'clock I thought I better call. I mean, I was already dead. So I came up with this great story: "We were at Farrell's and when we went to leave, the car had a flat. I tried to call, but everybody was waiting to use the phone. Then I got the AAA and had to wait outside for them for an hour and a half. But they never came, so I had to fix the tire myself because everyone had to go home. Then, when I was fixing it, the car fell off the

jack." I mean, it went on and on and on. Well, Mom believed it! I didn't tell her the whole thing was made up until about a year later, and she said, "It was such a wild story, I believed it! Oh, you little monster!"

Stealing

Stealing is another honesty issue that came up in most of the families we studied. Like lying, it has to be handled with "kid" gloves. Many of our parents discovered their children stealing sometime between the ages of eight and twelve. But they did *not* respond by shaming their children and telling them how terrible these acts of dishonesty were. What they *did* do was view this childhood filching for what it was: a moral misstep—not a precursor to juvenile delinquency.

Young children may steal because they need to feel more control or power, or they feel badly about something else and want to lift their spirits by lifting someone else's property. Older children may need to capture the attention of their peers, so they steal clothes or other status symbols that fill those needs. Kids who have been neglected or rejected by their parents may actually desire to get caught in a desperate effort to finally get someone to pay attention to them.

What you have to do when these incidents occur is try to determine where the unacceptable behavior is coming from; there may be some deep-seated problems that are of a much greater magnitude than the item stolen. If the infraction is merely a childhood mistake, which it usually is, take the appropriate measures. For example, if your child "steals" a book from the library and stashes it under his bed because he likes the pictures, it is not a capital crime, but he does have to face the music. This is unacceptable behavior, period. And the sentence should be: Have *him* return the booty to the librarian (*not* the drop box) with an apology, and pay the fine out of *his* piggy bank—not yours. The last thing you want to do is lessen the importance of the misdeed by making excuses for him.

We'll end this section with a story of how good upbringing fosters the healthy conscience that pays off in the end:

> When Gina was six years old, she found a dollar on the floor at McDonald's. I told her she couldn't keep it; she had to give it back to the clerk. She didn't want to, but I told her someone lost that money and might be coming back for it. So she gave it to the clerk. When she came back [to the table] she was so mad! She said, "The lady put the money in her pocket—and she didn't even thank me!" Well, I didn't think that was the best lesson in honesty, but I told Gina that she still did the right thing. I guess it sank in because during her junior year she took a trip to Europe and wouldn't you know, she found more money on the ground; this time it was four hundred dollars! All her friends started chanting "Party! Party!" but she went to the nearby currency exchange office and tried to give it back. They wouldn't take it! She kept trying, saying—just like I did that day when she was six—"Someone might be back for it." Well, they refused to take it, so Gina finally kept it and paid for everyone's cooking lessons and then gave the bus driver a big tip. *Voila!*

Humility

When our competitive, success-oriented world extols "pride in achievement," how do you instill in your children the virtue of humility? One way is to do what our parents did: Swiftly remind kids who act as if they are the center of the universe that helping others takes priority over fulfilling petty personal desires. One parent suggested this to her ten-year-old, who, upon reaching fifth grade, was becoming preoccupied with her own popularity:

> Get in the habit of saying this little rhyme Nana taught us when we overinflated ourselves: "There are more important things in the world besides me, but if I'm only looking at me, I cannot see thee." And she had another one she would use to mock us out if we got too big for our britches: "I love myself, I think I'm grand, when I go to the movie, I hold my hand." *Call* kids on this self-centered stuff! If you don't, they really *will* start believing they're God's only gift to the world, and *then* try getting them to listen to you! Good luck!

Along the same vein, another parent regularly reminded her overly competitive thirteen-year-old of the following idea that, like some of the others we have seen, might be most beneficial pinned to bedroom walls: *Life is about sharing and helping others, not winning prizes for ourselves.*

The best way to instill humility over self-centeredness is to teach *gratitude.* Teach children to be *thankful* for what they have, an old precept that in recent times has seemed to vanish. One parent said about gratitude:

> The problem is—and it's most obvious around Christmastime—kids get too much. Too much of everything—too much food, too much candy, too many toys. We're spoiling the hell out of them! How can they be grateful when everyone keeps piling on the gifts, one after another, faster than the kids can open them? They barely get one present ripped apart and they're handed three more! Pretty soon they're so overwhelmed by the confusing mess,

which by then has lost all semblance of meaning, that they get cranky and throw *everything* aside.

Another parent explained the payoff for teaching kids gratitude:

> I knew we had done something right when, one day, I brought home the rugby shirt Tom had been talking about buying and he said so sweetly, "You didn't have to do that, Mom." My eyes got teary. I mean, it just touched my heart. What a nice kid we ended up with! I said to him, "That's all right, Honey. I wanted to." He thanked me—and I knew he meant it.

Generosity

What are we teaching our children when we turn down the Girl Scout selling cookies at our door or we walk briskly past the Salvation Army bucket at Christmas? Such acts of frugality are unfortunately the rules, not the exceptions, in our society. If they weren't, we would not need the bell-ringing volunteers—they would be in the office processing our checks! Though most people can certainly afford a quarter for the poor, they are so intent on buying that umpteenth gift for already oversatiated kids that they can't break stride to drop a coin in the can. Here is a perfect—but missed—opportunity to teach children generosity.

Likewise, if most people who enjoy the outstanding programming on viewer-supported television will not even get up from the couch to make a donation during a pledge drive (nonpayers make up *90 percent* of the viewing audience), what message are they sending the children seated next to them? "Hey, Mom, you gonna call?" "Oh, no, Parsimony, we can't afford it."

The magnanimity effective parents show their children and others stems from love—the type that does not ask for anything in return and that does not "meet halfway." The following are several ways the experts taught their children to show love and generosity:

- To teach a child the true nature of giving, urge her to share not those things she has lost interest in, but the things she loves the most, like her dolls or ice cream. Because these things bring her so much enjoyment, gently suggest how wonderful it would be to share that joy and help another child experience the same bliss. Focus on the *result* of giving so the gesture does not feel like a loss. Demonstrate enthusiasm by sharing your own items with your child's playmate and show how much pleasure *you* gain from it: "Oh, Heather, I'm so glad you like my knitting yarns! Aren't they pretty colors?"
- Have your young child participate in a walkathon or other activity where the proceeds go directly to other people. She can't help but feel the joy of goodwill and generosity, which is an entirely different feeling from that of receiving. The pleasure associated with doing good for others is satisfying and habit-forming.
- At Christmastime, have your child select toys and clothes he is no longer using. If he doesn't think he can live without them, do what one mother did: Open up the toy chest and closet and separate the items into categories. Ask him when he last played with a partic-

ular toy or wore an old item of clothing. Here's what she recommended:

> Pull out three sweaters and ask if he thinks he'll stay warm with only two. If he's young, don't expect him to give anything up. So reason with him. Tell him how much a warm sweater would mean to a needy child. If he still doesn't get it, take him outside without one for a few minutes to make your point. See how long he lasts before giving in.

- Keep a family charity box in the house. A mother told us she kept hers on the kitchen counter and when it got a bit light, she would bring it to the dinner table and ask if anyone would be willing to contribute a little more for those in need. She said:

> If you don't keep bringing these things up, kids quickly forget about the other guy out there who needs help. They need reminding all the time, and I always thought the best time was when we were about to feed our own faces.

- Teach your children to constantly be aware of giving, not just at holiday time. Mrs. Thompson taught her children to start thinking about Christmas in January:

> When the kids were little and they found a penny or little trinket, I'd have them wrap it for a Christmas gift for the poor. We did this all year long. It got them thinking about giving instead of keeping things for themselves all the time. There started to be some

> competition among the girls over who had the most gifts by the end of the year. That was fine. That's the kind of competition I like.

Service

Service to local communities, schools, or volunteer organizations was of prime importance to the parents we interviewed. One, in particular, set a shining example for her children. Mrs. Wells was the president of the National Junior League, president of the PTA, chairperson of the Casey Program for black foster children, and volunteer food server at Samaritan House for the homeless one night a month—including Christmas evenings. Her son, Steve, followed in her footsteps and at twelve began working for the town mayor, taking notes at city council meetings, and continually participating in volunteer organizations, including one fund-raiser that surpassed all goals:

> We sold pizzas door-to-door. I was only fifteen and didn't have a car, so I hit the phone books and called everyone I knew to get orders. I asked my mother to help me deliver over a hundred pizzas that night. It was way more than anyone else and a lot more than we expected to do. I know it was because I saw my mother involved in volunteer programs all my life.

Another top student also did exceedingly well on his school fund drive, going far beyond the call of duty and breaking the food collection record by over 50 percent. Charley's goal as head of the drive was to collect ten thousand pounds of food. But after it began, he decided to up the ante to fifteen thousand pounds, an amount never before achieved at his school.

> Everyone said it couldn't be done—including me. So I didn't see any great risk in saying I'd shave my head in front of the entire student body if we reached our goal. I guess I underestimated them; I made them an offer they couldn't refuse. When the last pound was collected, our principal stopped classes to have a special assembly so I could have my head shaved. And I did. Mom wasn't too happy about my hair but she got over it; she knew it was for a good cause.

Another form of service included "Sub for Santa." One couple explained that one evening they saw an ad in the local paper asking for donations of toys for poor families. Though they did not have much extra money themselves at that time, they purchased several toys and delivered them to the needy people's homes. Said one mother:

> It was a good lesson for Chip. When we brought over the toys, we were often invited inside these people's homes. Chip saw how fortunate he was to have the home he did. Once he said as we left, "God, Mom, did you see how poor those people were? They really needed us, huh?"

Another student's parents sent him on a summer church trip to work at a mission in French Guiana and Martinique when he was fifteen. Though the student came from a comfortable background, he quickly learned to sleep and eat with the native people of these impoverished areas. His father had done no less when he was his son's age, traveling to the indigent East End of London to go door-to-door helping the needy.

Education

Needless to say, all the successful parents we spoke with valued education. But two in particular told us clearly why it is so important. The first was a corporate president of a large health organization who had his secretary hold all calls while we interviewed him in the middle of his busy day. As we walked into his stylish executive suite overlooking the busy financial district below, it was obvious to us that he was a man who had climbed the corporate ranks to the top. Talking with him and his wife (who had driven the twenty miles from their suburban home to participate in the meeting), we learned that setting goals and backing them with determination were the keys to their success. Here is his view on education, which both he and his wife felt was the most important value of all:

> When he was as young as three, we were asking Joe what he wanted to be. I remember his first idea was to be a doctor. Fine. I told him to be a doctor he would need to learn chemistry, math, science, and Latin. Then a while later he wanted to be a pilot. When I asked him why he changed his mind, he said, "Doctors have to work on Saturday and I'll miss my cartoons!" [Laughter all around.] At least he was thinking! The point is—and we always told Joe this—choose a vocation and begin to prepare for it by educating yourself. It doesn't matter if you change your mind later; begin to prepare as soon as you decide on a goal. When you make a change, start again to get the education you need to secure that position in life. Switching vocations is okay because it

> gives you a broader education. What matters is, what you do today determines what your future will be. Later, when Joe got older and changed his mind on anything, we'd ask if it was because he still wanted to watch Saturday morning cartoons! That always got a rise out of him.

The other parent we talked to was a single woman who lived in a modest home in the inner city. Financially, she was at the opposite end of the spectrum from Joe's parents, but she believed just as fervently that education was absolutely crucial. Her daughter had won a full scholarship to college in large part because of that belief.

> I told Rosa to study because I didn't want her to end up like me, working as a retail clerk for eight dollars an hour. I had no education and no skills, so I had no future. But she did and I wanted her to make the most of it. So I'd take her to work with me sometimes, and let her see what it was like to take orders from bosses and wait on customers all day. I wanted her to know it didn't have to be like that if she got an education; that was the *only* thing that would give her a decent future—and now she's on her way, thank God.

MONEY

By definition, "money" is not a value, but in our society, we see it as something even more laudable. If we didn't, why would we worship it, relentlessly pursue it, gamble it, and when we accumulate what we think is enough of it, flaunt it for all to see?

The money issue is bandied about the schoolyard, too.

Some kids have fancy clothes, others wear hand-me-downs. Some parents are doctors, others are janitors, so their incomes and assets vary greatly. Kids are well aware of these disparities, and are not above announcing, "Well, *my* Dad's a *lawyer!*" or "*We* have a *boat!*"

Let's start with the notion that though today's children adore the green stuff, they have a poor understanding of its purpose and have at best only the vaguest connection between hard work and earning money. According to Fred Gosman, author of *Spoiled Rotten,* the work ethic of bygone years has gone out the window. The parents we interviewed agree. Said one father:

> Today's kids see low achievement as "happenin'." With Bart Simpson as a role model, what do you expect? The "grunge" look is in. Grunge *thinking* is in. Flip that baseball cap around backward—like your motivation to succeed—drop your pants halfway down your butt, and have no idea who the secretary of state is.

Unfair characterization? Not if you walk through malls all across America as we did. You'll see these kids everywhere—except behind the counters working!

Statistics show that these pampered kids, whom parents demand so little of, grow up to be dependent—if not parasitic—creatures with no drive and no understanding of the value of hard-earned money. According to the U.S. Census Bureau, currently over 50 percent of the twenty- to twenty-five-year-olds in this country still live at home. By the year 2010, it is estimated the figure will climb to nearly *80 percent.* What will it be around, say, 2050? Will *everyone* be crashed out in front of Mom's tube all day, refusing even to go to the corner store for a quart of milk? "Not now, my *show's* on!"

Avoid teaching your child responsibility-free living by using the following suggestions from the successful parents:

- Explain to younger children the relationship of work to income. Show them that everything from their doll to the day's groceries is tied directly to your efforts at work. Take children to work from time to time, and when there, give them a small but menial task to perform in return for an appropriate wage. See what happens after ten minutes, and see the new appreciation they have for work and money.
- Explain what is involved in the money cycle: You help your company supply a product or service that fills a need, a customer pays the company for it, and you, in turn, receive some of the money as a wage. No "free lunch" for anyone. One mother told us how she drove home this concept to her six-year-old:

> It was Walter's big entrepreneurial venture, so I wasn't going to wreck it for him. Only I wanted it to be a learning experience. He and his buddy, Scott, come running in all excited, screaming that they wanted to open a lemonade stand. I don't know where they got the idea, but their eyes were bugging out of their heads. They just had to have a stand—and they wanted it *right now!* I said okay, and the next minute Walt was rummaging through the fruit drawer, grabbing up my good lemons. "Wait a minute, kiddo!" I said. "You're going into business, great. But you don't get free lemons and run off to make a

> killing." His face dropped. They thought they were out of business already. I told them they could do their lemonade stand, but the lemons would cost ten cents apiece and they could pay me out of profits. That was okay. Then they went nuts again, running all over the place looking for a card table and a sheet. Maybe I taught them something about finances, who knows.

- When children enter grade school, they can usually grasp the concept of a family budget. Have meetings to discuss the state of your finances and the allowable expenditures for your child. One mother described how amazed her seven-year-old daughter, Jeri, was when she explained the realities of money:

> When I told Jeri I didn't have the money for whatever it was she wanted, she came up with this bright idea: "Just write a check, Mom." I could see she had no idea you had to first put the money in the bank before you could do that, so I pulled out three months' worth of bills—the mortgage, the utilities, everything—and showed her each cancelled check and the declining balance in the book. She couldn't believe her eyes.

Another parent we met had her twelve-year-old actually write the checks for a couple of months so she got a first-hand feel of how much money it takes to run a household.

EARNING AND SAVING

Parents are sometimes uncertain about whether or not to pay an allowance, pay for chores, or control what their kids spend money on. Even among the successful parents we spoke to, there was some debate about these issues. What we have outlined in this section is a general consensus of what worked best for teaching the value of money. There was, however, full agreement that parents must be careful not to attach great power to money by using it as a disciplinary tool and withholding it for misbehavior or awarding it for good grades. Behavior and money should remain unrelated because children who connect money to performance may soon learn to overvalue it. When money becomes central in their lives, they can easily misconstrue it for love or, conversely, see the absence of money as disapproval. Praise and respect are the tools for showing feelings—not money.

The parents we met found that the best way to help kids develop an understanding of money and industriousness is to offer them opportunities to work around the house, beginning at a young age.

Earning

- Designate daily or weekly jobs such as taking out the garbage, clearing the table, feeding the cat, or folding the laundry, and make it part of a regular routine that you post for everyone to see. Point out to your child that your work is your responsibility to the family and his household jobs are *his* responsibility to the family. The parents we talked to vociferously agreed that a child should not get the idea that every chore has a fee for service attached to it, but rather, they should receive a more general monetary compensation for being a working participant of a cooperative family.
- Some parents gave a weekly allowance (see page 242) in return for such cooperation, while others had a

more casual side agreement or, as one parent put it, an I'll-scratch-your-back agreement, where it was understood that children could have the money they needed when they needed it, provided they held up their share of the bargain. It turned out that in either case the children received about the same amount of money.

- If your child would like to earn some *extra* spending or saving money, suggest she earn it by doing *nonroutine* work such as painting or gardening that you would ordinarily pay someone else to do. Give her a job that can be done in a short time and that is not boring or laborious. When she completes it, she will be satisfied with herself and eager to try another task later.

Saving

- Piggy banks are nothing new, but Triple Pigs is. Though only one parent came up with the name, several subscribed to the three-tier saving system that another parent characterized as "Save a little, spend a little, give a little." Here is how the first parent explained the system:

> It basically worked this way: I gave my daughter three piggy banks of different sizes, the largest for spending, the next largest for saving, and a way smaller piggy for charity. I allowed her to commingle the first two somewhat and borrow from the savings to make a special purchase. The rule was, until the charity bank was full—and it was really only about 10 or 20 percent of the others—Julie had to wait to buy herself a gift. If you think she had a hard time figuring out which bank to fill up first, she didn't.

When children get into the saving habit, they can follow it with a bank account—and at quite a young age. The true experts did not hesitate to explain to kids as young as five the concept of savings and interest. For most of them, the topic was quite appealing, and was made even more so when their parents added a dime of their own money to every dollar they saved.

- As stated above, many of the successful parents did not subscribe to the idea of an allowance and preferred giving children the funds they needed when their purchases were justified. But the parents who did give an allowance found there were some distinct advantages to it. One explained it this way:

> An allowance is an automatic budget trainer if you stick to it. It teaches your child money management in that the money he receives is going to be all he gets that week, so he had better save some of it if he hopes to make a purchase. As soon as you give in and give him extra money, you undermine the system.

- Delayed gratification is a primary character builder. The time interval between the wish and the realization of that wish is like gold: If something is too easily acquired, it rapidly loses its value. But if there is some wishing and waiting involved, a child will decide if the item is really worth it, and if it is, he will appreciate it that much more.

One student recalled the seemingly endless wait for something he wanted very badly:

> When I was seven and my brother was nine, our father said we could have the ten-speeds we wanted, but we would have to save for them. So we saved like maniacs. I got a paper route and Jeff cut lawns. We saved for months and months. It seemed like years, but then one day, there they were. They just appeared. Dad had taken our savings [which he had been holding] and I'm sure threw in a lot of his own money, and surprised us. There they were, these two matching beauties! We couldn't believe our eyes. I remember riding around and around our circular driveway for hours that day, and when we were done, we wiped the bikes down and slept with them at the feet of our beds. Then, the next day, we started it all over again, riding those things for hours. We loved those bikes, and I'm sure it was because we had worked so hard to get them.

- A child's sense of independence is greatly enhanced when *she* makes *her* choices for *her* purchases with *her* money. It is fine to offer to match your child's contribution with your own, but otherwise limit your involvement. If you are asked for help, turn the ball back to your child and say, "It's your money, you know best what to do with it." Here, again, the sense of mastery over one's life is more important than making the "right" choice.

CHAPTER 6

SUPPORT SOCIALIZATION

A child may do well scholastically, behave properly at home, and adhere to a strict code of morals, but if he sits by himself in the corner of the schoolyard every lunch hour, what is the quality of his *life*? What does he feel as he gazes over at laughing children sharing sandwiches and stories? Isolated from the rest of the world, how can he ever know the joy of human relationships?

If social skills are weak, chances for success in life are weak. The following story demonstrates how one boy's chances went from poor to none:

> I was having a great time at my twentieth high school reunion—until we sat down for dinner. On the table was a class roster listing everyone's address and current occupation. When you opened it up, the first page was headed *Deceased.* I immediately recognized the name John Carlton. When I turned to my classmate and pointed to the name, she said in kind of a whisper, "He jumped." "What do you mean?" I asked. "He jumped off the Brooklyn Bridge. Suicide." Suddenly, it all registered. I knew Carlton from elementary school. Even then the guy was a misfit. Nobody liked him; he was shy and always by himself. He never tried

> to play softball or anything with us. And in high school he just blended into the woodwork. I barely noticed him. When you did see him, he was never talking to anybody. God, what he must have been suffering all those years! Lonely as hell. I guess he couldn't take it any more. Or he got tired of being so damn unhappy. I felt terrible after I heard what happened.

Learning interpersonal skills is critical to successful interaction with others—starting right from infancy and moving through adulthood. A child who never learns how to enter a play group—or doesn't know how to behave once she's there—may have equal difficulty making friends in grade school, or joining a college sorority or a business organization later.

No child need suffer social exile. Anyone can be taught to be *friendly* and *empathetic*—the two main attributes of a good friend—and they can be taught to be personally attractive, affectionate, and socially responsible.

The effective parents' objectives in socializing their offspring were twofold: First and most important, they wanted to assure that their children led happy, meaningful lives instead of gloomy, lonely ones. Second, they wanted them to grow up to be of service to their families and communities. To accomplish these goals, they knew certain basics had to be in place.

Before a child can engage in healthy socialization, she first has to believe she is worth having as a friend. This involves self-esteem, which we covered previously. You will see again in this chapter how important it is. Next, she needs exposure to people of all ages where she can observe skilled social behavior in action and its effect on others. Finally, she must put what she learns into practice and reach out to make friends—embracing those people and activities that are beneficial, and rejecting those that are harmful. These are the issues we will discuss in this chapter, but before we do, let's look at what a socially successful person is:

- She fits into society comfortably. She is personally attractive, she's liked and makes friends easily, she makes a contribution to the world, and she is concerned about the welfare of others.
- She makes a good impression on strangers. They become interested in her and want to get to know her. When they do, she does not let them down. Because of her own sense of security, she is able and willing to meet their emotional needs, and does not have unreasonable expectations of them in return. She is not worried about *getting*; she is concerned with *giving*.
- She communicates through good listening and talking skills. Without verbal fluency, a child cannot express herself in a group or exchange ideas and information, which then leads to frustration and aggression, as we'll see later in this chapter.

You can see how these traits build upon each other and why we have placed this chapter after the other key elements of child rearing, all of which must be in place for socialization to succeed. How will you know you have done a good job teaching social skills? You will see a variety of signs: Your youngster will be willing to share his toys or play with a friendless kid without being reminded; he will become socially perceptive and be able to read other children's moods and feelings by watching their facial expressions or tone of voice; he will be able to talk to people in different situations and respond to their needs; he will make suggestions that other kids respond to; and most of all, his friendships will blossom because he is affectionate and trustworthy.

DEVELOPING EARLY SOCIAL SKILLS

See if you can figure out what is wrong with this scenario: Parents and kids are bundling up, preparing to leave a friend's home after a visit. As they get to the door, the father says to his six-year-old son, "Well, Steven, aren't you going to say good-bye and thank Mrs. Potts for dinner?" Seems like the normal thing for a parent to do, doesn't it? It's what most parents do when they want to teach their children proper social etiquette. But that does not make it right.

Let's take a closer look at this example. Four things are wrong: One, the parent openly reprimanded his child in front of other people; two, he did so *before* the boy did anything wrong; three, he *assumed* the boy was incapable; and four, he forgot his main teaching tool: role modeling. He told his son to say good-bye even before he said it himself! If this boy was watching his father for clues to proper social behavior, he certainly didn't get them.

Like the other key parenting elements we have discussed so far, children learn social conformity by observing their parents, siblings, friends, and strangers in various social settings, and then internalizing and mimicking those protocols. Give them opportunities to see you and others demonstrating good social skills. The true experts had several suggestions to accomplish this:

- Have your child participate in extracurricular activities, such as those we mentioned in the previous chapters (Cub Scouts, 4H, Little League, library reading groups, stamp clubs, model building clubs, religious youth groups, and the like), all of which expose children to other new children and adults.
- When kids approach adolescence, help them learn about their multicultural social system and their function in it. Introduce them to social institutions and volunteer organizations that serve the community, such as those our students worked in: crisis centers, nursing homes, homeless shelters, soup kitchens, and day care centers—often right alongside their parents.
- Expose young adults to literature, magazines, and television programs that have social significance and cover a vast array of essential issues every American should be versed in: World War II, the civil rights movement, biographies of artists, writers, explorers, presidents, and scientists who made significant contributions. In reference to important biographies, one parent told her nine-year-old son:

> Even though you're still a kid, you're a person like these people are. They were kids once, too, but I bet if you could talk to them, they'd tell you that when they were your age, they were already thinking about how they could make contributions and make a difference in the world. They probably didn't know what they were going to do, but they knew they were going

> to do *something* worthwhile. Their parents taught them to think that way. The time for you to start thinking about your life and what kind of person you want to become is right now.

As we progress through this chapter, remember the following rule, which applies to all the skills we have discussed so far: *Social skills need practice.*

And none need practice more than *manners,* which we will discuss first, followed by the two other key components of early socialization, *negotiation* and *cooperation.*

MANNERS

If we look again at the story of Mrs. Potts and Steven, we can amend the scene slightly to what it should have been. Instead of sending the subconscious message, "You are incompetent and discourteous," Steven's father could have set an example of good manners. As they were heading for the door, he could have said, "Well, Mrs. Potts, that was a lovely meal. Steven and I certainly enjoyed it, didn't we, Steven?" Dad exhibits good manners. Child learns lesson. No shaming takes place. What Steven's father forgot in the first scenario is a cardinal rule of parenting: *To raise considerate, thoughtful children, parents themselves must be considerate and thoughtful.*

Explain the rationale behind manners—the reason you write a thank-you note or why you wait until everyone is served before diving into your food. Without such explanations, manners may be confusing. Of course, some customs are "just because" types that people adhere to mainly to promote smooth social interaction. To a seven-year-old, though, it doesn't make much sense to leave perfectly good spaghetti sitting there when he could be twisting it around his fork.

NEGOTIATION

Negotiating resolutions to problems is an indispensable skill that gives a child a way to get her needs met. She may want to trade her broccoli for peas, exchange a toy truck for a playmate's airplane, or join a ball game that's just starting. To accomplish these things, she needs to know how to bargain, which means offering something of value in exchange for what she wants. If she can convince her schoolmates that she is a fast runner and good fielder, she'll probably get that coveted spot in the outfield.

Here are a variety of tips the successful parents suggested to teach negotiation skills:

- Strike simple bargains with your child, ones that don't violate preset limits. Offer deals such as, "If you do all your chores this week without me having to remind you, we'll go out for pizza Friday night." This is not bribery, like offering candy to a screaming toddler in a grocery store is; it is merely a reward for following through on an agreement.
- Teach negotiation by demonstrating it. Let your child see you making deals with others. Tell another child or spouse, "If you fold the laundry, I'll fix dinner tonight." Explain to the repairman, within earshot of your child, "I'd like to use your company, but I can't wait all day for you to arrive. Could we please make an appointment either between eight and twelve or one and four?" Make the give-and-take clear.

- Encourage your child to make her own decisions when appropriate. Instead of saying, "We're going to the park to play on the swings today," a single father we interviewed told us what he would say:

> I would say, "We can go to either the park or the library. If we go to the park, you'll have to clean your room now because you won't have time before dinner. If all you want to do is check out a book at the library, you can clean your room when we get home. Your choice." My advice is, when they ask you to help them with this type of decision, don't get caught up in the warm, fuzzy "parenting thing"; it does more harm than good. Tell them they're capable of figuring it out themselves. Switch gears and say something like, "It's your playtime, so it's your decision," and leave it at that. They'll figure out what to do.

- Let your child take the consequences for poor decisions; it will markedly improve her negotiation skills. Mrs. Parker told us about the time her sixteen-year-old daughter, Cheryl, thought she had won a negotiation, but as it turned out, her decision caught up with her:

> I told Cheryl her miniskirt was too short for sitting in class, but of course she argued it wasn't. "It'll ride up on you at that ridiculous length," I told her. "You'll be pulling it down all day." But I didn't get through to her and it wasn't my problem anyway. Sure enough, like clockwork, about ten in the morning, I get a call at work: "Mom, can you bring my jeans over to

school?" I already had the jeans in the car and brought them over on my lunch break. I knew she was going to call.

COOPERATION

Good teachers know the value of team efforts, where each student takes responsibility for a certain part of the project. Such projects require give and take (negotiation) and proper attitude (manners). While one student researches one topic, another may outline important points or plan diagrams and charts. Another member of the team may be the writer, while another compiles the work into a unified whole. Any student who fails to negotiate with other members or behave in a friendly manner will quickly be replaced.

The following are some of the ways the successful parents taught their children a team orientation.

- Have your young child help plan activities at home. For example, even a six-year-old can make a rough list of napkins and cups required for a party. Have her shop with you and pick these items off the grocery shelf herself. Mrs. Berwick explained one incident that arose from such involvement:

    > Making Betty the cohostess turned her into a social butterfly. I didn't have to worry about getting her to set the table; I couldn't get her away from it! She thought it was her party. She was so into it that one time she met some guests at the door and showed them right to the dinner table while the rest

> of us were having drinks in the living room! When I walked through the dining room to get some ice, there were Madeline and Bill sitting there by themselves!

- If you plan to take a trip, make your older children responsible for reservations or figuring out a logical route to your destination. Said one father:

> Think how much more fun it is for the kids in the back seat when they get an opportunity to participate. Stanley loved to say, "Okay, Dad, take Highway 40 to 89 up ahead, or get off at the next off-ramp." And think how relieved you'll be to hear, "Hey, there's our hotel, just where it's supposed to be!"

- As mentioned above and in the last chapter, volunteer work is of prime importance, especially in teaching children cooperation.

> Dawn and I helped serve over a thousand meals at St. Anthony's hall one Thanksgiving. Everybody chipped in and everybody did the dirty work—scrubbing potatoes, setting up chairs, helping the older people get to their seats, cleaning up. There were no prima donnas at St. Anthony's.

Other team activities that require cooperation include: preparing the soil and selecting and planting the seeds for a vegetable garden; putting on a neighborhood variety show in the garage; or working with a community group to help revitalize a run-down part of town.

MAKING FRIENDS

Kids between five and ten years of age *practice* making friends. They are not sure who they want as friends—or who wants them—and they are not sure how the process works, so they try different things and different kids. Usually these relationships are short-lived and not very substantive, but they are part of the skill-building process that helps kids form genuine relationships as adolescents.

When children enter into their first fickle engagement, though it is only a precursor to the real thing, it is often their parents' first real dilemma—and heartache. This bittersweet phase of the parent/child relationship finds "babies" not needing parents as exclusively as they once did. It can't help but hurt as parents think back to the times when their children wanted them and only them. But as painful as it might be, parents must heed another critical rule many fail to grasp: *Parents' goal must be* separation *from their children, not* attachment *to them—and the earlier the better.*

This is one of the most treacherous pitfalls in parenting, and it is one where parent and child often reverse roles. When infants are first born, they cling to their parents for love and sustenance. But as they grow up and start to pull away, it's the parents who do the clinging. Resist this reverse dependency and teach your child to make friends at a very young age—starting at two or three. It will greatly improve his chances for meaningful relationships beyond the family—one of the primary purposes of child rearing in the first place!

If your children's socialization is on track, your role as guardian will shift. Kids will progressively see their family as more of a home base to which they can return when necessary. Like birds, they'll flutter around and start peeking out of their nest more and more until one day, they abandon it altogether. Don't panic; rejoice! You've raised healthy kids!

BEST FRIENDS

Children need partners in their first flights of fancy from the nest. Developing a best friend relationship is a major step in their socialization. It moves them beyond the confines of the family to a place where they can share the intimacies, problems, and joys they can't share with parents or siblings. By confiding in a friend, children can dissipate anxieties that often come from within the family itself. But they have the same problem adults do when it comes to meeting new people: No one wants to make the first move. Help your child past this stumbling block by explaining that other children would enjoy meeting her but they are too scared to make the overture. This is most important because it takes the onus off her and it shows her she is not the one with the problem. Once she is clear on this, she will reach out to kindle friendships, as this father did when he was a youngster:

> I loved Elvis Presley and so did my friend, Cliff. That was the link that got us together. How did I know he liked Elvis? One day when we were in fifth grade, I saw him wearing a pink Elvis Presley belt with musical notes on it. Remember those thin belts they wore with the buckle on the side in the '50s? I went up to him and told him I liked Elvis too. That's all it took—that one dumb Elvis belt! We've been friends now for some thirty years. I remember how we used to stare

> at Elvis's picture on his album covers and try to comb our hair like him. The only problem was, when my hair started getting long enough for a ducktail, my mother would send me down to the barber to get what they called then a regular boy's haircut. That meant *short*—and trim the sideburns! I always came home with whitewalls—and never looked anything like Elvis.

Best friends make long summers times of great joy. Comrades plan strategies to build a fort, put on a neighborhood play, or bake cookies for a sidewalk sale. They afford each other opportunities to care deeply about a nonfamily member—a major step in the development of a conscience. You can help bond the relationship by openly accepting the friend into your home and encouraging activities both kids will enjoy.

But beware—youthful relationships are capricious, so you've got to be ready to soothe hurt feelings when the friendship falls apart—and it usually will. As we said, kids practice making friends—sometimes just for the sake of practice, other times because they need an ego boost or reassurance that they are attractive or popular. The downside is that once the mission is accomplished, the child who thought she had a lifelong friend realizes it was all a ploy; she was "just for practice."

To help relieve the stress of a collapsed friendship—often the first deeply felt emotional hurt a youngster experiences—be careful not to downplay the importance of the rejection. Instead, relate a time when you too were abandoned by someone you trusted. It will help soothe the pain.

When Darcy came home brokenhearted about her breakup, I told her about the time my best friend, Shannon, said she'd meet me in front of Jefferson High at three o'clock. It was May and we were all going up to the lake after school to go swimming and meet some cute guys. As I'm driving down to school at about twenty to three, who do I see going the other way? Shannon and the gang! And they were already following the guys! They were whooping and hollering out the window, heading up to the lake to have a great time—without me. Good buddy Shannon couldn't wait the bloomin' twenty minutes for her best friend to show up. I was crushed and I didn't speak to her for a month! Anyway, when I was done with my story, Darcy scoots over and puts her arm around me—as if this happened yesterday—and says, "Don't worry, Mom. She didn't mean it." I didn't know whether to laugh or cry. But I could see she felt a lot better.

Shyness

As children branch out, they meet new children with personalities that are different from their usual playmates. This interaction is healthful because it requires *adaptation,* another key component of socialization. Planning and encouraging such interaction for your child often prevents—or is a good antidote for—shyness, a condition that all children have to some extent but that can grow into a severe neurosis if not checked early.

When a shy, withdrawn toddler meets a slightly older, more expressive child, for example, he is likely to come out of his shell, especially if there are no other kids around to interfere with the one-on-one interaction. If he has been overprotected, meeting a more courageous child can have a corrective influence on him and open the door to more aggressive play. The following is an example of what effect new kids can have on each other:

> I had such a phobia about snakes. I couldn't even look at one on television. This wasn't the greatest thing for my eight-year-old because it made him scared of creepy crawly things, too. Then one day, he brought home an alligator lizard! Oh, it was a beautiful thing! It looked just like a miniature alligator. I don't know why it didn't bother me, but it didn't. Robby caught it in the field while playing with a neighborhood boy who loved spiders and snakes and all. The boy showed him how to sneak up behind the lizard and grab it up behind the jaws so he wouldn't get bitten. Once he did it, he was over his fears, and he started bringing home field mice and tree frogs. That boy was good for Robby.

A shy child may face another problem other kids usually don't face: bullies. Aggressive children often pick out shy ones as easy targets for abuse, so prepare your child with some strategies to ward off the unwanted attention. Role-play with him and teach him to stand up confidently and tell the offender, "Don't bother me!" or "Get away from me!" It is when victims cower that bullies see their tactics work.

One seventh grader stood up to the bully but went a little too far in the process. Here's his mother's story:

> I guess the one good thing about the incident is that we saw Joe finally overcame his shyness and was beginning to blossom. But what a blossom! He was smaller than the other kids and always getting picked on by this one boy. Finally he was pushed to the limit and couldn't take it any more, so he "moons" the kid. Quiet little Joe shows his bare butt in the

middle of the schoolyard! The problem was, he also mooned the nun on yard duty! They wanted to suspend him from school, but I intervened and said, yes, Joe showed poor judgment, but he was driven to it by this boy. They finally agreed, and after a stern reprimand, they let him stay in school.

ADOLESCENCE AND PEER PRESSURE

Children who are unable to cope with the pressures of adolescence were most likely raised in either authoritarian or permissive households, both of which leave kids ill equipped to form their own identities. As we discussed in Chapter 3, overcontrolling parents don't respect their children, and they don't trust them enough to make their own decisions. The result? By the time they reach adolescence, kids are stunted and unable to fend for themselves, which leaves them searching for support from their peers. Likewise, children from permissive homes are susceptible to peer pressure because their indulgent parents taught them that self-discipline and self-reliance were not necessary. In both cases, children seek from their peers the guidance they never received at home.

But they get shortchanged in the deal. When weak children seek approval from peers, they are slapped with a stinging dose of reality: Their peers are even *more* critical and disapproving than their parents! Now where do they turn? To *compliance*—and to problems.

The students we studied did not find themselves in such dire straits. As preadolescents, they exhibited three distinctive characteristics that benefited them when they entered adolescence: One, they had learned to be outwardly *friendly* to everyone, regardless of what group they may have belonged to; two, they were *confident* and not looking for approval since they already approved of themselves; and three, they were *perceptive* and had a knack for responding to their classmates' needs in a way that made them attractive and desirable to be around. When they entered adolescence, their parents took further steps to assure a smooth transition from childhood to adulthood. Here are some of the most important of those steps:

- Stress the value of personal attractiveness—not beauty. See that your child maintains herself physically and show her that she can work on problem features like acne or oily hair, which, in this squeaky-clean society of cover girl ideals, are a kiss of death socially.
- Adolescents erroneously believe they are constantly being watched by their peers, when the truth is that such scrutiny is largely imagined. One mother explained this to her daughter:

  > Your friends are just as worried about making their own mistakes as you are. They don't want to draw attention to themselves either. I know you feel like you're the only goldfish in the bowl, but you're not.

  Point out to worried kids that their anxiety is wasted energy that could be better put to use opening up to the real world—a world that is not nearly as critical as they fear.

- Hold practice conversations at home to prepare your adolescent for meeting new people. Have her take the lead in a discussion of current affairs or political/social issues, and treat the session for what it is: *practice.* Don't try to camouflage the effort or pretend you are just helping round out her education. Openly state that being informed is an integral part of socialization.
- Encourage your child to discuss subjects of interest to his peers, such as the sports they like or the school subjects they are interested in. By asking questions and asking for opinions on *their* interests and needs—not his own—he demonstrates his ability to be a good friend. There is nothing more *un*friendly than talking about yourself all the time.

> I suggested to Doug that after he got friendly with another fellow, if he ever saw that this boy had a problem or concern that he probably didn't feel comfortable talking to his parents about, he should empathize with the boy. Show interest by taking the boy aside and probe a little further about the issue he's brought up. This is what good friends are for. It's what so many people want in a relationship but never find.

- To cement relationships, recommend that your child follow up his initial meetings with personal phone calls and invite the new acquaintances to join him on excursions or to plan other activities. As we mentioned, he will find that if he makes the first efforts to be a friend, the friendship will be returned.

IDENTITY

The paradox of adolescence is that while maturing teens have a compelling need to distance themselves from their parents and assert their *in*dependence, they become highly *de*pendent on their peers for approval. Most teenagers rate themselves against their peers: The more they are like them, the more comfortable they feel.

In their search for identity, teenagers compare everything. At the onset of puberty, bodies, minds, and clothes are the hot topics. The opposite sex is getting more interesting. Boys buy their first jockstraps and boast that they "need" to shave. Girls buy bras and get their periods. Gossip is rampant. Who's cuter? Who's developing fastest? Who's making out with whom? Who's a nerd? Who's a jock? *Who am I*?

One of the hallmarks of adolescence is a grossly exaggerated need to look precisely the way one is supposed to look. And thus begins an obsession with the mirror. Developing teenagers practice postures, devilish smiles, "too-sexy" looks, hair flips, and muscle flexes. Then, when they think they have finally decided on what to wear for the day (always a tenuous decision), they head back to the mirror to obsess a while longer and make sure the ensemble "works."

Looks and Clothes

If you are fourteen and show up at the mall in jeans and sneakers when everyone else is in shorts and sandals, your day is basically wrecked. If you're lucky enough to spot the gang before they see you, you may save yourself untold horrors by slipping down a hallway and zipping back home to change. One student told us about a friend of his who, one Friday night, switched back and forth from straitlaced Levi's

Dockers and penny loafers to shredded blue jeans and motorcycle jacket:

> By nine o'clock, he gave up. He called and said he was going to bed, he didn't feel like going out anymore. He was a good guy, but his problem was, he didn't know if he was a punk, a preppy, a goober, or a biker.

There is really no harm in this musical chairs identity so long as attire is not too outlandish—especially with girls. Several mothers told us that provocative, sexy dressing was out until their girls left home at eighteen "by which time they either have a brain or they don't," said one mother. Another parent told us about a period when his son was about fourteen and insisted on wearing his torn Van Halen shirt every day, rain or shine. They eventually arrived at a mutually agreeable plan that he could wear whatever he wanted at home, but when they were out in public, he was going to have to dress quasi-normally. His son agreed and made a follow-up deal that when they went shopping for his clothes, he could do the selecting.

> We told Rob that since we were paying for his clothes, we would decide what the budget would be and what the limits of outrageousness were. Within those limits, he could do pretty much what he wanted. I do remember, though, taking back a pair of those ten-pound black military boots with the two-inch-thick rubber soles. He wasn't going to go around like a skinhead—and he wasn't going to ruin my kitchen floor!

Another problem arises around the issue of looks, and it is not related to clothes because attire won't make any difference: Some kids don't fit the beauty mold no matter what they do. What if your daughter is a bit on the pudgy side or your six-foot string bean of a son tips the scale at a mere 130 pounds while his acne keeps getting worse? Answer: *bad news*. The game gets tougher to play. A great wardrobe and perfect hair are not enough. Good grades and good athletic ability are not enough. Life is bleak for imperfect kids who desire perfection. More than any other time in their lives, they need you to help them through this period of uncertainty. Here are the steps that worked for the effective parents:

- Remind your adolescent that though it does not seem like it with all society's emphasis on beauty and perfection, her other assets are much more valuable. The "don't-judge-a-book-by-its-cover" adage was never more appropriate, so use it. A father we interviewed asked his fifteen-year-old daughter a few mind-opening questions whenever she started complaining about her average looks:

> Are the cutest girls as good as you in soccer or math? Are they as friendly as you are? Any of them on the conceited side? Would they be as good a friend as you would be? Do you really think their hallowed popularity means anything if that's all they've got—popularity—and for the wrong reasons? Think about it, Nadine, you've got a lot going for you. Let's get off the looks kick.

Mr. Twitchell said these "quizzes," as he called them, did not work overnight and at first "went in one ear and out the other." But eventually they were effective in bringing Nadine around to thinking about more substantive issues than looks.

- Avoid hypocrisy. You wouldn't make fun of your child, so don't criticize yourself or belittle your own body every time you gain or lose weight. Don't draw attention to physical imperfections if looks aren't supposed to matter.
- Being skinny and stereotypically beautiful is not genuine beauty and it doesn't last forever anyway. Make a list of people who are not cover girls but who are successful and happy despite their normal looks. You might ask your daughter what one mother asked hers:

> What's more important, wasting energy fretting over hairdos and boobs, or developing meaningful relationships with an eclectic mix of people who think a little deeper than that?

When adolescents' personalities eventually begin to stabilize and they develop a better sense of who they are, they begin to feel the urge to move farther out of the nest. But they are not ready to fly off into the sunset quite yet; they need a safe replacement for the sound footing they are leaving, so they hop down to another limb to a different type of nest: the "in group."

IN GROUP

Adolescents gain a sense of security from a peer group that validates their independence, their movement away from their parents. But *independence* does not mean *individuality*—far from it. Group members pay the price to join the ranks. Here in the peer group differences are discouraged. Support for each other through sameness is paramount, and to advance such homogeneity, cliques exert enormous pressure on their members to conform. Because of their emotional turmoil and urgency to belong, most youngsters are willing to pay that price of acceptance. If they aren't, it's tough to get into one of the groups of punkers, jocks, preppies, computer nerds, or poets.

If an adolescent ventures into a clique group, she better be ready to ride the bronco for a while. She will have to prove herself by showing how identical she can be or by offering new contributions vis-à-vis her wit or her interest in topics popular to the group. If her offerings don't pass muster, she may be seen as a liability instead of an asset, someone who makes the group look bad in the eyes of others—the most egregious offense a member can make.

You can see why the issues we discussed in Chapter 4 are so vitally important to surviving adolescent peer pressure. A strong self-image permits a child to select a group of friends not out of fear but out of choice. There is nothing wrong with your child wanting to join a healthy group of well-rounded kids who have like interests, but the problem with any group, club, party, or esteemed organization is an age-old one: The groups that appear to be the most desirable are often the hardest to join.

If your child comes home dejected because of her failure to join the group of her choice, her exclusion may be the result of poor social skills. Sometimes the group itself is socially incompetent and doesn't recognize her interest in joining or doesn't have the wherewithal to ask her. Here's how you can help:

- Remind your child that some groups merely look exclusive; their main purpose is to put up the facade of seeming difficult to get into. If she can see through this front, she may want to look for a group that is not so concerned about appearances. One mother, whose daughter was considering such a group, asked her simply, "Are you really sure you want to be a 'clique clone'? I would rethink joining that group if it were me."
- Explain the capricious nature of cliques. Tell your child they are often short-lived, ephemeral, trendy groups whose identity is so tenuous that they may be here today and falling apart tomorrow. Sally's mother told her:

> Cliques aren't too terribly different from fashions. I can't believe guys once wore polyester *leisure* suits. You know, the baby blue with the navy contrasting stitching? So lovely. Oh, and those disco shirts they wore unbuttoned to the navel. And the gold chains! Yuk! Things that don't have real substance go out of style. Then we look back and wonder why we were so excited about them in the first place. Your father was so uninterested in clothes that I got sick of looking at him in the same navy blue polo shirt all the time, so I bought him a pink one. What a waste of money *that* was.

- Consider with your child the various other groups and activities that are available. Discuss her interests and goals regarding joining a group. Point out that the "cool" groups have to expend a lot of energy on image and biases, and may not have nearly as much fun as a normal, easygoing group of kids who worry less about looks and more about enjoying activities together.

- Explore the possibility of your child starting his own group. If he's interested in science, encourage him to invite other interested students to form their own club. If he loves literature, help him start a monthly book club where members can discuss a particular work. That's what this student did:

> We were the poets. We had to be different, ya know? Greg, Eric, John, and I went down to Goodwill and bought these old tweed jackets that we thought were *too* intellectual for words. Nobody admitted it, but let's face it, we were all trying to look like Hemingway! Our thing was to sit under the old oak tree during lunch and discuss Thoreau. I know, "gag." We were pretty much of a clique ourselves, but hey, our stuff was what got published in the *Phoenix* [literary magazine]!

Hanging Out

The days of "coming over to play records" are over. First of all, there aren't any records anymore. Second of all, there's nothing "happening" at home. Malls and fast-food restaurants are where the action is; they seem to be the hip meeting places for teens to share views on pop music, sports heroes, school projects, or parental restrictions (one of which is probably hanging out at the mall). There is nothing wrong with your kids "hanging" with their friends if you approve of the location and they come home when they are supposed to. Teenagers need their privacy and their camaraderie, but parents have a right and an obligation to know what is going on and where. Even if they protest, kids know your concern means you care.

> If you make it clear that you are only concerned about their welfare—not their conversations—kids will appreciate the concern. Claudia said to me once, "Ya know, Mom, [my friend] Maria never has to check in with her mother, even when we're out kinda late. I don't think her mother really cares where she is. It's kind of a pain to stop and call you all the time, but I'm glad you want me to. You're a good mom, Mom."

When our parents were not quite sure how they felt about a hangout or activity, they didn't hesitate to contact the parents of their children's friends to discuss it. If they concurred that the location was not the best, they had that much more ammunition—and they proved they were not the only "unreasonable" parents in the crowd.

There is another benefit to staying in touch with other parents whose values you share: You can form a brain trust and devise strategies to change your kids' plans to ones you approve of. When you put your heads together, you'll have a fighting chance to outwit kids who, at this age, can pull some pretty clever maneuvers to outwit you.

> I had no idea Jackie was doing some of the things she was doing. If kids really want to go somewhere, it's pretty tough to stop them. I mean, when Jackie was fourteen and we lived

in New Haven, she went all the way to New York one Friday night to one of those wild clubs where they slam dance and the band guys fly off the stage into the crowd. I had no idea! She ended up at Smith anyway and her grades were always terrific, so when I finally found out about this, there wasn't a whole lot I could say.

NEGATIVE FRIENDSHIPS

Delinquent kids don't come out of the womb "bad." They often have abusive parents or parents who cannot express their love adequately, so they are forced to seek approval elsewhere. Such unhappy children are so starved for love they often will do anything to get it—including drugs, sex, and real crime. The problem for you is that "naughty" friends can provide a new kind of excitement that is hard to resist for a fifteen-year-old. Here's the hard-and-fast rule regarding undesirable relationships: *Try to stop them.*

Certainly, you want your child to select his own friends, but you have a parental responsibility to assure the selection is beneficial. As your child reaches adolescence, you will see that some associations have to be discouraged and it will take you about ten seconds to determine which ones. Keep in mind the reasons your teenager selected such a friend: intimacy, excitement, nonconformity, peer acceptance, sex appeal, antidote for boredom—none of which are adequate. With the possibility of serious trouble lurking, this is *not* the time to allow a great deal of freedom. You are still clothing and feeding your child, so you deserve to know where she is and who she's with—and you have to approve of both.

Friends should exert a corrective rather than negative influence on each other. To insure this is the case, take note of a number of things the successful parents did:

- The most obvious way to guard against negative alliances is to carefully select the neighborhood you live in. Once there, protect your rights. Most parents we met vehemently opposed having their children bused from their own neighborhoods—the ones they had worked hard to afford—to designated schools situated miles away in unsafe neighborhoods.

> Our local elementary school is right there [points out the window]. It is literally a three-minute walk for Kent. But I was told he must go to another school clear across town because of quotas and some harebrained affirmative action program. We moved here because this is where we want to raise our children and this is the community we think is best for them. Then I heard something equally unbelievable: The only way you can keep your child in this school is to *lie* and say he has an *emotional* problem—like we're getting—[laughs] and that he can't be that far away from his parents. You've got to have a signed letter by a psychologist, if you can believe that.

- Pay attention to the schools your child will be attending. The parents we met took great pains to research the best school districts and even interview administrators before they moved to their neighborhoods.

One mother from Honolulu said she put her child in a private school when she discovered the local public school instructors used pidgin English, a broken, choppy form of mixed dialects and incorrect diction, in the classroom.

- Select your own adult friends wisely because their children are going to be socializing with your children. Several parents built their and their children's social lives around their places of worship.

> When Milt and I moved to Torrington from the city, we didn't know a soul. But as soon as we joined the temple, we started meeting lots of nice people. At first we were invited to a few dinner parties; then we'd reciprocate and have those couples and their kids over to our house. I'd say within a couple of years we had a group of about thirty or so friends whom we saw regularly. Then, when the kids were around ten, they all went to Hebrew school together and attended each other's bar mitzvahs. None of this would have happened if we hadn't joined our local synagogue.

- If your child selects a friend with questionable qualities, put your communication skills to work to express your concern (not annoyance) about the possibilities of problems with this friend. Make it clear that you are not prying into her social life or trying to control her, and remind her that you were her age once, so you know what this type of relationship can lead to. As writer Sam Ewing said, "Parents who wonder where the younger generation is going should remember where it came from."

- Calmly voice your objections to your child's new friendship, remembering that whatever you are objecting to is probably just the thing that attracted her to her friend in the first place. Be specific. Relate to her what can happen from such an association, or better, what *did* happen to someone you knew as you were growing up. That's what this parent did:

> I told [my son] Frank about this guy in our neighborhood, Jim Parks. He was a wild man. He used to steal cigarettes from his mother at thirteen. I remember the packs, they were Kent. Then the next summer he stole her car and showed up at our softball game. He jumped the curb and spun a 360 right in the middle of the infield! Once I saw him take a guy's motorcycle over the hill. When he came back, he was doin' about sixty and *standing* on the seat without holding onto the handlebars. The guy was nuts. Then I lost track of him until years later someone mentioned his name. "What happened to Parks, anyway?" I asked. "Overdosed on smack just like everyone said he would."

- If you make your concerns known and then back off for a while to observe, you may see the relationship dissolve on its own because you will have gained the respect of your teenager by *not* restricting the friendship outright and not casting aspersions that your child will feel obligated to defend. The last thing you want to do is give the relationship more potency than it originally had.
- If none of the above measures are effective in discouraging your child from having a delinquent

friend, you'll have to draw the line in the sand: The kid is off limits, association with him is not allowed, and he is not permitted in your house, period.

> There was a period there one summer when Lita would run out of the house when she heard this "boyfriend" of hers zooming up the street on his Harley motorcycle. I don't know where she found this guy, but he apparently wasn't too big in the brains department. He had dropped out of high school and played in some band, and the one time I met him, he reeked of beer. That's all I knew about him and that's all I needed to know. I told Lita she was forbidden to ride on that thing after I saw her jump on it one day and take off in her cutoffs and bare feet. But when he kept coming around, I laid down the law: "No hairy guy and no motorcycles, or no car and no parties for the rest of the summer." I knew she might have weaseled out to a party now and then, but at least I made my position clear. And it didn't matter anyway because after she pouted for a few days, she came in and told me I was right, the guy was a loser and she had dumped him.

Forbidding a relationship is a last resort, but it's a "resort" your child will find more comfortable than the one known as juvenile hall—or the emergency room.

THE BIG ISSUES

A seventeen-year-old slugs down shots of Jack Daniel's and beer chasers at a parentless party, then heads home with a carload of revelers. Only they never make it. What the police report terms an "accident" is anything but. The car "traveling at a high rate of speed," as the report reads, veered over the center line and crashed head-on into a family of four, not due to an accident, but due to the lethal combination of liquor and youth.

Another teen at the party stayed behind to try a new high: a toke of crack cocaine, or perhaps a spoon of China White heroin (both of which are becoming increasingly common in suburban America). The euphoria is such a relief from his fears, frustrations, and lousy home life that he returns to the drug again and again, only to become hopelessly addicted. And this is only half of the equation. Sex is now a deadly game, too.

As of this writing, the number-one killer among men aged twenty-five to forty-four is AIDS, contracted from unclean needles or unprotected sex. Many of those people contracted HIV while still in their teens. From 1981 to 1992, an astounding 47,300 cases of AIDS were reported among young Americans ages 13 to 29. The number of HIV-infected people worldwide is now so vast that it is estimated not in the hundreds or thousands, but in the *millions,* with the rate of infection escalating *six times faster* for women than for men. This is not an issue just for gay men or drug users but an epidemic of such massive proportions that without question, someone carrying this deadly disease will one day come into close contact with *your* child. The question is: Will it be sexual contact? Answer: That depends on *you.*

In this era of permissiveness, promiscuity, and relaxed moral standards, your adolescent will, at times, feel great pressure to do things that are not in his best interest. Will he have the resolve to resist them? The answer is an emphatic "Yes"—but with some "Ifs" attached.

Your adolescent will be prepared for the big issues if you maintain open *communication,* if you teach him how to *think,* if you appropriately *discipline* him, if you instill a high sense of *self-esteem,* and if you live by a clear set of *values.* If you follow these five key elements, upon which this final key of socialization is dependent, you will have done everything you could to raise a great, resilient kid. Will it be enough? It was for the parents we met.

With this in mind, let's discuss how they handled the first of the widespread social problems kids everywhere face today: drugs.

DRUGS

When your sixteen-year-old wants to go to an unsupervised party with a questionable group, you will have to deny permission without a lot of debate while making it clear that you made your decision not because you don't want her to have a good time, but because you love her. This has to be *explicit,* not implicit, as Sandy's mother explains:

> There was not much Sandy could argue about when I'd tell her I loved her and didn't want to see her put in a dangerous situation. I knew that if all she heard was, "You can't go because I said so!" there'd be plenty to rant and rave about, not to mention the fact that it's disrespectful, if not infuriating, to pull rank on her like that. I asked her once, "How would you feel if I couldn't care less where you go and what you do, whether you make it home in one piece or

> not?" Right away she responded, "I'm old enough to know right from wrong," which was just the opening I needed. "Then why can't you see how *wrong* this party is?" She didn't have much of a comeback. I told her I respected her opinion and I knew her friends were going to this party, but in this particular case, the right thing to do was do something else.

It is a lot easier for a teenager to say "No" to her peers when she has her parents to "blame." You are a crucial ally in the fight against peer pressure. If your teenager's peers know she is free to do whatever she wants, it is tough to back out of uncomfortable situations.

No matter what you do, at some point your teen will not only be exposed to drugs, she will find herself in a high-pressure situation where it will seem a lot easier to give in than take the flak for "wimping out." It is then that your widely publicized rules can serve as scapegoats for a cornered kid. "I don't feel like getting tossed out of my house just to prove to you guys I'm cool." "If my parents catch me high I lose my car and my allowance. It's not worth it."

Your child has to be assertive when facing tough situations. The dean of one school, who saw every type of adolescent problem, offered this advice:

> Kids have to be prepared to take the risk of being ridiculed and made fun of for being straight, being nerds, because that's the way other kids make themselves look good. Immature kids mock the good kids because they *don't* feel good. The problem cases who end up in my office all have one thing in common: They have a pressing need for approval; they need all the support they can get to make

sure they're validated and that their way is the right way. To them, the best way to do that is to chastise others, which they think reduces the threat the dissenters pose to their belief system. Kids facing peer pressure need to be courageous enough to be different. If they'd stop to think about it for a minute, they'd realize what the real consequences of acting responsibly are: losing their popularity with *irresponsible* kids. Where's the loss?

The parents we met used several methods to help their children fight peer pressure. All of them are important to remember when dealing with a life-threatening issue like drugs:

- Teach your child to use the widely publicized phrase, "Just say no." It may not be quite that simple for most kids, but it's a good place to start. Will friends abandon a youth who shows good judgment? If they do, they're the "losers." One father had this to say about friends:

  > If friends are truly friends, won't they accept your decision to abstain if that's what you want to do? Don't real friends want the best for each other? Which deserves more respect, caving in to peer pressure and poisoning your body with junk, or standing firm on your beliefs? Which shows the most individuality? Which shows the highest regard for yourself? Which is really the coolest, the hippest?

- Help your child see peer pressure as an illusion. Priscilla's mother said to her:

Pretend your friends are not there when making choices. What would you do if no one was around, no one knew you? What if you were like an invisible person or everyone faded away except you and the drug peddler? No one could see you, no one could judge you. What decisions would you make then if your popularity wasn't a factor? I've got a feeling it would be a whole different ball game.

- Discuss drugs openly and regularly. One father told us that in his home, drugs were common "table talk," both at family meetings and mealtime:

I wanted the subject fixed in John's brain. I knew he was going to encounter drugs no matter what we did, so when he did, I wanted him to be prepared. I wanted my words, "People will say 'try it,' " to echo inside his noggin whenever someone tried to push him into trying something. I knew he'd think twice if he'd heard the warnings enough times.

- Prepare your child for the inevitable. *Practice* the likely scenario with her, including back-and-forth dialogue, so she will be equipped with the right responses to counter such pressure. This is role-playing again, and it works.

"Come on, Linda, lighten up. Get high."

"I'm high on life, girls. I'm in the clouds with the angels already."

"You're too straight. Try a snort of this coke. You won't believe how great it is."

> "I'm running a ten-miler tomorrow morning with Bill and Pete. I'll never make it if I stay up all night on that stuff."

- If you experimented with drugs yourself or knew those who did, share this information with your teenager. Relate your own experiences warding off pressure to conform as you grew up. Tell your child about those who started with social use and went on to use hard drugs regularly. Explain the short-lived high and the miserable lows you or those you knew felt after trying drugs. Said one father:

> I got through advanced statistics by the skin of my teeth. But I'd hate to go through *that* again. My roommate in college came up with the clever idea of going to bed when we got home from school, then get up about nine in the evening and take a few bennies [benzedrine] so we could stay up and study all night, and then walk right into our stats test the next morning. He proudly called it "Waiting 'til *past* the last minute" to cram. So we took four beans [benzedrine] apiece, drank two pots of coffee, and shook our way through the test the next day. I was sick for three days after coming down from that crap and I've never touched coffee again either.

- Inform yourself on the current drugs of choice. Learn what their effects are and how chemical dependency works, and how a teenager's behavior may change when using drugs. Contact local law enforcement agencies and find out how drugs are being distributed and what to watch out for. Talk to drug crisis centers about prevention—or intervention if there is already a problem.

- Copy articles about people—executives, teachers, sports stars, doctors—who succumbed to pressures, got hooked on drugs, and lost their families and businesses. Find stories about kids who ended up in mental institutions or thought they could fly out second-story windows after taking LSD (another drug that is experiencing a resurgence in popularity). Discuss the physical and mental horrors of withdrawing from narcotics and how people are ravaged by the effects of crack and smack.
- Help your adolescent dispense with the myth that "everybody's doing it." Remind your teenager that she is not the only one being tempted to try drugs—a temptation definitely not worth giving into.
- As with every other issue we have discussed, tell your child you are always there for her. Here's what one mother said:

> If you are confronted with drugs, come talk to me. I will not reprimand you and I will not discipline you. I will talk to you as a concerned friend because that is what I am. This is not Friday night drinking anymore; this stuff can ruin your life. I love you and want you safe.

Most kids fall victim to drug abuse because they are undervalued at home. By ingesting drugs, they hope to get a quick fix of self-esteem, but it wears off as fast as the drugs do.

Because you have total control over your child's validation, you absolutely can prevent this problem. A child with a strong self-image will not collapse under peer pressure. Even peers who do use drugs respect a person who has his head on straight—and is not afraid of *being* straight.

SEX

"Oh, Mom, you're so old-fashioned. *Everybody* is having sex," say today's kids.

While it is not true that "everyone" is having sex, it *is* true that adolescent sexual activity is more prevalent than ever before and is starting at younger and younger ages. Studies show that children as young as thirteen and fourteen regularly engage in sexual intercourse. By eighteen, almost *half* of all teenaged girls in minority groups and about a quarter of white girls have been pregnant, sometimes more than once. A large percentage admitted they engaged in sexual activities not because they wanted to or because they were in love, but because they were pressured into it by peers or boyfriends.

It is no secret that as adolescents mature, they become increasingly interested in the opposite sex. What *does* seem to be a secret, though, is what the natural progression of that interest should be. One purpose of early dating is to practice for "real" relationships later. Kids need to find out who they are compatible with and what they are looking for in a relationship. Having sex can only get in the way of that discovery. Said one school psychologist:

> The decision to be intimate can have traumatic results for children whose lives can become obsessed with sex as a way

> of obtaining the emotional love they need. Rarely can a pressuring partner supply that love, nor is he or she usually interested. A student who gives in to sex may think he or she is being loved and, in turn, may show devotion and love back. But in most cases, the partner is exploiting the other's emotional weaknesses and using the other for his or her own gratification. No child believes this, but all children should be told this by their parents.

Sure, it is possible that a boy may *think* he loves his "girlfriend" today (usually as he's unbuttoning her blouse), but by tomorrow things may look decidedly different—at least to *him.* She's still "in love," waiting by the phone for his call, while he's off to the ball game trying to charm another girl into giving him her phone number. This is the nature of adolescent "love," and children playing this adult game need to know it.

Teenagers need to understand the stages of adolescent dating as well. "If they jump from childhood directly into an adult relationship they are ill prepared for," said one father, "they miss the whole dating ritual and all the emotional growth that comes from it." The psychologist added, "Kids having sex is like throwing the switch on a fuse box that isn't wired to handle the load—the fuses blow."

Adolescents need to know the real-world, adult risks they face when playing around with sex. Today the game is too often Russian roulette—with all the cylinders loaded. Of those teenagers who are having sex, about one third don't use contraceptives. Pure ignorance and machismo account for this grossly irresponsible behavior. In the old days, such stupidity resulted in venereal disease or the burden of an unwanted pregnancy. Now you can *die,* after a wrenching, horrific illness. And if you're a girl, your chances of contracting AIDS are over *ten times* that of boys—an awfully risky way to try to keep a boyfriend from dumping you.

The other problem with immature relationships, as they relate to socialization, is that they isolate kids from their peers, parents, and schoolwork. Said one mother:

> Teenagers who become wrapped up in emotionally charged "love affairs" miss the most vital time in their lives, a time when they should be opening up and enjoying all kinds of new experiences and people.

Adolescents need to learn about sex early, *before* they enter puberty. Just the thought of these "talks" puts most parents into a state of panic. Relax. You will be surprised (or perhaps, delighted?) at how much your child already knows—and how much he has all mixed up! You'll then see how important it was that you got started when you did. Here are the basics:

- The growth spurts that accompany puberty vary greatly, so when your child is between the ages of nine and ten, start talking about sexual matters related to physical development. For girls, signs of puberty such as breast development and pubic hair may appear by then, so if you have a daughter, reassure her that while not all girls develop on the same time schedule and most get their first menstrual period between eleven and thirteen, she should not worry if she is early or late. (Amazingly, over 50 percent of mothers don't explain menstruation to their daughters and over 90 percent don't discuss sex at all!) If you have a son, he will enter puberty around the age of twelve, so explain the mechanics of erections and wet dreams before then. These are rapid, radical changes for children who suddenly feel adult impulses and undergo physiological changes. *Save kids confusion and embarrassment by discussing what is about to take place* before *it takes place.*

- Safeguard your child against disease, pregnancy, and the emotional hurt that comes from immature sexual activity by *talking*, and talking early. Another mother said:

> Don't beat around the bush. You are going to have to talk about *organs* sometime, and the time is now. With the help of a "birds-and-bees" book, or a good magazine or educational show, you can much better explain the mechanics of sexual intercourse, how females get pregnant, and how diseases are transmitted.

- Keep an ear open for hints of curiosity from your child. She may come to you with a simple question, and when she does, answer *that question* for the moment. The mother continued, "Don't take this as an invitation for a full dissertation on sex, or the issue she brought up will get muddled in the confusion."
- Explain that sex is a good, natural thing that bonds people together and affirms their love for each other. It may sound old-fashioned (probably because it is), but remind your child again that sex is for adults who are in a special, long-lasting relationship and who

have established a deep, mature caring for one another. Puppy love and teen crushes do *not* come under this heading.

- Balance your discussion of sex. Don't pull a veil of secrecy over it just because your parents did, but by the same token, don't act as if you know all there is to know about the subject. Ask your child for his views. Ask what he means when he says, "I know about that." He may have only a vague, general concept of what you are talking about or he may have his details mixed up. One parent said, "My nine-year-old actually thought condoms were for making water balloons because that's what his buddy used them for."
- Remind your children—girls *and* boys—that when they give up their virginity, they can't get it back. The act of intercourse should be reserved for a special, deeply felt bonding that requires maturity and time to develop, a relationship that is *for keeps,* not *for fun.* Teach your children to use the most important two-letter word of all: "No!" Remind them that the physical closeness may be exciting, but giving in to sexual pressures—or exerting them—is not a sign of maturity. What makes people really attractive is *abstinence,* as the following mother knew:

> I wasn't at all happy about Marilyn's health ed teacher using a banana to demonstrate how to use a condom. I was even less happy when the surgeon general got up in front of a country suffering miserably from the burden of teenaged pregnancies and advocated condom distribution to high school students. What I didn't hear her talk much about was *chastity.* It

> was like the word was stricken from the English language. Abstinence, chastity, self-control—what happened to *self-control* in this society?

- As you did with drugs, help your child come up with responses to anticipated lines. Since you were there once yourself, it shouldn't be hard to prepare him for the obvious "Oh, but I love you so much"—a line you have no doubt heard (or used?).

With an issue like sex, your job is to *inform* and then *trust.* Share your own experiences here, as you did with drug issues. You can't go on dates with your children and you can't dictate morals, as we have seen. But if you use the parenting skills we have discussed in the other chapters—especially those involving self-esteem—your children will grow up respecting their physical and emotional well-being and will arrive at adolescence in a position of personal strength and dignity that will help them make independent choices about what is right for them.

APPENDIX 1

PARENTING SKILLS QUIZ and REVIEW

The following review quiz corresponds to the issues discussed in each chapter. You may use it in several different ways.

First, you may want to test your overall parenting strengths and weaknesses before reading this book. This may give you an idea of what you want to focus on as you read each chapter.

Second, you may want to test your comprehension of the material you have read.

And third, you may find that the quiz is useful as a quick reference guide when various issues arise.

No matter how you utilize the following quiz, bear in mind that there is no "passing" or "failing" score. There is simply *clarification* of what the successful parents often found were very difficult issues.

Notice as you select your answers that there are sometimes only subtle differences between the correct answer and the other multiple choices. What is designated as "correct" is what parents felt was the best way to handle that issue.

CHAPTER 1. COMMUNICATE

1. When kids say something unthoughtful out of frustration, you should (a) ask for an explanation, (b) ask for an apology, (c) not worry about it.
2. If they're not paying careful attention, how do most parents usually communicate? (a) Heart-to-heart talks, (b) short lectures, (c) criticism and judgment.
3. When you are listening to your child, your main goal should be to (a) let her have her say, (b) understand the meaning behind the words, (c) ask her to listen back.
4. What is the main reason for the communication gap? (a) Parents talk too much, (b) kids won't keep quiet, (c) kids won't listen.
5. If your kids learn to come to you for the little things when they are little, they learn (a) to rely on you, (b) to come to you for big problems later, (c) that you are keeping tabs on them.
6. We use communication mainly to (a) relate to one another, (b) express our emotions, (c) make a good living later in life.
7. What has the greatest effect on what we hear and say? (a) Our state of mind, (b) societal influences, (c) the subject matter.
8. The worst effect of parents' emotional outbursts on kids is (a) shutdown of communication, (b) resentment, (c) parents' loss of popularity.
9. When children witness verbal abuse between their parents, the worst consequence is that they (a) become angry, (b) feel guilty, (c) become sad.

10. The average meal is usually a time (a) to discuss topics of interest, (b) for parents to relax, (c) for negative communication.
11. Helping kids verbalize thoughts (a) shows you care, (b) makes them feel better, (c) is a form of harassment.
12. When an adolescent is silent, (a) softly try to start communications, (b) assume he has a problem, (c) leave him alone.
13. How do you show willingness to communicate? (a) Facial expressions, (b) starting a conversation, (c) walking quietly into a child's room.
14. Which is the most important for a younger child? (a) Talking to her, (b) being available to listen, (c) helping her figure out her problem.
15. It is best to (a) let your child talk freely to you whenever she wants, (b) set a date to talk later, (c) get to the root of the problem immediately.
16. For discussing issues, dinnertime is (a) bad, (b) ideal, (c) fine for most things.
17. It is the kids, not the parents, who are uncomfortable discussing sex. T____ F____
18. If you had to pick one, which is usually most important? (a) Listening to try to understand your child's concern, (b) talking calmly and rationally to help, (c) assuring your child that her problems are not as bad as they seem.
19. When kids have a minor problem, it is better to (a) help them solve it, (b) just let them vent, (c) have a talk.
20. Of the following, which is not that important for good communication? (a) Paying attention, (b) body posture, (c) participating in the conversation, (d) all are important.

21. The main problem with "you" messages is that they lay blame and are accusatory. T____ F____
22. To avoid making your child feel guilty, it is best not to tell him how his behavior affected you. T____ F____
23. When it comes to resolving a problem, you should (a) always make the final decision in the end, (b) compromise your position or collaborate, (c) seek an outside opinion.

Answers and Page Numbers

CHAPTER 1. COMMUNICATE

1. c p. 27
2. c p. 27
3. b p. 28
4. a p. 29
5. b p. 30
6. b p. 33
7. a p. 33
8. b p. 34
9. b p. 35
10. c p. 36
11. c p. 38
12. c p. 40
13. a p. 43
14. b p. 44
15. b p. 47
16. a p. 50
17. F p. 50

18. a p. 53
19. b p. 54
20. d p. 55
21. T p. 57
22. F p. 62
23. b p. 63

CHAPTER 2. ENCOURAGE INTELLECTUAL DEVELOPMENT

1. Rote memorization and the three R's are still the most valuable part of education. T____ F____
2. Being able to absorb and recall data is more important than just "thinking creatively." T____ F____
3. Most schools teach kids not "what" to think, but "how" to think. T____ F____
4. Arts education in America is (a) overemphasized in place of the basics, (b) barely exists, (c) is now about equally balanced with other studies.
5. What is the solution to the problems in the educational system? (a) More funding, (b) parents' involvement, (c) more class days.
6. Creative thinking is best combined with (a) critical thinking, (b) painting and music, (c) creative writing.
7. To reach intelligent conclusions, children do *not* need to (a) observe, (b) categorize, (c) passively accept information from teachers, (d) question information from teachers.
8. IQ is basically innate and unchangeable. T____ F____
9. Which is *not* true? Appropriate stimulation (a) increases the size of the brain, (b) makes kids smarter, (c) does not affect IQ.
10. Intellectual growth happens best in (a) calm, quiet environments, (b) active environments.

11. Overstimulation can be just as harmful as understimulation. T____ F____

12. Which is probably the most important part of early intellectual development? (a) Playing with toys, (b) having friends, (c) reading.

13. The national average is seven hours of TV viewing per day per person. How much TV did the successful children in this study watch? (a) 2.2 hrs/day, (b)4.8 hrs/day, (c) 6.8 hrs/day.

14. It is okay to keep reading material beyond comprehension range. T____ F____

15. At what age should parents start taking their children to the library? (a) Eighteen months, (b) thirty months, (c) forty-eight months.

16. If you discover your child reading under the covers with a flashlight, you should (a) look the other way, (b) talk to his teacher, (c) remove the flashlight.

17. It is best not to help kids with answers when they get stuck. T____ F____

18. You should end teaching sessions when kids are (a) ready to stop, (b) tired, (c) enthusiastically learning.

19. When your child is involved in an activity, you should (a) let her play quietly in her own world, (b) engage her in conversation, (c) introduce a new playmate.

20. Older children should use (a) broad generalized language, (b) specific language, (c) less language.

21. Using "mind games" and other teaching aids is (a) good for developing linguistic skills, (b) too much pressure for most kids, (c) makes kids competitive.

22. The important thing about mathematical intelligence is (a) the relationship between the numbers, (b) memoriz-

ing certain basics like times tables, (c) understanding calculations.

23. To help a child in school, parents should spend more time correcting homework and less time in PTA meetings. T____ F____

24. It is best if kids, not parents, talk to teachers about assignments and tests. T____ F____

25. What is a good, basic organizational tool for study planning and goal setting? (a) A mission statement, (b) a desk calendar, (c) an electronic planner.

26. Parents should not be too involved in homework and let their child suffer the consequences. T____ F____

ANSWERS AND PAGE NUMBERS

CHAPTER 2. ENCOURAGE INTELLECTUAL DEVELOPMENT

1. F p. 68
2. F p. 68
3. F p. 69
4. b p. 69
5. b p. 69
6. a p. 71
7. c p. 73
8. F p. 74
9. c p. 75
10. b p. 77
11. T p. 80
12. c p. 83
13. a p. 83

14. T p. 85
15. a p. 86
16. a p. 88
17. T p. 91
18. c p. 94
19. b p. 96
20. b p. 97
21. a p. 99
22. a p. 101
23. F p. 105
24. F p. 107
25. b p. 111
26. F p. 113

CHAPTER 3. DISCIPLINE

1. Which parenting style was used most in the past? (a) Authoritarian, (b) permissive, (c) balanced.
2. Which parenting style is used most today? (a) Authoritative, (b) permissive, (c) authoritarian.
3. Between authoritarian and permissive parenting style, which is the most effective? (a) Authoritarian, (b) permissive, (c) neither.
4. It is important to try to be "popular" with your child. T____ F____
5. Distracting a child instead of saying "No" is wise. T____ F____
6. Militaristic discipline (a) is good to a point, (b) makes kids emotionally weak, (c) makes kids emotionally strong.

7. If your child continually neglects his responsibilities to his pet, you should (a) take over the duties yourself, (b) assign them to another sibling, (c) give the pet away.
8. You should (a) obtain your child's concurrence with rules, (b) set rules without having to explain the reason for them.
9. You should decide upon rules and disciplinary plans of action (a) before a family meeting, (b) during a family meeting where everyone can discuss it.
10. Family meetings should be held (a) when an issue comes up, (b) when everyone agrees to a time and place, (c) at least once a month.
11. One reason to have family meetings is so children can (a) learn what business meetings will be like, (b) air their grievances, (c) learn punctuality.
12. Which is better when rules are violated? (a) Give one warning before disciplining, (b) take action immediately.
13. Rules and regulations improve a child's sense of freedom. T____ F____
14. For disciplinary measures to be effective they need to (a) be strict, (b) have a distinct beginning and end, (c) make perfect sense to children.
15. Once disciplinary measures are imposed, it is a good idea to forgive a child as soon as possible. T____ F____
16. By the time a child reaches adolescence, written contracts agreeing to specific behavior (a) are not very trusting, (b) are necessary, (c) are a sign of overparenting.
17. If your teenager comes home past his curfew, you should (a) give him one more chance, (b) immediately set a new, earlier curfew, (c) take away the car.

18. There are some limited instances when publicly scolding a chid is beneficial. T____ F____
19. Withholding affection is too severe a disciplinary measure. T____ F____
20. Parental suspicion can cause children to be (a) jealous, (b) deceitful, (c) trusting.
21. In most cases, a light spanking is the best way to discipline a toddler. T____ F____
22. The best thing to do about negative, attention-getting behavior is (a) determine calmly what is causing it, (b) react to it immediately.
23. If a young child says something bad about a new sibling, the first thing you should do is (a) have a quiet talk, (b) take some kind of disciplinary action, (c) not respond.
24. When a new baby arrives, other kids need (a) to help, (b) more play time, (c) more attention.
25. In today's society, it does not hurt to "overprotect" a little. T____ F____
26. If you openly show affection while disciplining, you (a) send a mixed message, (b) make clear the behavior, not the child, is bad, (c) undermine the measure.
27. Children believe internally that their parents discipline out of (a) fear, (b) love, (c) instinct.

ANSWERS AND PAGE NUMBERS

CHAPTER 3. DISCIPLINE

1. a p. 117
2. b p. 117

3. c p. 118
4. F p. 122
5. F p. 123
6. b p. 124
7. c p. 125
8. a p. 127
9. a p. 127
10. c p. 130
11. b p. 130
12. b p. 131
13. T p. 133
14. b p. 136
15. F p. 137
16. b p. 137
17. b p. 138
18. F p. 140
19. F p. 142
20. b p. 146
21. F p. 146
22. a p. 149
23. c p. 150
24. c p. 150
25. F p. 152
26. b p. 154
27. b p. 155

CHAPTER 4. INSTILL SELF-ESTEEM

1. The majority of children have (a) a low, (b) a high, (c) an average sense of self-esteem.
2. To maintain a good self-image, children need (a) friends, (b) validation, (c) limits.

3. What percentage of young girls are happy with their appearance? (a) 29 percent, (b) 49 percent, (c) 69 percent.

4. Which promotes high self-esteem most? (a) Reasoning with kids, (b) sticking to rules "just because," (c) good grades.

5. What is the first things kids feel when verbally or physically abused? (a) Rage, (b) confusion, (c) resentment.

6. Telling a child she is "the best" (a) is fine if she *is* the best, (b) helps her self-image, (c) is too pressure-laden.

7. "Feeling good" about kids makes them feel good about themselves. T____ F____

8. Saying "No" too often frustrates children. T____ F____

9. Which builds character the most? (a) Restrictions, (b) delayed gratification, (c) chores.

10. Confessing your own shortcomings (a) undermines you as a role model, (b) is a good idea, (c) is scary for a child.

11. Kids who are insecure about performance need to be (a) consoled, (b) told to "just do it," (c) challenged more often.

12. Exposing kids to new things they are uncertain of (a) scares them, (b) builds autonomy, (c) causes regression.

13. Self-esteem is something a parent bestows on his child. T____ F____

14. Setting up challenges so kids can win (a) is a good idea, (b) gives a false sense of security, (c) is deceitful.

15. When a child is faced with a decision, parents should (a) say, "You decide," (b) do nothing, (c) give hints as to the right decision.

16. Trying to protect your child from failure (a) is natural and right, (b) strengthens self-esteem, (c) weakens self-esteem.

17. Pointing out successful people such as sports stars gives kids the idea that (a) high levels of success are out of reach, (b) you need natural talent to succeed, (c) success takes a lot of work.
18. You should put the definitions of *procrastination* and *perseverance* on your child's wall. T____ F____
19. Visualizing success before starting is a New Age idea that does not really work. T____ F____
20. Regardless of the effort put forth, it is best to give your child at least some praise. T____ F____
21. Children should be forced to look at their imperfections. T____ F____
22. Praise should be (a) specific, (b) general, (c) ongoing.
23. When up to bat, a child with high self-esteem will (a) just take swings, (b) try for home runs, (c) think about the team.
24. When a child is anxious about an activity, it is best to (a) encourage her, (b) praise her in advance, (c) let her quit.

ANSWERS AND PAGE NUMBERS

CHAPTER 4. INSTILL SELF-ESTEEM

1. a p. 160
2. b p. 163
3. a p. 165
4. a p. 166
5. b p. 166
6. c p. 168
7. F p. 170

8. F p. 173
9. b p. 173
10. b p. 175
11. a p. 176
12. b p. 178
13. F p. 180
14. a p. 181
15. a p. 183
16. c p. 184
17. c p. 184
18. T p. 186
19. F p. 187
20. F p. 188
21. T p. 189
22. a p. 191
23. a p. 192
24. c p. 194

CHAPTER 5. TEACH VALUES

1. If you had to select one culprit for today's lack of values, it would be (a) teachers, (b) parents, (c) TV.
2. In the past twenty years, teenage suicides have (a) declined, (b) doubled, (c) tripled.
3. Teenage suicide has increased because of lack of a belief system. T____ F____
4. Kids rarely adopt the exact views of their peer group. T____ F____
5. To resist peer pressure, kids need (a) their parents' set of values, (b) an internalized code of ethics, (c) counseling.

6. It is a good idea to discuss other families' values. T____ F____
7. Values are so important, we should structure our lives around them. T____ F____
8. Conservatives coined the term "family values." T____ F____
9. Kids should be taught that life is about serving others. T____ F____
10. Criticizing misbehavior involving poor judgment is (a) necessary, (b) unnecessary, (c) harmful.
11. Children should try to adopt their parents' set of values. T____ F____
12. Moral values are best expressed (a) by parents' actions, (b) in words, (c) through religion.
13. Instead of being reactive, be (a) quiet, (b) proactive, (c) fairly aggressive.
14. Get ideas across through (a) short lectures, (b) literature, (c) TV.
15. Asking your child if he would like to join the Cub Scouts is a good idea. T____ F____
16. Parents should openly admit their own moral mistakes to their children. T____ F____
17. Teaching kids about a Supreme Being or God is a good idea. T____ F____
18. If a youngster asks if Santa is real, (a) tell him the truth, (b) tell a white lie to avoid spoiling the fable, (c) write to the North Pole.
19. Very young children are not capable of intentionally distorting the truth. T____ F____
20. When younger kids steal, parents should (a) make kids pay the penalty, (b) call the police, (c) not say too much.

21. Christmas is the one time most children learn the meaning of gratitude. T____ F____
22. Generosity is about "love and be loved," "give and take." T____ F____
23. Kids should be asked to share the things they love the most, like toys, ice cream, and the like. T____ F____
24. Children have only a vague idea of the connection between money and (a) love, (b) work, (c) success.
25. Money is an effective tool for modifying behavior and parents should use it more often. T____ F____
26. It is a good idea to pay children for (a) household chores, (b) extra work, (c) excellent grades.
27. Children should (a) be able to save all their money, (b) donate some of their money, (c) spend whatever amount they wish on whatever they wish.
28. Young children can understand the concept of interest and savings. T____ F____

ANSWERS AND PAGE NUMBERS

CHAPTER 5. TEACH VALUES

1. c p. 199
2. c p. 202
3. T p. 202
4. F p. 203
5. b p. 203
6. T p. 204
7. T p. 205

8. F p. 207
9. T p. 208
10. c p. 209
11. F p. 210
12. a p. 211
13. b p. 214
14. b p. 214
15. F p. 215
16. T p. 216
17. T p. 221
18. a p. 223
19. T p. 226
20. a p. 227
21. F p. 230
22. F p. 231
23. T p. 231
24. b p. 237
25. F p. 240
26. b p. 241
27. b p. 241
28. T p. 242

CHAPTER 6. SUPPORT SOCIALIZATION

1. The best thing for joining a sorority, business organization, or club is (a) sponsorship, (b) money, (c) social skills.
2. Kids can learn to be friendly. T____ F____
3. One of the important things about social competence is the ability to make a good impression on strangers. T____ F____
4. It is better to (a) ask kids to say "thank you," (b) just say it yourself, (c) reprimand them lightly if they don't say it.

5. To teach children manners, (a) explain the rationale behind them, (b) reprimand them when they are impolite, (c) let them learn naturally.

6. Negotiating resolutions to conflicts is something young toddlers need to learn. T____ F____

7. Making "deals" is something young toddlers need to learn. T____ F____

8. Between the ages of five and ten, kids (a) form long-lasting friendships, (b) practice making friends, (c) usually avoid making friends.

9. Your goal as a parent should be separation from your child (a) only when he is ready, (b) the sooner the better, (c) at adolescence.

10. If your child is rejected by a friend, the best thing to do is (a) explain your own similar problem, (b) downplay the problem, (c) distract the child to another activity.

11. To help a shy child, find a playmate who is (a) older, (b) younger, (c) also shy.

12. Shy children should learn to (a) stand up to bullies, (b) avoid bullies, (c) seek help from teachers when confronted with bullies.

13. The scrutiny teenagers fear is usually (a) imagined, (b) real, (c) justified.

14. If children try to learn about subjects of interest to a peer group in order to be admitted, it (a) is conniving, (b) shows too much interest in joining, (c) is a good idea.

15. When it comes to clothes, kids should (a) wear what they want, (b) avoid provocative dress, (c) buy them on their own.

16. Peer groups (a) encourage, (b) discourage individuality.

17. If a child cannot get into a peer group, he should (a) start his own, (b) persist until he does, (c) seek help from teachers.
18. If you are not sure about the appropriateness of your child's hangout, (a) call the police, (b) call another parent, (c) call the hangout.
19. You should try to stop your child's negative friendships. T____ F____
20. You do not need to be overly concerned with "big" issues like AIDS and heroin use, which are mainly inner-city problems. T____ F____
21. When peers try to pressure kids into something they don't like, the kids should "blame" their parents as a way out. T____ F____
22. Teaching kids to "Just say No" is an old-fashioned, ineffective, conservative idea. T____ F____
23. Kids often start taking drugs because they are (a) bored, (b) undervalued at home, (c) looking for fun.
24. What percentage of teenaged minority girls are pregnant by age eighteen? (a) 10 percent, (b) 25 percent, (c) 50 percent.
25. It is best to start talking about sex when your child is age (a) nine to ten, (b) eleven to twelve, (c) thirteen to fourteen.
26. If, when discussing sex, your child says, "I know about that," (a) accept him on his word, (b) question him, (c) go on anyway.
27. Telling children they can never get their virginity back (a) is a little old-fashioned, (b) may make them think twice, (c) is too personal.

28. In this day and age, which should you emphasize most? (a) Condom use, (b) abstinence.

ANSWERS AND PAGE NUMBERS

CHAPTER 6. SOCIALIZATION

1. c p. 245
2. T p. 245
3. T p. 246
4. b p. 247
5. a p. 249
6. T p. 250
7. T p. 250
8. b p. 254
9. b p. 254
10. a p. 256
11. a p. 257
12. a p. 258
13. a p. 260
14. c p. 261
15. b p. 263
16. b p. 266
17. a p. 268
18. b p. 269
19. T p. 270
20. F p. 275
21. T p. 277
22. F p. 278

23. b p. 281
24. c p. 282
25. a p. 284
26. b p. 286
27. b p. 286
28. b p. 286

APPENDIX 2

A QUICK GUIDE to the IMPORTANT ISSUES

Since this book is intended for parents of children of all ages, we have highlighted here the key issues of each chapter and indicated the age group each falls into.

We have coded the various age groups as follows:

(P) for preschool ages zero to six; (S) for school ages seven to twelve; (A) for adolescent ages thirteen to eighteen; (AA) for all ages.

Remember, though, children vary. Some mature faster than others, so particular issues may or may not apply to a child at any given time. The following is designed only as a general guideline, as is all the information presented in this book. Be sure to consult a competent professional regarding problems or concerns you or your child may have about any of the issues we have discussed in this book.

CHAPTER 1. COMMUNICATE

Page

25. (P) Toddlers have a hard time getting attention.

25. (A) Adolescents need to share joys and sorrows with parents.
26. (P) Talk to infants.
27. (S) Preteens say things they don't mean.
27. (S), (A) Growing kids retreat into their own worlds where they don't have to listen to parents.
28. (AA) Respect kids' right to privacy and to not talk.
29. (A) Parents talk/lecture too much rather than listen.
29. (AA) The communication gap: Parents and kids don't know how to talk to each other.
29. (AA) Can you hear what your child is saying? Are you listening with an open mind?
32. (A) Generation gap—clothes, music—is your teenager allowed to express herself?
33. (AA) Control your emotions.
34. (AA) Speak calmly and rationally.
35. (P), (S) Spouses should avoid arguments and verbal abuse in front of young children.
35. (AA) The "polite rule": No yelling allowed.
36. (AA) Talking turnoffs: criticism, accusations, and the like.
38. (P) Don't coax or help toddlers finish sentences.
41. (AA) Accept silence, which is normal. Don't insist on talking.
43. (AA) Make communication possible with the right attitude and expressions.
44. (AA) Be available for talking.
45. (P) Toddlers need to be heard.
47. (A) Preplan times for talking; make dates for quiet time alone.

50. (A) Uncomfortable subjects: Inform yourself; discuss openly.
53. (AA) Avoid lectures; depend on listening.
55. (AA) Learn to listen and respond. Participate, use posture, and keep an open mind.
60. (AA) Avoid "you" messages; use "concern" messages.
62. (S), (A) Explain the effect of your child's behavior on you.
63. (S), (A) Compromise, "give in," when appropriate; collaborate on solutions by listing options.
65. (A) Avoid mixed messages and be specific.

CHAPTER 2. ENCOURAGE INTELLECTUAL DEVELOPMENT

Page
68. (S), (A) The three R's and rote memorization don't teach kids to think.
69. (A) Teenagers have poor mathematical skills because of poor analytical/creative reasoning ability.
69. (S) Today's sixth graders don't know who Beethoven is.
70. (A) It is never too late to improve study habits.
71. (P), (S) Provide a home atmosphere that fosters creativity and free-flowing ideas.
72. (AA) Foster creativity through dancing, singing, and drawing.
72. (AA) Don't correct children when they are expressing their creativity.
73. (AA) Welcome new ideas.

73. (S), (A) Children must combine creative and critical thinking.
74. (P) Myth: Whatever IQ you are born with you are stuck with.
75. (S) Intelligence is more than an IQ score.
76. (AA) Focus on your child's potential, not his IQ.
77. (P) Children's brains grow in response to a stimulating environment.
80. (AA) Pay attention to cognitive growth spurts.
80. (P) Let your child guide you. Avoid overstimulation.
81. (AA) Parents must provide an intellectually enriched environment.
83. (P) Reading is the most important aspect of early intellectual development.
83. (S) Parents' reading habits directly influence kids reading habits.
85. (S) Keep reading material challenging.
86. (P) Introduce your child to the library—the most important institution.
86. (P) Build your child's desire to read; get her interested in books.
91. (AA) Build your child's intellectual competence by encouraging independent thinking; don't help her think.
92. (P) Adhere to the eight "Do's" of intellectual development.
92. (P) Establish a learning environment.
96. (P), (S) Develop children's cognitive function by having them speak about the activity they are engaged in.

97. (S), (A) Ask mind-opening questions on outings and field trips.

97. (S) Have kids use specific language and avoid "lazy" thinking.

99. (AA) Use humor, puns, and mind games to give a mental workout.

101. (S), (A) Teach the relationship between numbers, not just numbers.

105. (S), (A) Get involved with school, teachers, and the PTA.

110. (A) Teach organization and goal-setting.

112. (A) Help your child avoid wasting time; supervise study.

113. (A) Teach your child to study effectively.

CHAPTER 3. DISCIPLINE

Page

118. (AA) Allow freedom within specific guidelines.

118. (AA) Encourage self-reliance over servility.

122. (P) Don't give in to demands.

122. (P) Firmness is not meanness.

123. (P) The less discipline kids receive, the less respect they have.

123. (AA) Firm discipline makes for relaxed kids.

126. (AA) Authoritative style is reasonable, without guilt.

126. (AA) Avoid both authoritarian and permissive parenting.

127. (A) Relinquish control as children grow.

128. (S), (A) Anticipate problems and discuss them at family meetings.
131. (S), (A) Impose rules and stick to them.
132. (S), (A) Treat kids with the same respect as grown-ups.
134. (S), (A) Stand firm when kids test limits.
137. (A) Use contracts.
140. (AA) Critical remarks hurt kids.
142. (S) Withholding affection is an effective consequence.
145. (S), (A) Natural consequences teach self-discipline.
146. (P), (S) Spanking is sometimes necessary.
149. (P), (S) Understand what is causing negative behavior.
150. (P), (S) Kids often misbehave out of frustration.
151. (S) Don't overparent.
152. (S), (A) Avoid stereotyping kids.
154. (AA) Discipline without anger.

CHAPTER 4. INSTILL SELF-ESTEEM

Page
160. (AA) The majority of children today suffer from low self-esteem.
162. (AA) Self-esteem is the lifeblood of mental health.
163. (AA) Everyone needs to be approved of.
163. (S), (A) Insecure children may become emotional cripples.
163. (S) Without parental reinforcement, self-worth cannot develop.
164. (S) Children with low self-esteem have distinct characteristics.

165. (A) Only 29 percent of adolescent girls like their appearance.
165. (AA) Parents' harsh verbal/physical abuse can cause low self-esteem.
166. (S) Verbal reasoning and discussion foster self-esteem.
166. (AA) Abuse causes confusion, shame, and fear.
167. (S), (A) Don't compare siblings.
170. (AA) It is not necessary to always verbalize love.
171. (AA) Defeats are learning experiences.
171. (S), (A) The effort is more important than the result.
171. (S), (A) Encourage kids to participate in activities.
173. (P), (S) Saying "No" to children builds character.
173. (AA) Kids need reassurance that they can succeed.
174. (S), (A) Relate stories about your own difficulties.
178. (P) Foster autonomy by introducing children to new people and activities.
183. (S), (A) Encourage kids to face challenges and to persist.
186. (S), (A) Avoid procrastination.
187. (S), (A) Have kids visualize success.
189. (S), (A) Praise must be earned.
191. (S), (A) Don't forget to praise when warranted.
193. (AA) The intrinsic or emotional rewards are the most valuable.

CHAPTER 5. TEACH VALUES

Page
199. (AA) Television distorts our view of reality and values.

201. (AA) Crime is glamorized on television.
203. (A) When parents are inattentive, kids turn to peers for values.
204. (S), (A) Stay up on current issues.
204. (AA) Parents' competitiveness prevents sharing real values.
205. (AA) Lives are built on values.
207. (AA) We need to rediscover family traditions.
207. (S), (A) Values are still transmitted by example.
208. (S), (A) Children must genuinely believe in values.
209. (S), (A) Learning moral judgment is a process.
210. (S), (A) Parents cannot dictate morals.
211. (AA) Parents can be both friends and police officers.
212. (AA) The Golden Rule is still valuable.
214. (A) Be proactive rather than reactive.
214. (AA) Use literature to teach morals.
222. (S) Avoid "serious" talks about God.
225. (P) Ask kids honesty questions.
226. (P) Lying and stealing are part of childhood.
229. (A) Life is about sharing and helping.
229. (S) Humility comes from gratitude.
231. (S) Teach children they do not "lose" by giving.
233. (P), (S) Young children can learn that life includes extending themselves.
235. (AA) Education is invaluable.
237. (S) Children need to learn the connection between money and work.
240. (S) Don't use money as a disciplinary tool.
241. (P), (S) Kids should learn to save, spend, and give money.

CHAPTER 6. SUPPORT SOCIALIZATION

Page

245. (S), (A) Kids must feel they are worth having as friends.
245. (S), (A) Good social skills are critical to success in life.
246. (A) Socially competent people meet other people's needs.
248. (P) Introduce kids to the world beyond the home.
249. (P) Children need to learn manners.
250. (P), (S) Negotiation and bargaining are important tools in school.
250. (S) Strike simple bargains with your child.
250. (S), (A) Let your children see you making deals.
252. (S), (A) Team projects teach cooperation.
254. (S) Turning away from parents and toward other kids is a sign of health.
255. (A) Healthy parents help their children branch out and abandon the nest.
255. (S), (A) Best friends help kids shoulder the pressures of growing up.
257. (S) Older kids can be a good influence on shy ones.
259. (P), (A) Avoid overcontrolling so kids can form their own identities and resist peer pressure.
262. (A) One hallmark of adolescence is looking "right."
264. (A) Explain there is more to life than looks.
267. (A) Peer groups that look desirable may not be.

269. (S), (A) Know where and with whom your child is hanging out.
271. (AA) You can influence who your child's friends are.
272. (S), (A) Voice objections to negative friends.
276. (A) Be your child's ally in the fight against pressures to do drugs and sex.
276. (S), (A) Discuss the perils of drugs and sex.
284. (A) Use heart-to-heart talks, not lectures.
287. (A) Prepare kids for life by informing and then trusting them.

APPENDIX 3

ABOUT the INTERVIEWS

Though we had the background, experience, and credentials to initiate a scientific study, we chose to take a journalistic approach to this project. We tried to select a wide cross section of families, but we did not attempt to have a scientifically valid random sample that was statistically significant. We relied instead on the recommendations, referrals, and judgments of school administrators and others who were interested in participating in this project.

Our goal was very clear: We wanted to find the common traits, strategies, and wisdom of highly successful parents. We chose to stick mostly with children who were high school seniors so we could explore a group who had proven a significant degree of accomplishment. On a few occasions, though, we were referred to students of college age or older. Occasionally, unusually promising younger kids were included if we felt their parents' contributions were noteworthy.

We were looking for a combination of beliefs and patterns of child rearing that, when melded together, formed a whole picture, or "gestalt," which defied scientific delineation. After running all our data through a qualifying sieve, we harvested the six key elements and the stories behind them.

The common threads woven throughout the parenting tapestry were visible not from statistical analyses, but from observations, hunches, and the insights that came from one-on-one, heartfelt, honest, open dialogue with parents who loved their children very much.

We found the families for this book after writing and calling school administrators, teachers, and parents across America, from the West Coast to New England, primarily around the urban areas of San Francisco, Los Angeles, San Diego, Hartford, Boston, New York, and Miami. We contacted educators from a roughly equal number of inner-city and suburban public schools and, to a lesser degree, rural and private schools.

Some of the parents we met were surgeons; some were laborers. Their educations varied, as did their family structures, with about a third of the children coming from single-parent families and the balance from two-parent households.

We met families from many ethnicities and religions, including African Americans, Asians, Caucasians, Hispanics, and Pacific Islanders. Individuals from the Buddhist, Catholic, Hindu, Jewish, Mormon, Muslim, and Protestant faiths were represented, as were a few agonistics.

We personally interviewed at length over eighty parents and students from families specifically recommended by educators, and spoke with about another fifty who were referred to us by the interviewees and others. Acquaintances, neighbors, family members, business associates, patients, and clergy knew kids who they thought met our criteria.

Our questionnaire continued to evolve as the interviews progressed. Some questions we found to be important, while others elicited little response. We used the questionnaire only as a general guideline since we wanted to determine what parents themselves felt were the key child-rearing issues, without unduly influencing them. Much of the time, only a small portion of the questions were covered, as parents veered off on tangents of their own or discussed issues of particular interest to them; we encouraged this.

To gain more spontaneous answers, at first we did not send the questionnaires in advance and only used them as work sheets during the meetings. Later, we switched to sending them before the interview so parents could ruminate about past incidents and anecdotes they felt would be useful to us. This proved to be more successful for obtaining the specific examples we were looking for because it gave parents time to prepare rather than forcing them to recall eighteen years of child rearing on the spot. We also assured anonymity and have changed names slightly to protect privacy.

When we met our subjects, we thanked them for taking the time to speak with us and explained the purpose of the interview again. Did our recording of the interviews or the fact that these families were selected as exemplary models distort their responses in any way? We don't think so. We assured them that the tape recorder was only to help us avoid writing everything down, and we asked them to simply ignore it. It seemed that all of them did, and no one asked that we not use it.

All interviews were done in person, except for a dozen or

so that were done by telephone. A few included both modes or brief follow-up telephone discussions. Our goal was to obtain data from the widest possible cross section and then synthesize it into meaningful patterns for other parents to follow. We believe we accomplished that goal.

About the Authors

ALAN D. DAVIDSON, Ph.D.

Dr. Alan D. Davidson received his undergraduate training in psychology at the University of California at Berkeley, and took his doctorate in clinical and developmental psychology from the University of Cincinnati. Since 1974, he has worked with thousands of parents and children in his practice in San Diego. During the last twenty years, Dr. Davidson has been president of the Academy of San Diego Psychologists, and has written more than eighty articles and presented dozens of seminars nationwide on human behavior. In 1992, he published his first book, *Guide to Competency-Based Interviewing,* and speaks nationally on various topics including personality, human potential, and creativity. He has appeared several times on national television *(Good Morning America, NBC Nightly News)* and is frequently seen on local television.

Dr. Davidson began his career as a teacher and consultant for juvenile hall, where he interviewed hundreds of parents and troubled children. He then consulted with Head Start, and worked with the principals and faculty of several elementary schools, where he developed a program to provide enriched environments for the children of military families. During this challenging assignment, he studied the problems of "intermittent parenting," where fathers were absent for long periods and mothers worked, and successfully developed programs to increase family stability.

Dr. Davidson also evaluated hundreds of children considered for different accelerated and "gifted" programs.

ROBERT E. DAVIDSON

For the last twenty years, Robert E. Davidson, a graduate of San Jose State University, has been a successful international businessman and corporate president. More recently, he was manager and chief copywriter for an advertising company chosen by *INC* magazine as one of the INC 500—America's five hundred fastest-growing companies. He is currently a marketing consultant and copywriter.

During his years as a corporate president, Robert not only wrote millions of dollars worth of advertising copy, he also interviewed over five hundred middle-aged baby boomers for another project. He discovered during these interviews that only a few people were inwardly successful, personable, and happy, while most others suffered from the anxiety and disillusionment of unfulfilled adulthoods.

Robert conceived the idea for this book: investigating what it was during people's formative years that directed them toward a course of personal fulfillment.